# How to Read Music

Alan Charlton

FLAME TREE
PUBLISHING

Publisher and Creative Director: Nick Wells
Project Editor: Polly Prior
Art Director: Mike Spender
Layout Design: Theresa Maynard
Production: Chris Herbert

Special thanks to: Toria Lyle, Sara Robson, Claire Walker and Lyndall Willis

17
9 11 13 12 10

This edition first published 2008 by
FLAME TREE PUBLISHING
6 Melbray Mews
Fulham, London SW6 3NS
United Kingdom
www.flametreepublishing.com

Music information site: www.flametreemusic.com



ISBN 978-1-84786-305-8



**Alan Charlton** is a composer, teacher and writer on music. He received a PhD in composition from the University of Bristol, studying with Raymond Warren, Adrian Beaumont and Robert Saxton. His music has been widely performed in the UK and abroad, receiving many prizes and awards for composition. He was the first Eileen Norris Fellow at Bedford School, where he currently teaches. He is the author of *Music Composition Workbook Volume 1* (Rhinegold Publishing) and a contributor to *The Illustrated Encyclopedia of Musical Instruments* (Flame Tree Publishing).

Printed in China

# Contents

# Introduction

Why is being able to read music important? After all, many excellent musicians have never learned to read music.

Many musicians finding learning to play by ear is perfectly adequate for their needs. However, there are times when you can't rely on your ear alone. These might be:

- if you want to learn music with lots of fast notes, thick chords and complicated rhythms
- if you want to make music with others in a choir, orchestra, wind orchestra, guitar orchestra or big band who read music from a score
- if you want to compose music and write your ideas down
- if you want to arrange music for different performers
- if you want a better understanding of music: how chord sequences work, how effective melodies are put together and how to combine different parts with each other, for example
- if you are a guitarist and can read TAB but also want to read staff notation.

This book will be helpful to anyone who wants to learn how to read music for whatever reason. Perhaps you can sing or play an instrument already or are learning an instrument.

You might be interested in composing or arranging music, or are just someone who wants to find out more about music. Whatever your reasons, you will find that this book will guide you painlessly through the process in easy stages. Whether you like classical, jazz, rock, pop, film and TV, folk or world music, this book will suit all tastes.

The book is broken into 12 sections. The most vital of these for reading music are those on pitch and rhythm. You will probably find that not all of the material in the book is relevant to your particular instrument, so you will be able to skip some sections. For example, before starting the section on pitch, check the range of your instrument with the section on page 372 to see which clef your instrument uses and which notes you need to learn. We have made every effort to make the exercises as fun as possible and we have tried to use popular melodies that hopefully you might recognize.

The exercises are playable on any pitched instrument. There are frequent keyboard and TAB diagrams to help you if you are a keyboard player, guitarist or bass guitarist.

Like learning to read, learning to read music opens up a whole new world of musical discoveries. Persevere, don't give up and soon you will be able to read even difficult music fluently. Good luck!

Pitch
Treble Clef
Bass Clef
Rhythm
Play Along 1
ACC Accidentals
Key Sign
Scales
Chords
Other Chords
Play Along 2
Comp

# Pitch

When you sing or hum a note, you are producing a pitch. If you hum a tune, the pitch goes up and down. If you want to write down the tune, you need a way of showing where the tune goes up and down and by how much.

In music, this information is written on a stave. A stave is a set of five horizontal lines spaced an equal distance apart. The higher up the stave a note is drawn, the higher the pitch of the note when it is played. Writing a note lower down on the stave will produce a lower note.

## Staves

Writing notes on a stave is called staff notation. Most musical instruments are pitched, so use staff notation.

# Staves: Lines

Let's look at the stave in more detail. It is made up of five lines. Notes can be written on these lines or between them. As with the stave, the lines towards the top of the stave represent higher notes, while those nearer the bottom represent lower ones. Each line represents a specific note, so it is important to be able to distinguish between them.

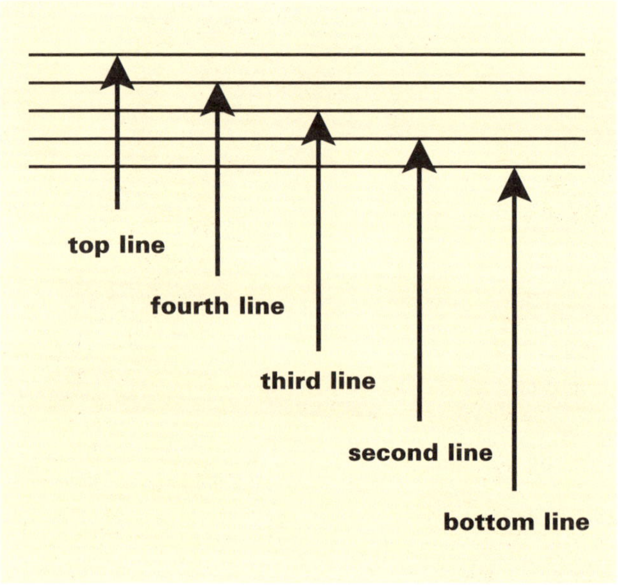

# Staves: Spaces

In between the lines are four spaces. Notes can also be written in these spaces. Again, the higher up the stave the space is, the higher the note it refers to. There are also spaces immediately above the top line and directly below the bottom line.

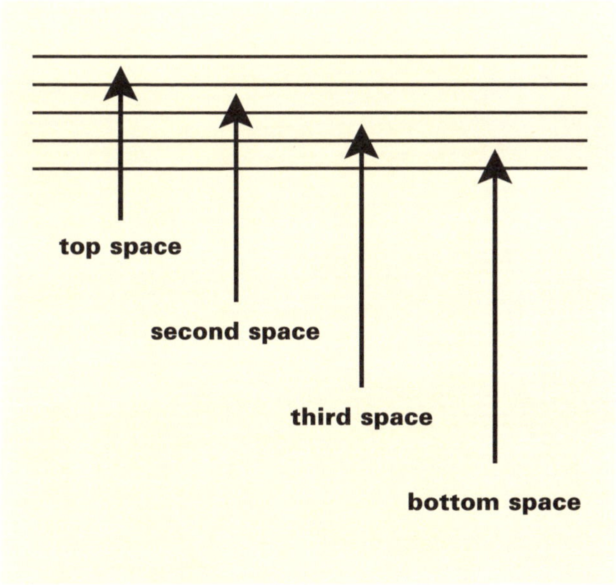

Pitch
Treble Clef
Bass Clef
Rhythm
Play Along 1
ACC Accidentals
Key Sign
Scales
Chords
Other Chords
Play Along 2
Comp

# Treble Clef

Although the lines and spaces represent musical pitches, a musician will not know which exact notes are meant until a clef is drawn on the stave.

A clef is a symbol that is drawn at the left hand side of every stave. Each clef has its own shape and is written at a particular vertical position on the stave.

There are two main clefs: the treble clef and the bass clef. The treble clef is used for higher instruments, whereas the bass clef is used for lower ones. Some instruments, such as the piano, use both.

The treble clef wraps around the second line and very loosely resembles a seahorse.

Common instruments which use this clef include:

- guitar, violin
- flute, recorder, oboe, clarinet, saxophone, trumpet, french horn
- children's voices, female voices, high male voices
- piano, keyboard, organ, bagpipes, tin whistle, xylophone and glockenspiel.

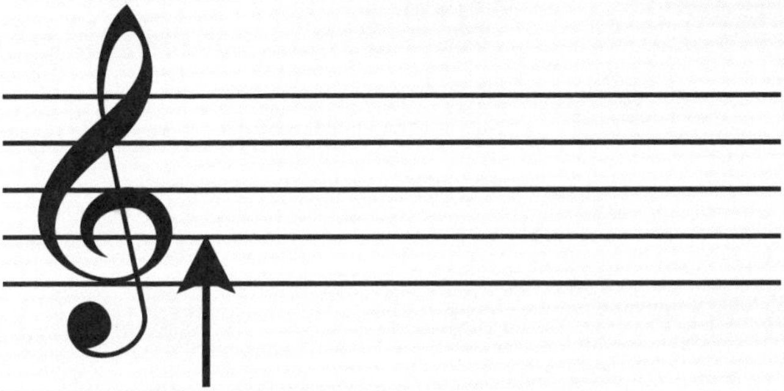

**The treble clef wraps around the second line**

# Bass Clef

The bass clef is used for lower instruments, those which often provide the bass line. The clef, which looks like an ear with two dots behind it, wraps around the fourth line up the stave.

Common instruments which use the bass clef include:

- bass guitar, cello, double bass
- keyboard bass, piano, organ, keyboard
- bassoon, trombone, tuba
- timpani, harp
- low male voices.

Some instruments use both treble and bass clefs:

- piano, keyboard, organ, harp, marimba
- cello, double bass
- french horn.

Some instruments use different clefs, such as the alto and tenor clefs. For a list of these, see page 370 of the Compendium.

**The bass clef has two dots either side of the fourth line**

# Noteheads

To represent a musical pitch, an egg-shaped symbol is drawn on a line or in a space in the stave. This symbol is called a notehead and is either filled-in or hollow. Neither type (filled-in or hollow) affects which note is meant.

Noteheads are the same size as the space in between the lines. To avoid confusion, it is important that, when written by hand, they are carefully positioned exactly in a space or centred on a line.

# Ledger Lines

If a pitch is higher or lower than the notes represented by the stave, extra lines called ledger lines are drawn and the notehead positioned on these in the same way. Ledger lines are the same distance apart as the lines on the stave. You can use any amount of ledger lines, although the more there are, the more difficult the music is to read.

# Noteheads are egg-shaped and come in two types:

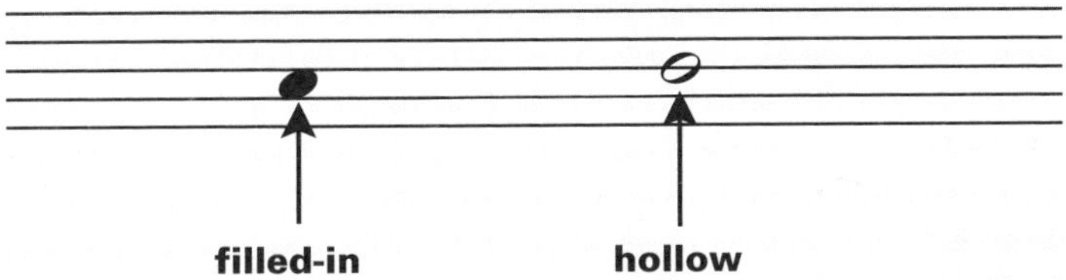


**When they appear on the staff, noteheads are written on a line, in a space or resting above or below a line**

**For notes that are too high or low to be written on the staff, short horizontal lines called ledger lines are used**

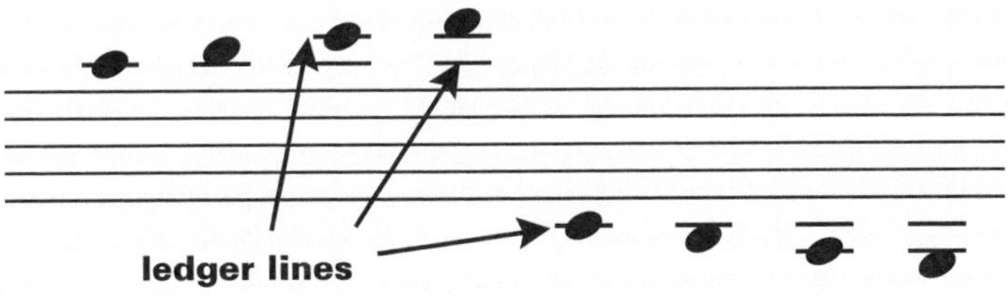

# Middle C

Which exact pitches do the treble and bass clef represent? A very important note in music is middle C. This is the C that is nearest to the middle of a keyboard. On most instruments that use the treble clef, middle C is the lowest C they can play.

Middle C is the lowest C on the violin, flute, oboe and xylophone. On low instruments such as double bass, bass guitar, cello, bassoon and trombone, middle C is normally the highest C the instrument can play easily.

Middle C is also midway between the treble and bass clefs: it is one ledger line below the treble clef and one ledger line above the bass clef.

Finding where middle C is on your instrument is very important as it will enable you to find out the notes of the treble and bass clef.

**Middle C is one ledger line below the treble clef**

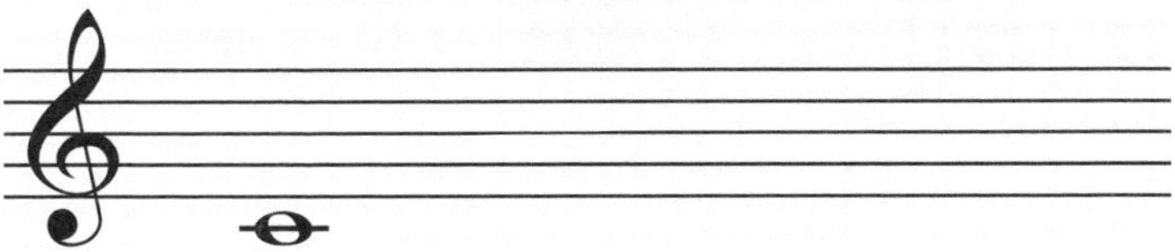

**Middle C is one ledger line above the bass clef**

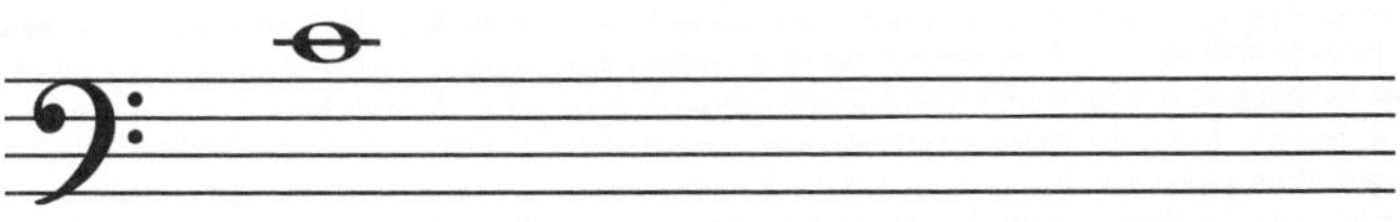

# The Notes of The Treble Clef

The following pages will introduce you to the notes of the treble clef. This section introduces two to five new notes at a time, shows you how to find them on your instrument and tests you on them through exercises where you fill in missing letters in words, write out notes on a stave or find words in a musical 'notesquare'. Two memorable phrases, or mnemonics, are given here to help you: '**FACE**' and '**E**very **G**ood **B**oy **D**eserves **F**ootball'. Learn these by heart and refer to them when you are stuck.

Next there is a series of short melodies based on three, five and eight notes designed to familiarize you with the different areas of the treble clef. Some of the notes covered here may be too low or high for your instrument, so just pick the exercises that apply to you.

Towards the end of the section, there are exercises based on ledger line notes below and above the stave. Again, these may be too low or high for your instrument, so just pick the exercises relevant to you.

# The Space Notes (FACE)

## The space notes of the treble clef

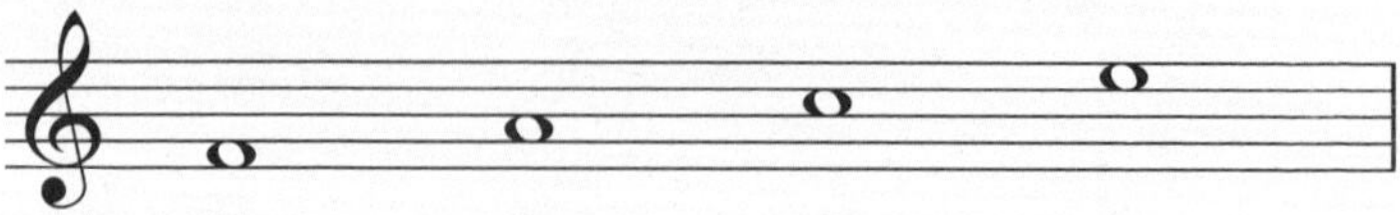

**F** (bottom space) **A** (second space) **C** (third space) **E** (top space)

## Finding FACE on your instrument

**First find middle C**

**Then find:**

the first F above middle C | the first A above middle C | the next C above middle C | the second E above middle C

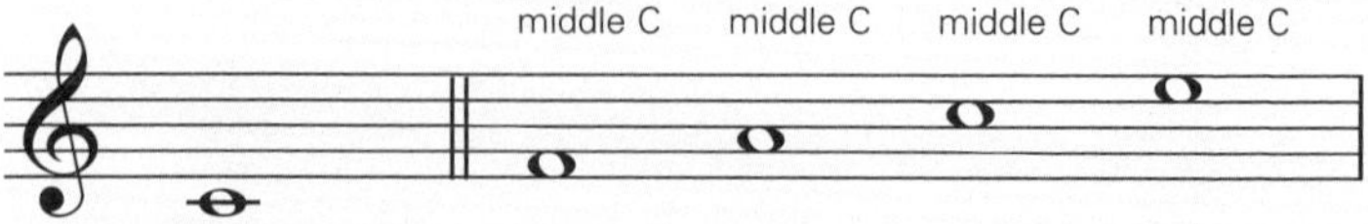

**middle C** **F** **A** **C** **E**

**Each note is higher than the previous one**

## FACE on a keyboard

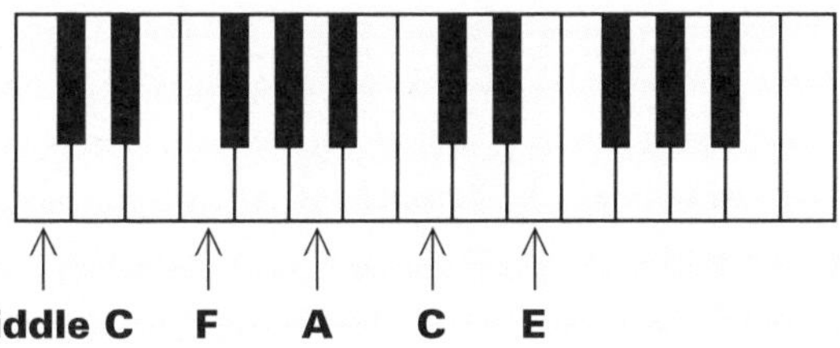


## FACE on a guitar (standard tuning)

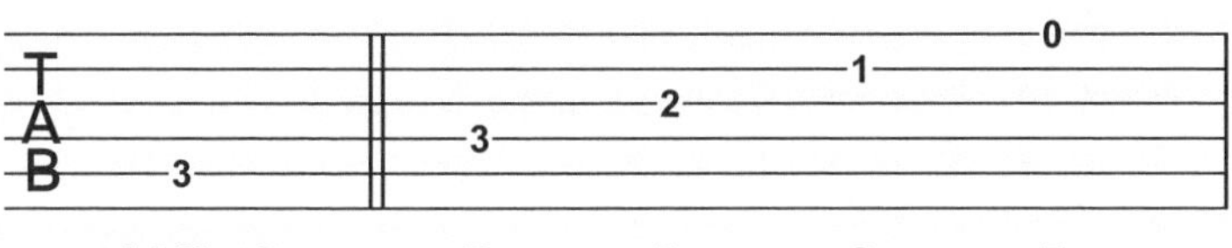

# Space Notes (FACE):
## EXERCISE 1

### Fill in the missing letters using the given notes

Example

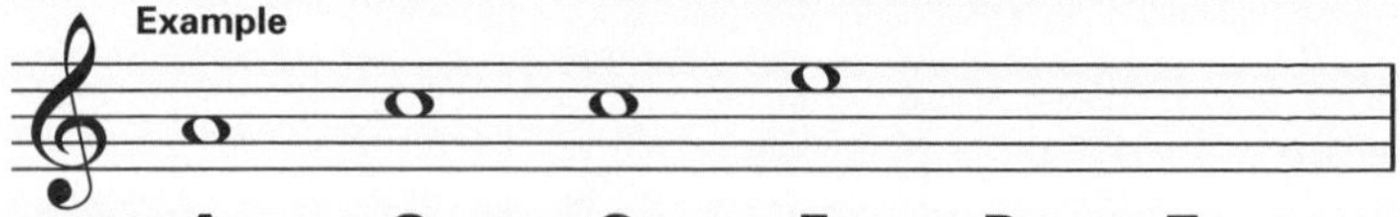

A <u>C</u> <u>C</u> <u>E</u> P T

_ R _ _ M

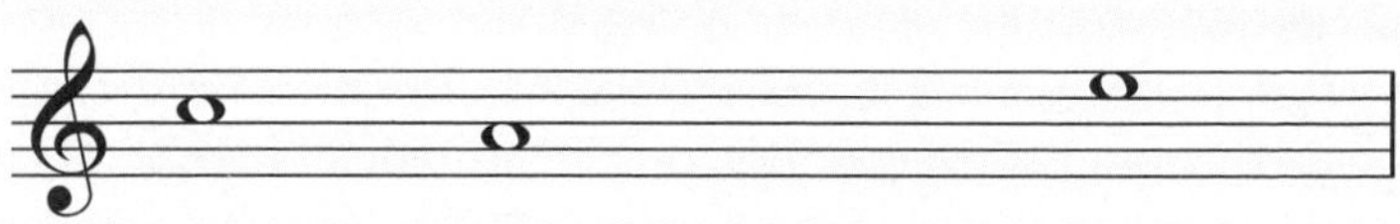

_ _ K _

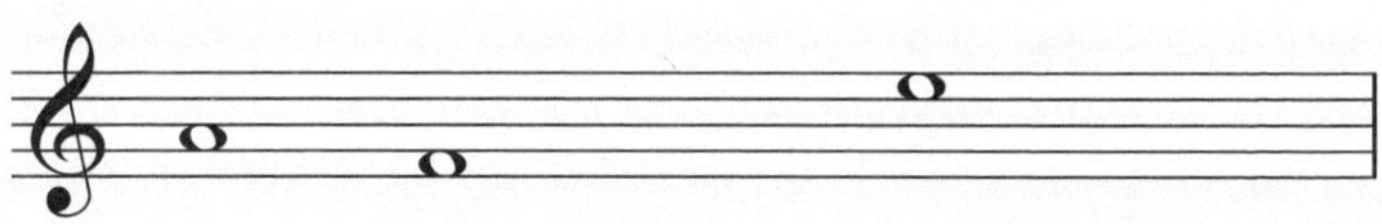

_ _ T _ R

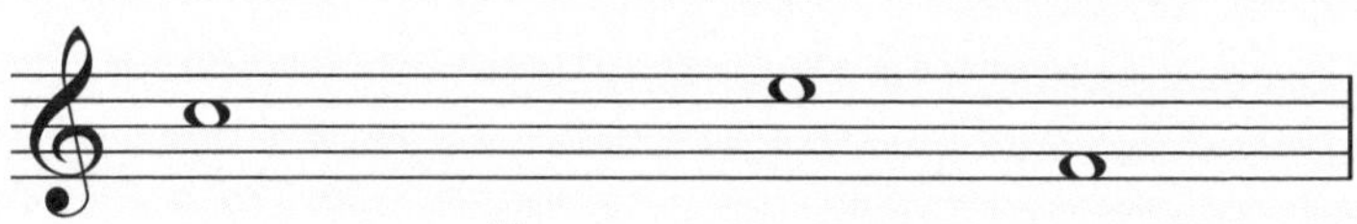

_ H _ _

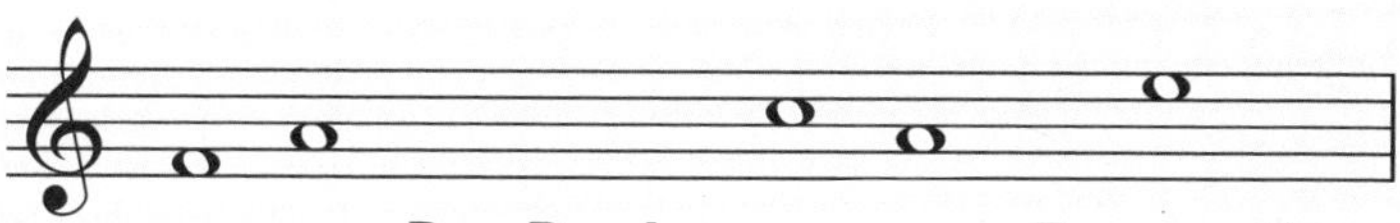

_ _ B R I _ _ T _ S

M _ G N I _ I _ _ N T

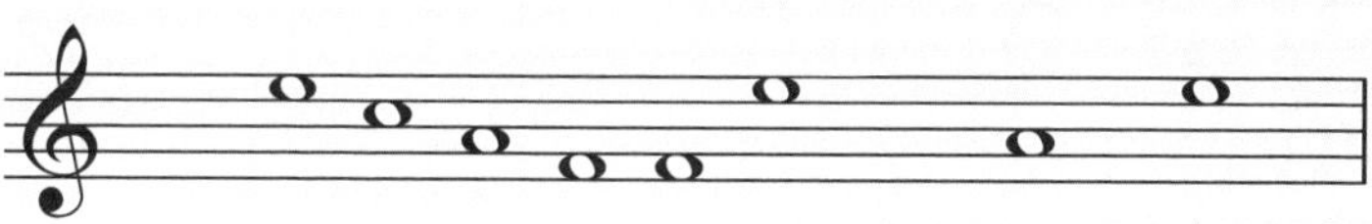

D _ _ _ _ _ _ I N _ T _ D

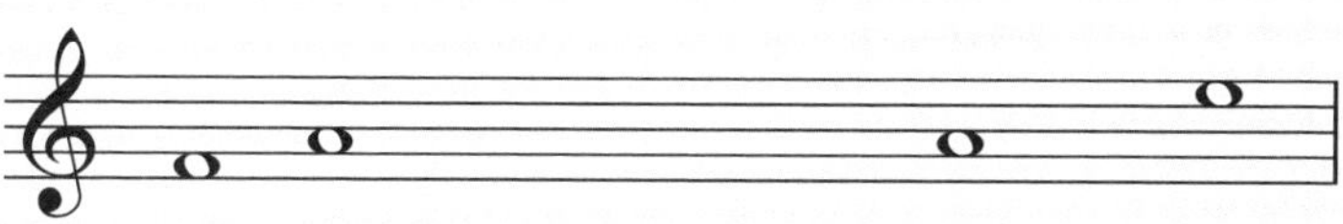

_ _ I R T R _ D _

_ O _ _ _ _

# Space Notes (FACE):
## EXERCISE 2

### Write the boxed letters as space notes on the staves

Example

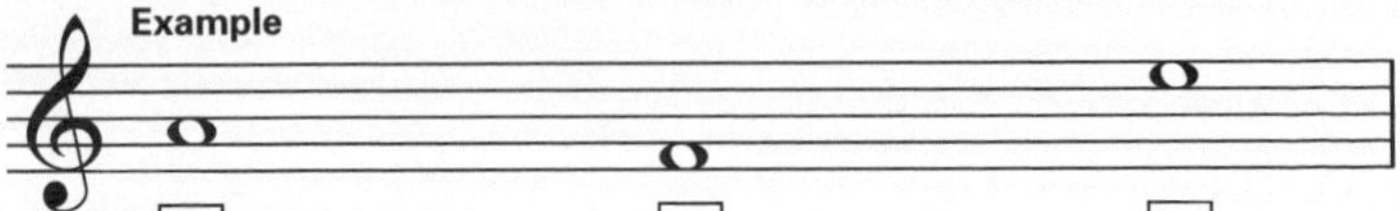

[A] L [F] I [E]

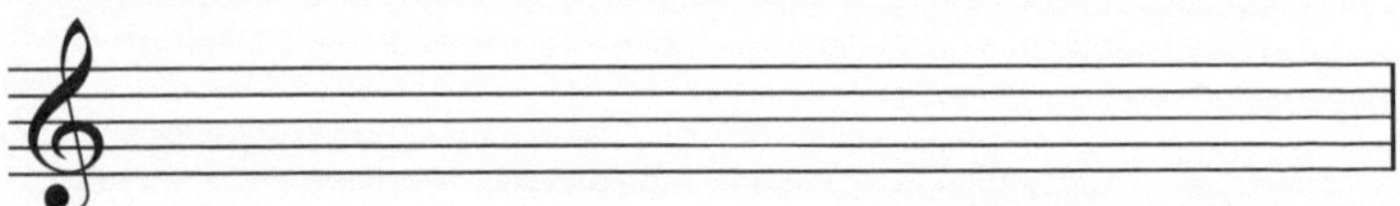

[C] R [A] V [E] S

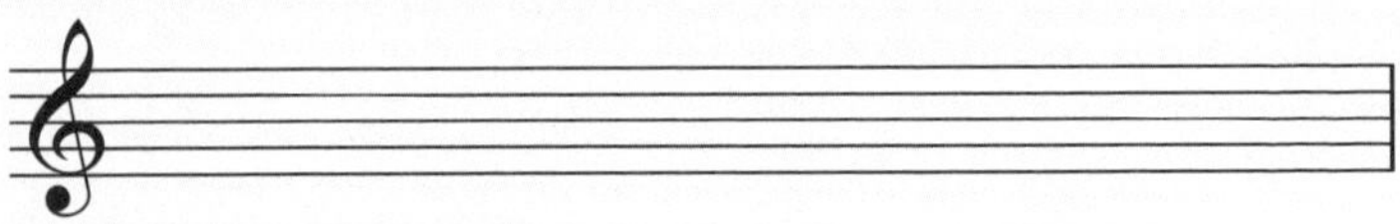

B [E] [E] [F]

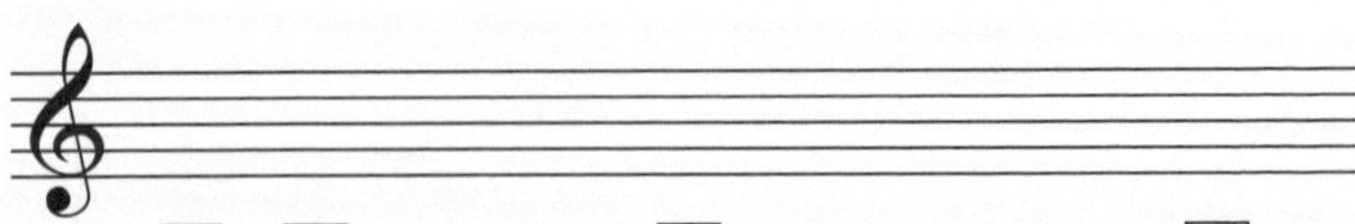

[C] [A] S S [E] R O L [E]

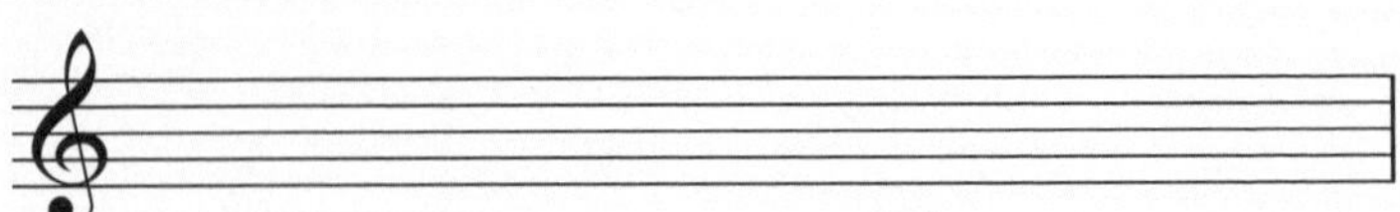

N [E] [C] [E] S S I T [A] T I N G

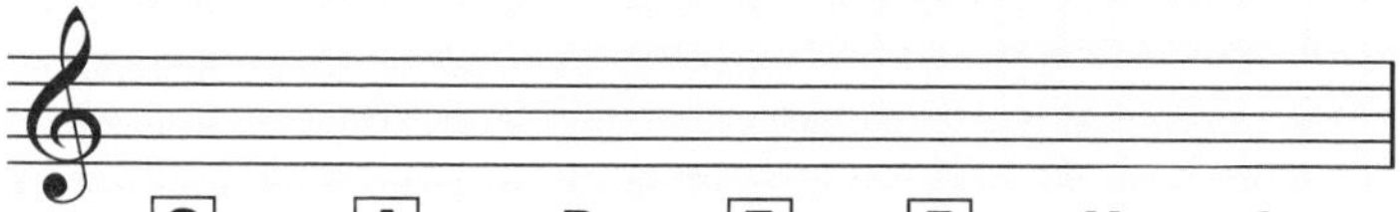

[C] [A] R [E] [F] U L

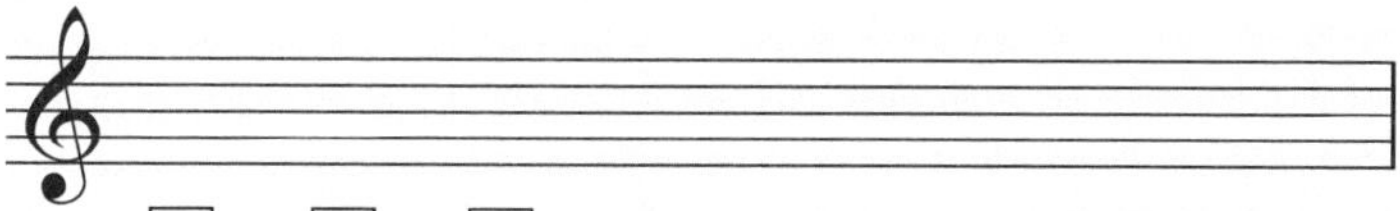

[F] [E] [A] S T I N G

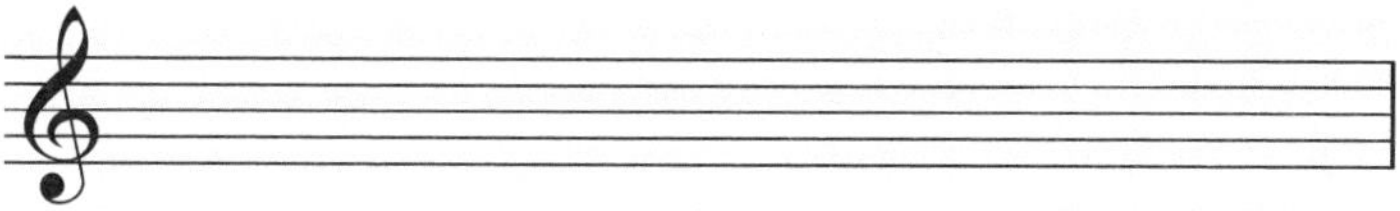

[E] S P [E] [C] I [A] L L Y

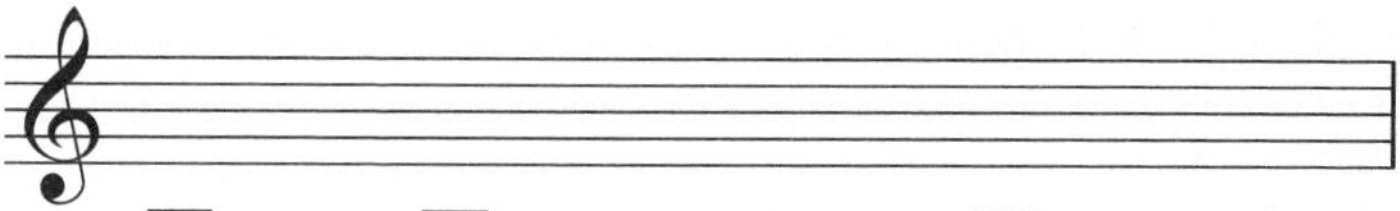

[A] [F] T [E] R

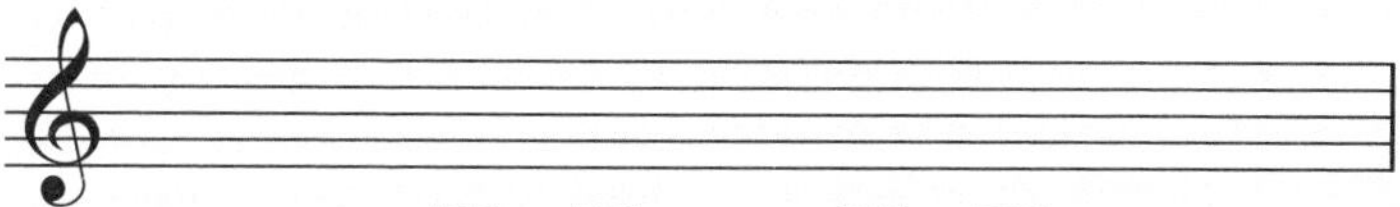

B R [E] [A] K [F] [A] S T

# D Below and G Above The Stave

## D below the treble clef and G above the treble clef

## Finding the same D and G on your instrument

**First find middle C**

**Then find:**

the first D above middle C

the FACE notes

the second G above middle C

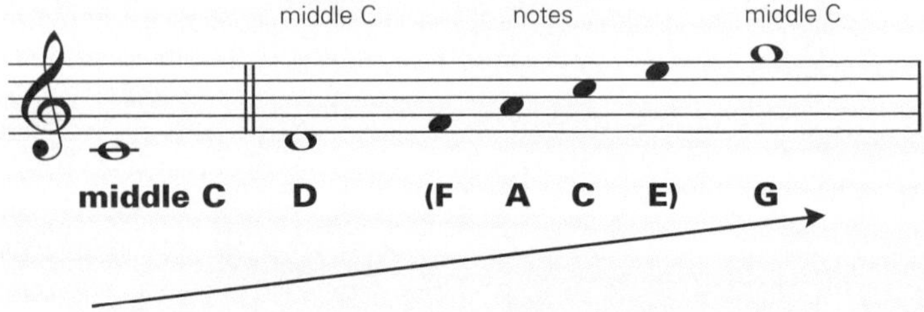


**Each note is higher than the previous one**

## D and G on a keyboard

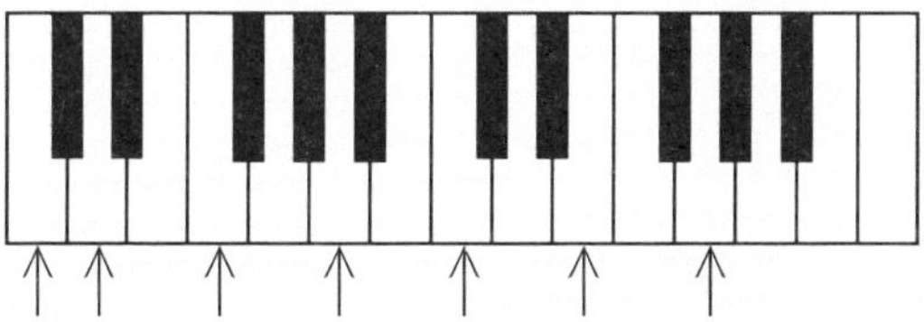


## D and G on a guitar (standard tuning)

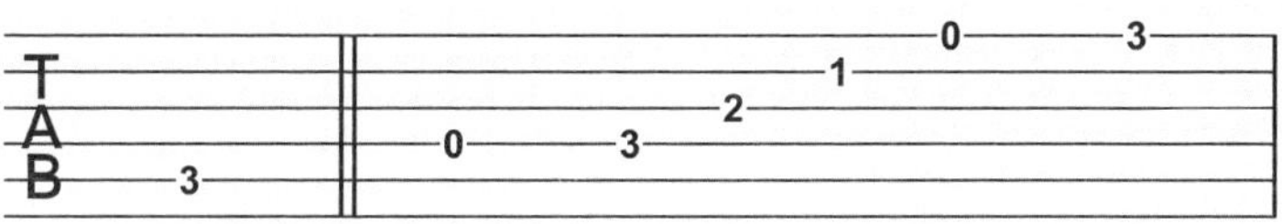

# D Below and G Above The Stave: EXERCISE 1

## Fill in the missing letters using the given notes

Example

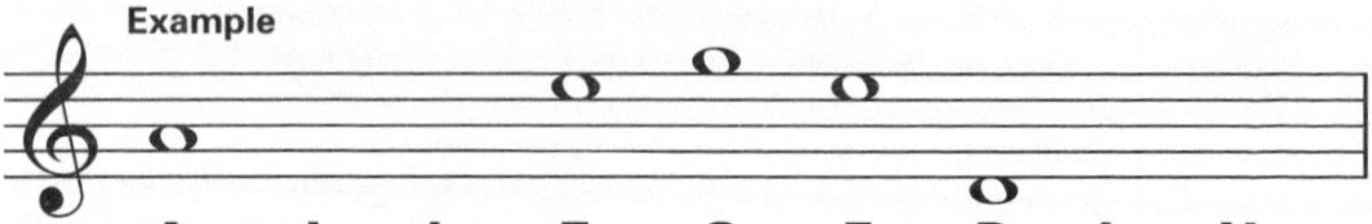

A L L E G E D L Y

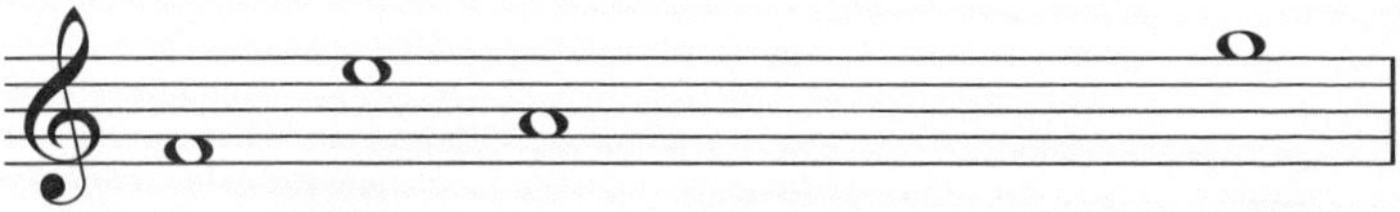

_ _ _ R I N _

_ R M _ _ _ _ _ O N

_ _ R _ I _ L _

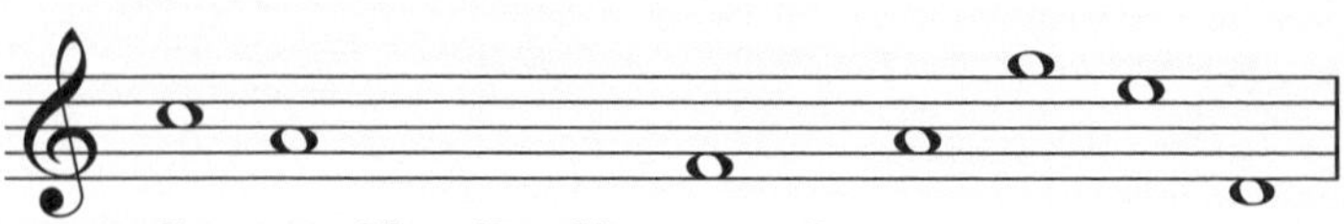

C _ M O U _ L _ _ _ _

M _ _ _ _ ’ S

_ I S _ R _ _ _ _ U L L Y

_ _ _ _ _ _ _ _

_ _ R _ _ N

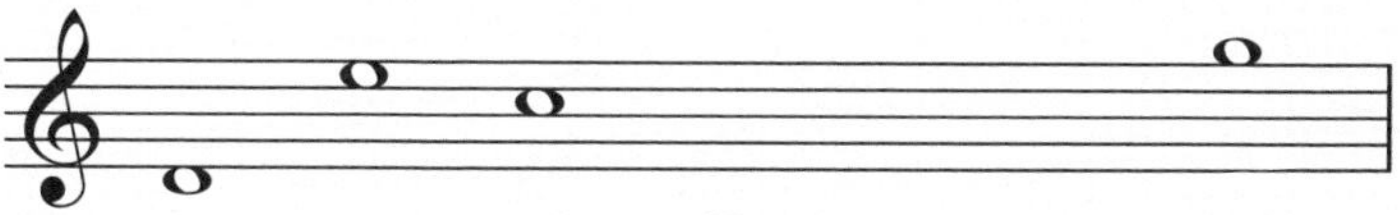

_ _ _ K I N _

# D Below and G Above The Stave: EXERCISE 2

## Write the boxed letters as space notes on the staves

Example

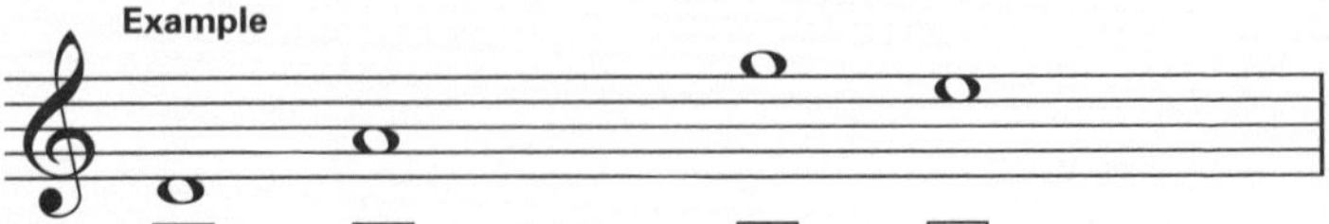

[D] [A] N [G] [E] R

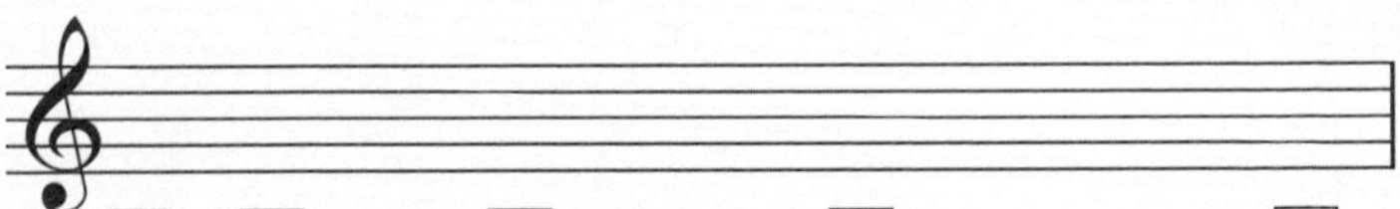

[C] [E] L [E] B R [A] T I N [G]

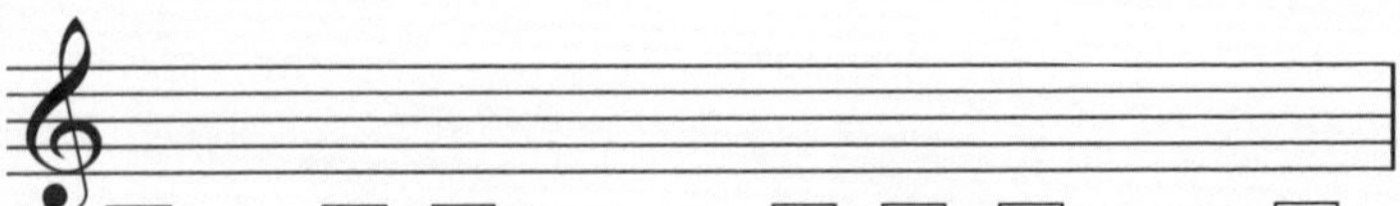

[C] H [E] [E] R L [E] [A] [D] I N [G]

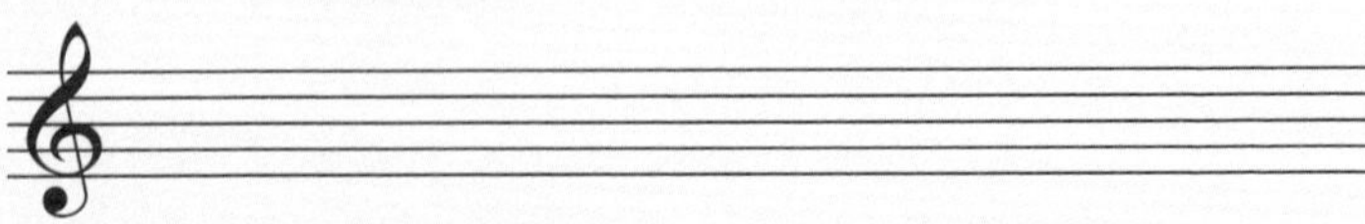

[D] I S [C] O U R [A] [G] [E] S

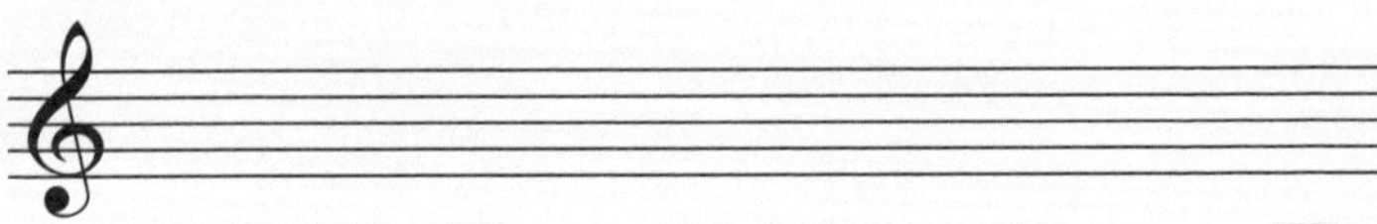

B R [E] [A] K [D] [A] N [C] I N [G]

A F F E C T I N G

D E R A N G E D

T E E N A G E D

R A G A M U F F I N S

D I S G R A C E F U L L Y

Pitch
Treble Clef
Bass Clef
Rhythm
Play Along 1
ACC Accidentals
Key Sign
Scales
Chords
Other Chords
Play Along 2
Comp

Pitch
Treble Clef
Bass Clef
Rhythm
Play Along 1
ACC Accidentals
Key Sign
Scales
Chords
Other Chords
Play Along 2
Comp

# The Line Notes (EGBDF)

## The line notes of the treble clef

| | | | | |
|---|---|---|---|---|
| **E**very<br>(bottom line) | **G**ood<br>(2nd line) | **B**oy<br>(3rd line) | **D**eserves<br>(4th line) | **F**ootball<br>(top line) |

## Finding EGBDF on your instrument

| | | | | | |
|---|---|---|---|---|---|
| **First find middle C** | **Then find:**<br>the first E above middle C | the first G above middle C | the first B above middle C | the second D above middle C | the second F above middle C |

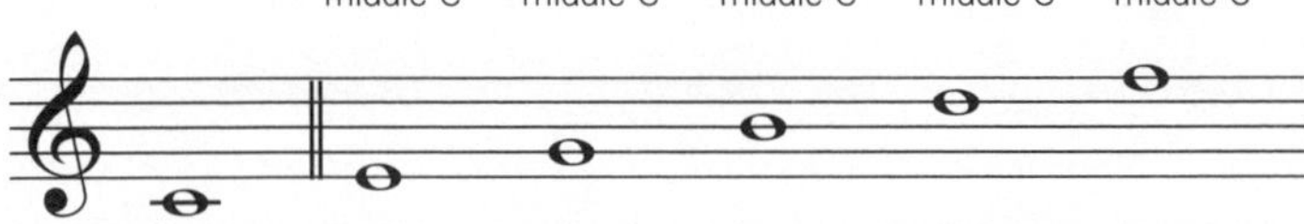

| | | | | | |
|---|---|---|---|---|---|
| **middle C** | **E**very | **G**ood | **B**oy | **D**eserves | **F**ootball |

**Each note is higher than the previous one**

## EGBDF on a keyboard

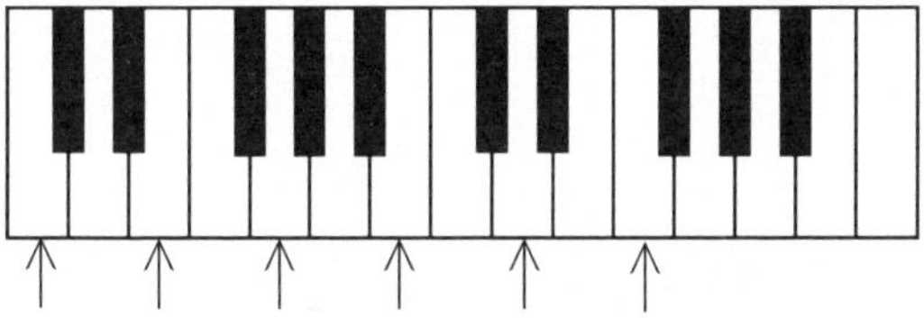

**middle C** **E**very **G**ood **B**oy **D**eserves **F**ootball

## EGBDF on a guitar (standard tuning)

**middle C** **E**very **G**ood **B**oy **D**eserves **F**ootball

# Line Notes (EGBDF):
## EXERCISE 1

### Fill in the missing letters using the given notes

**Example**

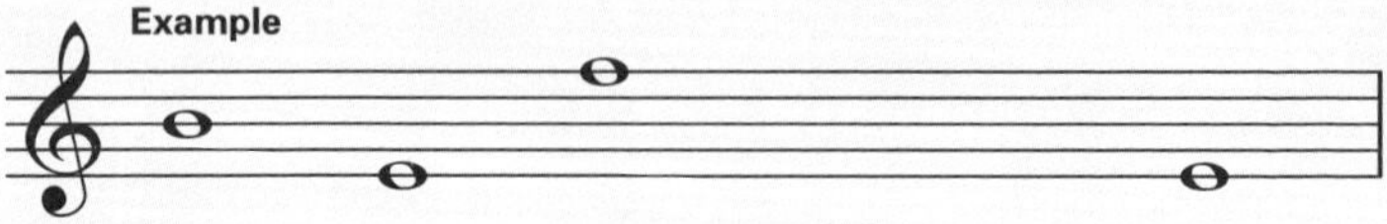

B E F O R E

_ _ _ _ I N _

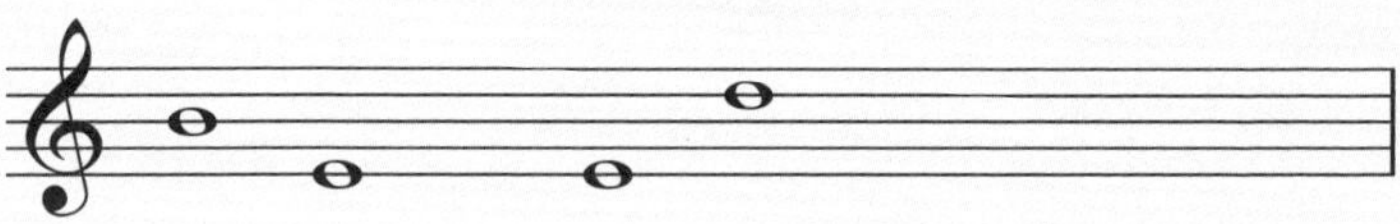

_ _ N _ _ I C T ’ S

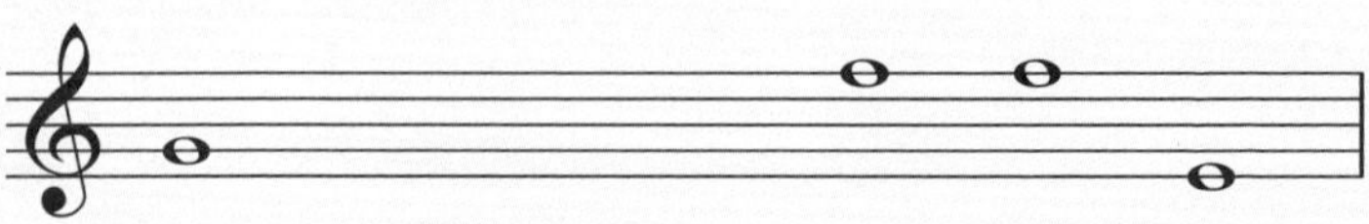

_ I R A _ _ _

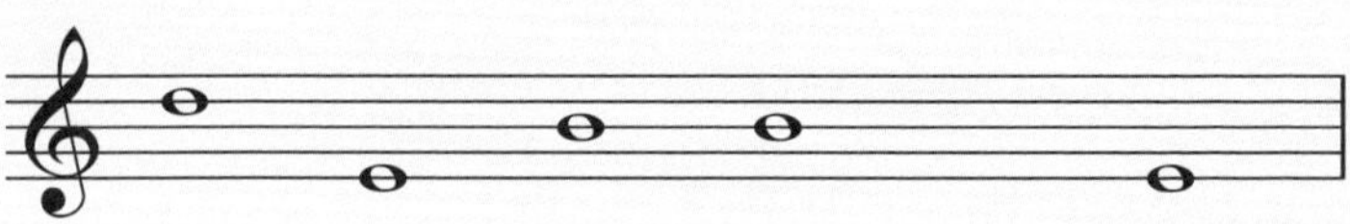

_ _ _ _ I _

_ _ _ R U _ _ I N _ L Y

_ R _ _ _

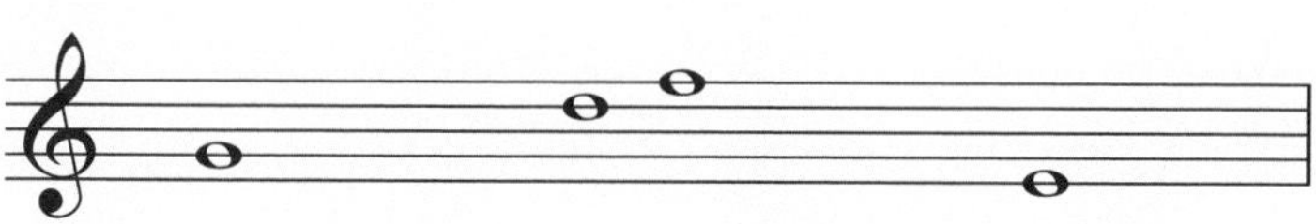

_ R A N _ _ A T H _ R ' S

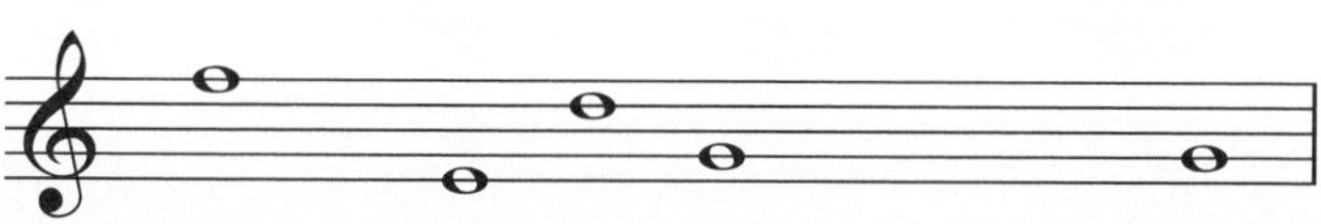

_ L _ _ _ L I N _

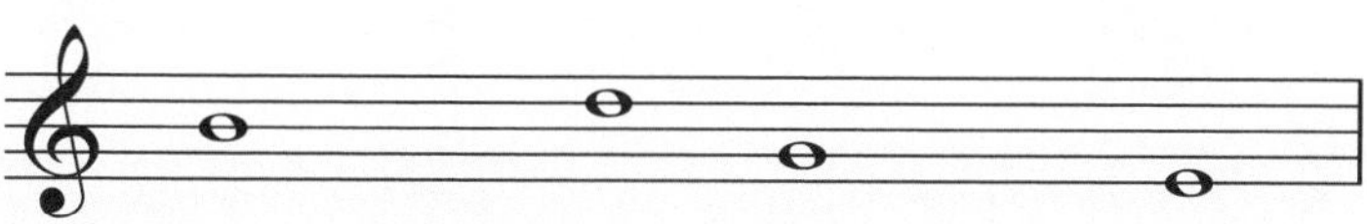

_ U _ _ I _

# Line Notes (EGBDF):
## EXERCISE 2

### Write the boxed letters as line notes on the staves

Example

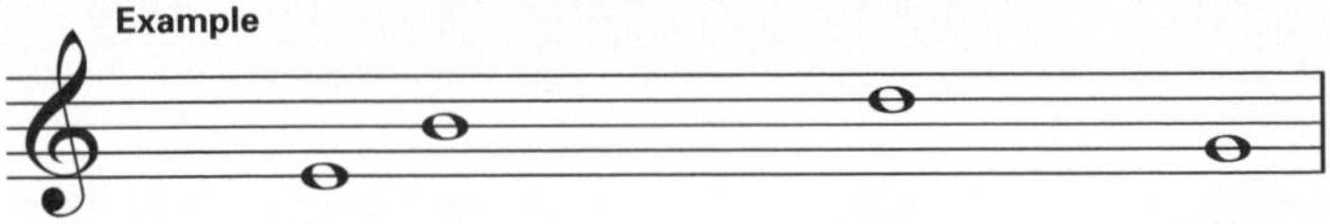

R **E** **B** U I L **D** I N **G**

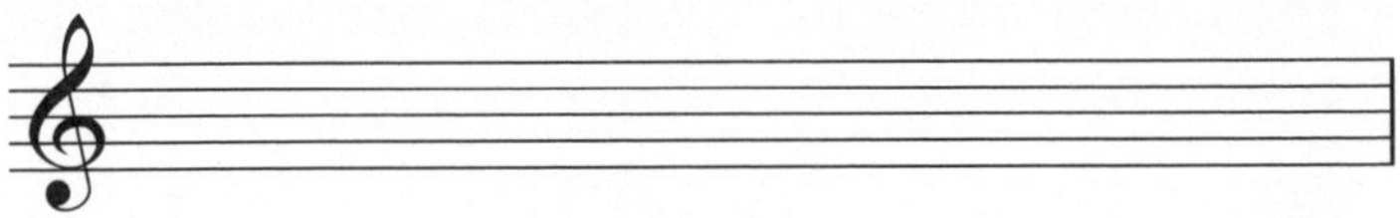

L O A **D** **B** **E** A R I N **G**

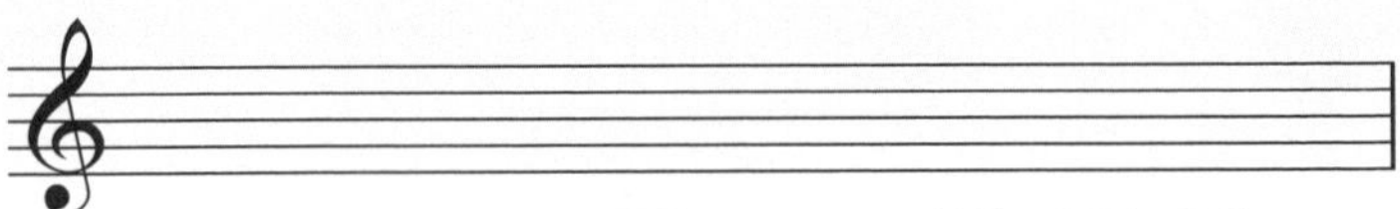

**F** O O T **B** R I **D** **G** **E** S

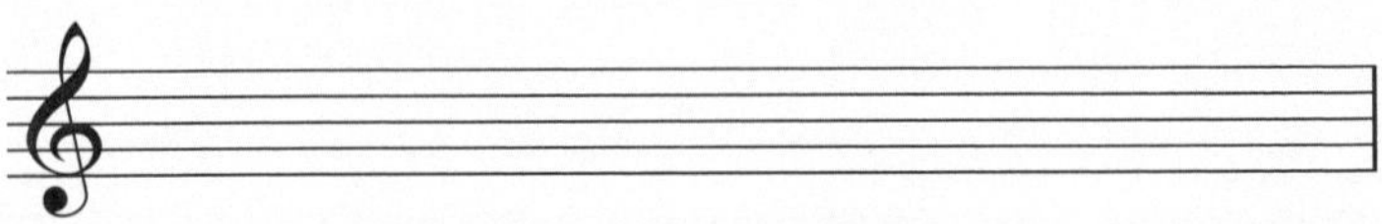

**E** N **G** **E** N **D** **E** R S

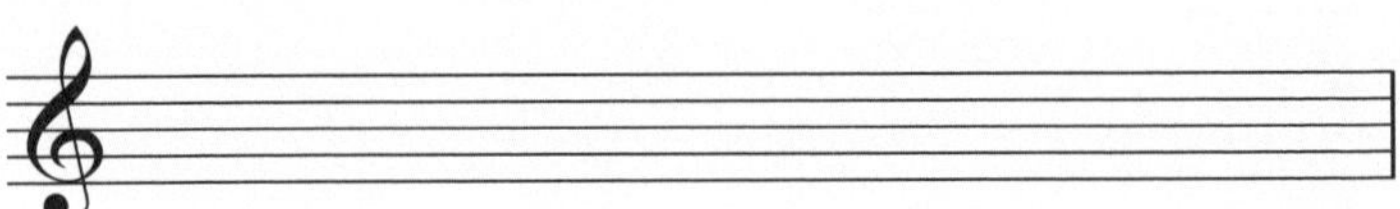

**B** **E** **F** R I **E** N **D** I N **G**

A F F A B L E

D E S I G N E R S

G A B B L E D

G O D F R E Y

B A F F L I N G L Y

# C Below and A Above The Stave

## C below the treble clef and A above the treble clef

## Finding the same C and A on your instrument

**This C is middle C**

**Then find:**

the 'Every Good Boy Deserves Football' notes above middle C

the second A above middle C

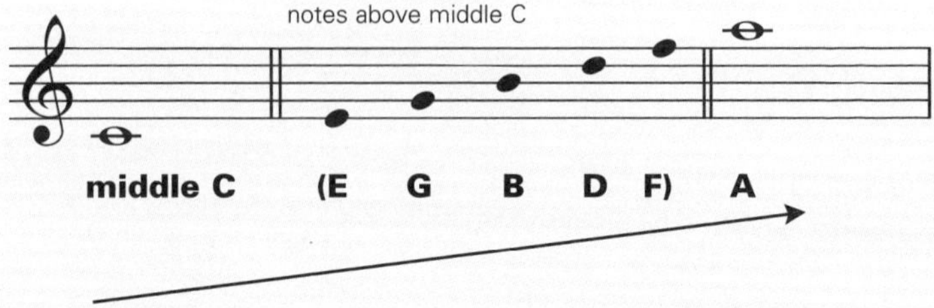


**Each note is higher than the previous one**

# C and A on a keyboard

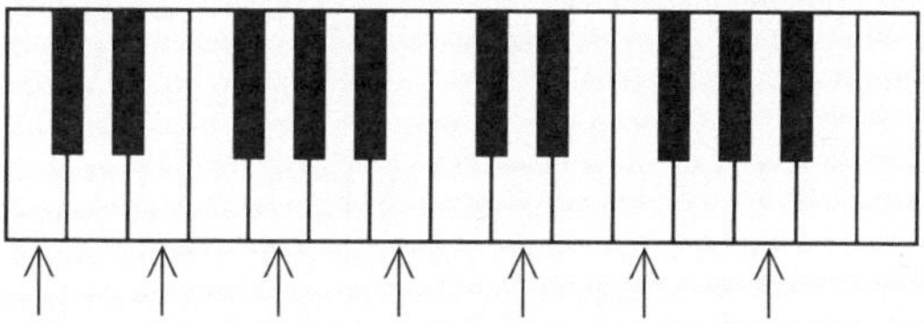

**middle C (E G B D F) A**

# C and A on a guitar (standard tuning)

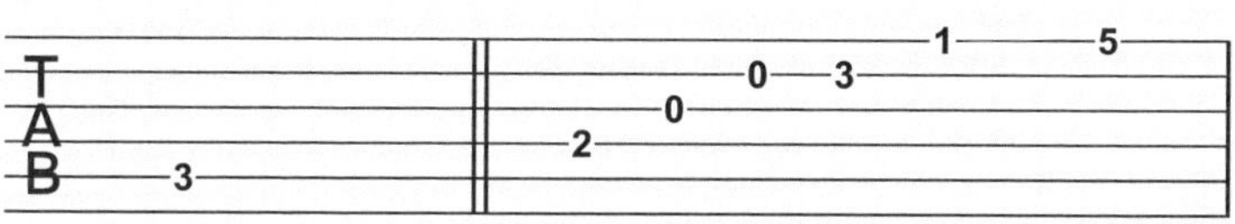


**middle C (E G B D F) A**

# C Below and A Above The Stave: EXERCISE 1

## Fill in the missing letters using the given notes

Example

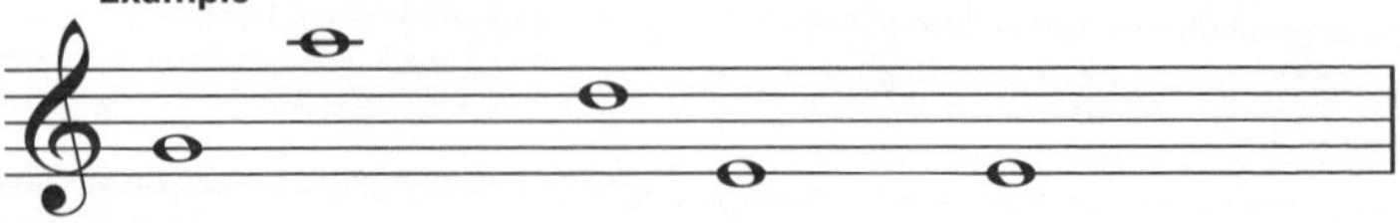

G A R D E N E R S !

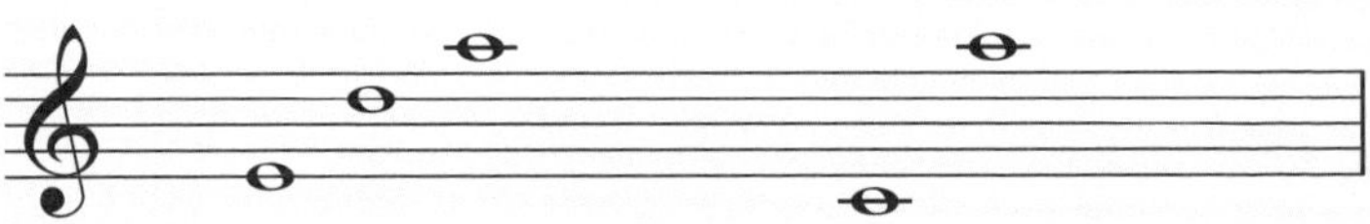

P _ _ _ N T I _ _ L L Y

_ L _ _ N I N _

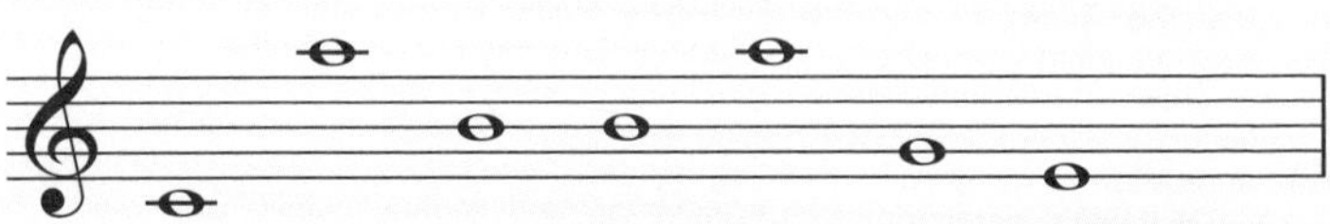

_ _ _ _ _ _ _ S

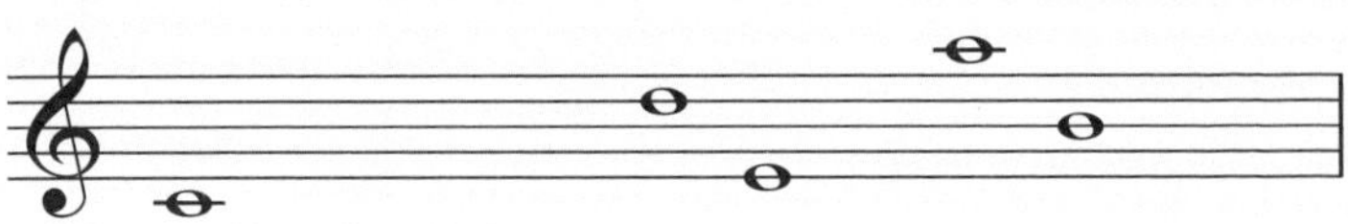

_ O N S I _ _ R _ _ L Y

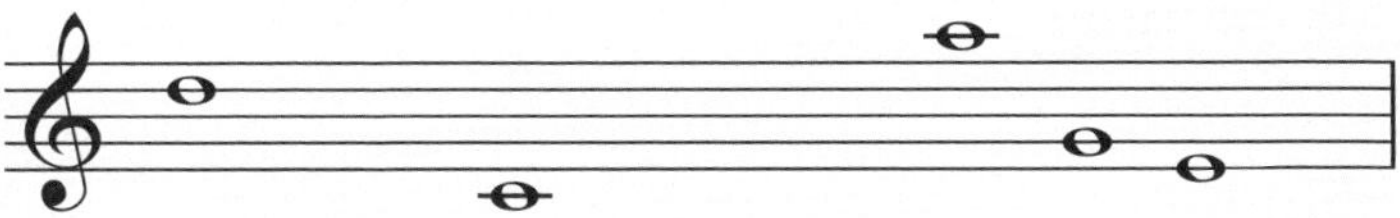

_ I S _ O U R _ _ _ S

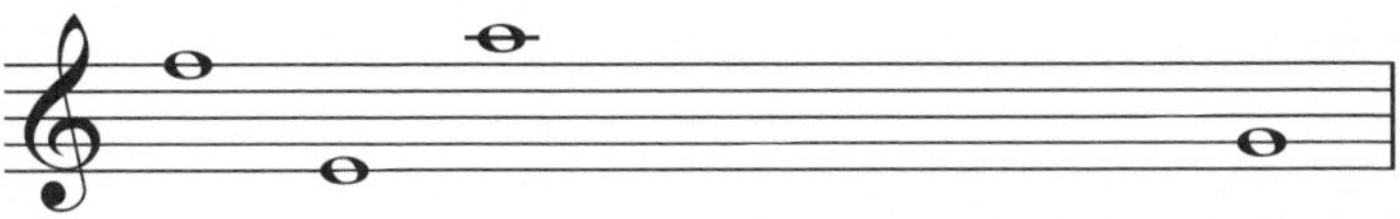

_ _ _ S T I N _

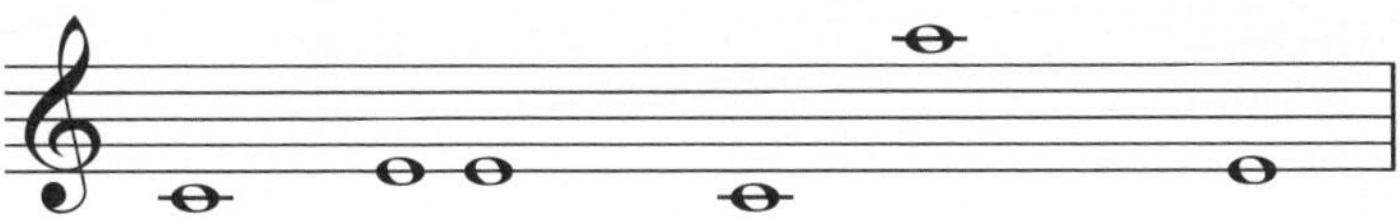

_ R _ _ P Y - _ R _ W L I _ S

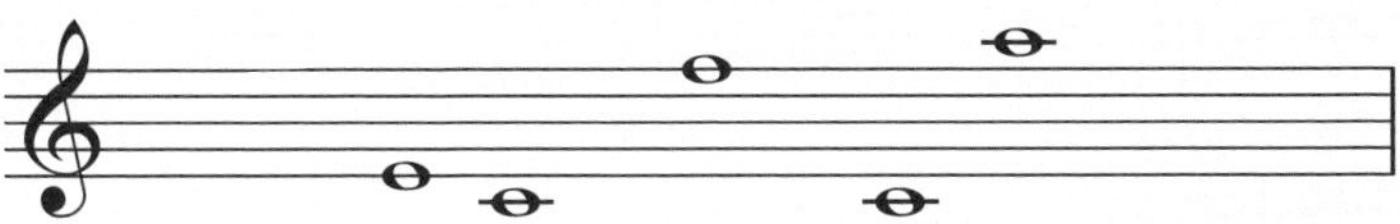

S P _ _ I _ I _ _ L L Y

_ L _ _ K _ L I _ S

Pitch
Treble Clef
Bass Clef
Rhythm
Play Along 1
ACC Accidentals
Key Sign
Scales
Chords
Other Chords
Play Along 2
Comp

# C Below and A Above The Stave: EXERCISE 2

## Write the boxed letters as notes on the staves

Example

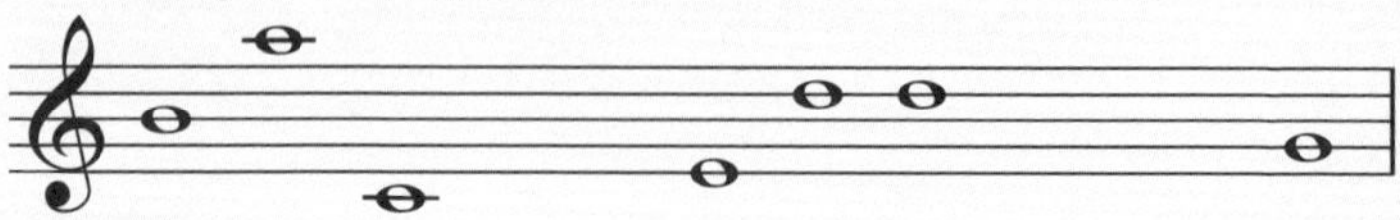

[B] [A] [C] K P [E] [D] [D] L I N [G]

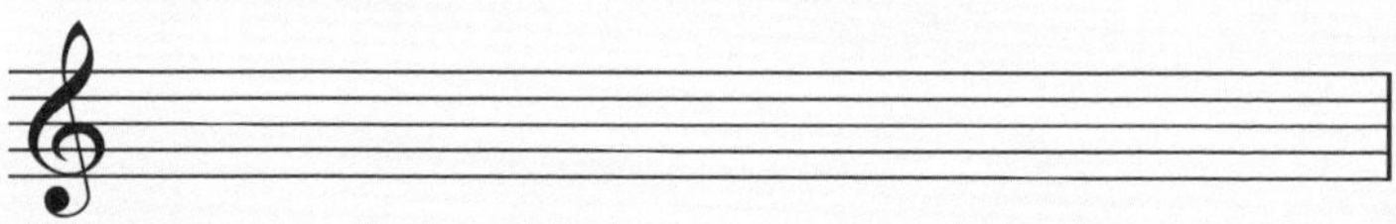

[F] R [A] N T I [C] [A] L L Y

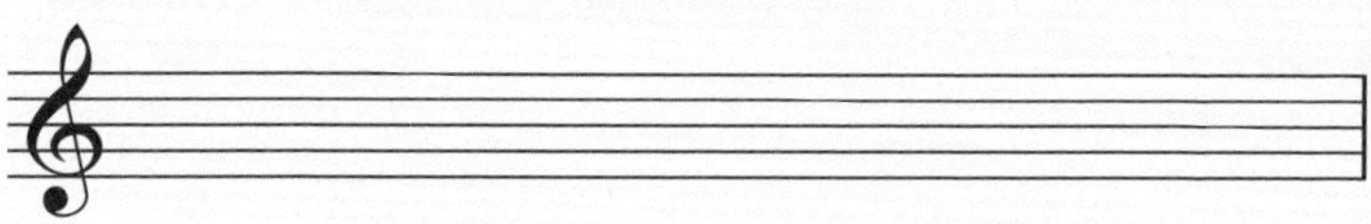

[F] R [A] N [C] [E] S [C] [A]

[A] [C] [C] [E] P T [E] [D]

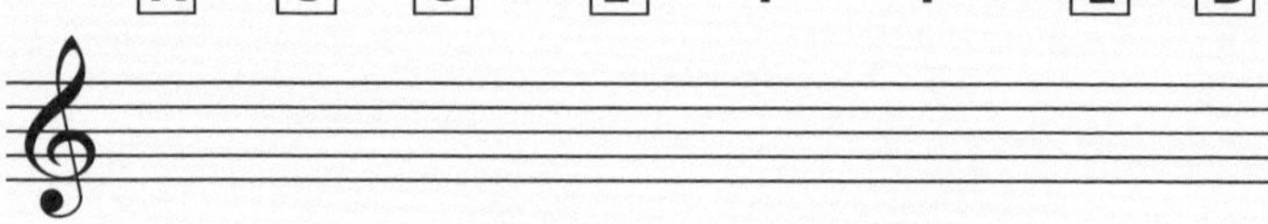

[D] [E] [C] L [A] N ' S

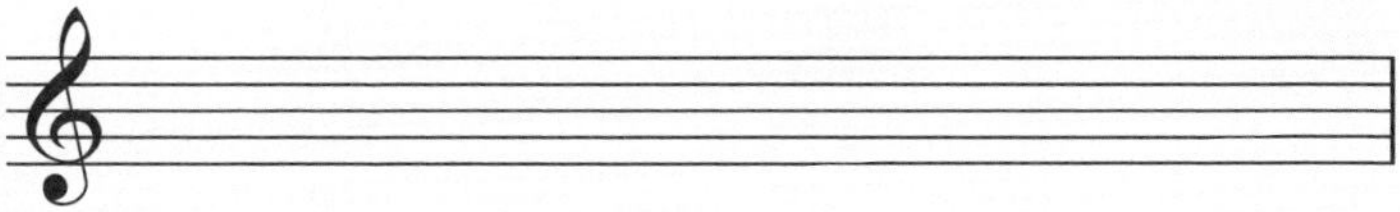

D R E A D F U L

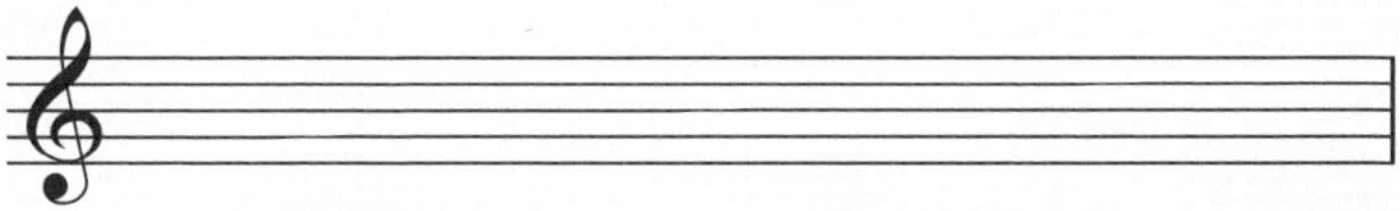

C E L E B R I T Y

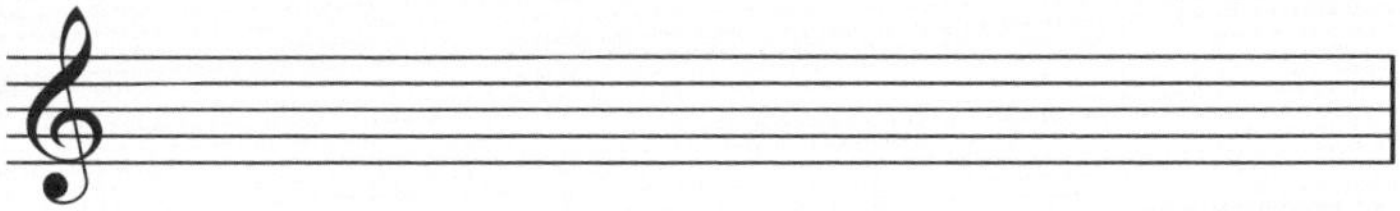

C H A L L E N G E

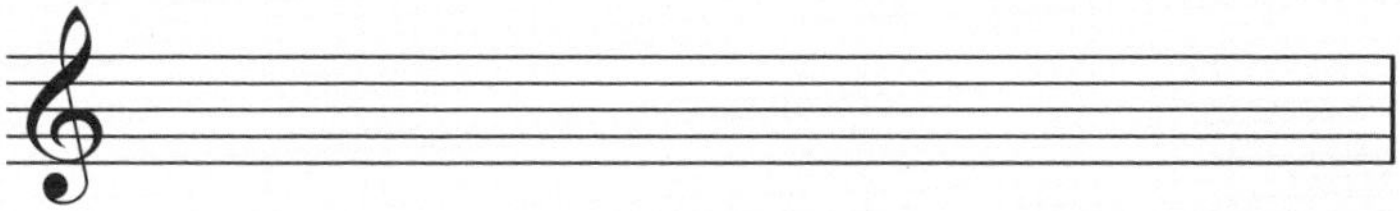

R E - E N A C T I N G

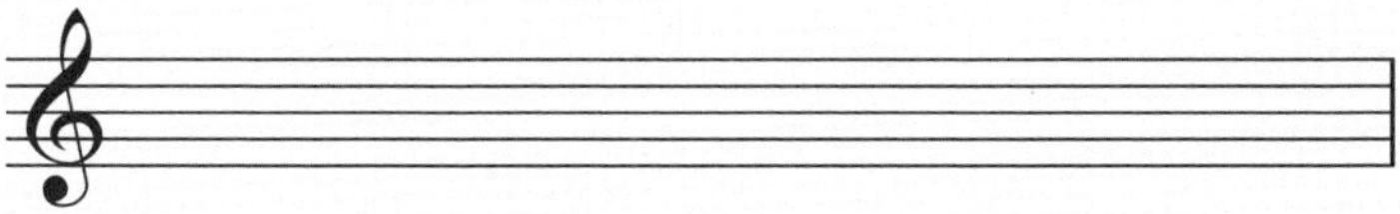

B L A C K A D D E R

# Putting Space and Line Notes Together

Since the space notes and line notes alternate on the stave, when they are both put together, they interlock neatly to form a scale of C major. A scale is a series of notes in which each note is a step above the one before. When they are all played one after another from lowest to highest, they form a smooth rising pattern that repeats every seven notes. The notes of a scale can be used to make tunes and chords.

The notes of C major contain just the white notes on a keyboard. None of the notes of C major have accidentals – broadly speaking, the black notes of the piano – which makes it an ideal scale to start off with when you are first learning music.

Different types of scales and accidentals will be explored later in the book.

# How line notes and space notes fit together

These are the notes of C major

Pitch
Treble Clef
Bass Clef
Rhythm
Play Along 1
ACC Accidentals
Key Sign
Scales
Chords
Other Chords
Play Along 2
Comp

# Octaves

By now, you will probably have noticed that some notes appear more than once on the stave. The note E, for instance, appears on the bottom line but also on the top space. Why is this?

If you play a scale from the lowest note on your instrument to the highest, you will find that each note reappears at regular intervals. On a full-sized piano, for instance, the note A can be found at eight different places on the keyboard. The distance between two successive notes of the same name is called an octave.

In the treble clef, you have so far looked at the notes of two octaves. Try to remember whereabouts on your instrument the two versions of each note occur: where is the lower C and where is the higher C? Generally speaking, notes below the middle of the stave will be low down on your instrument while notes above the middle of the stave will be in its middle or high register.

# Octaves

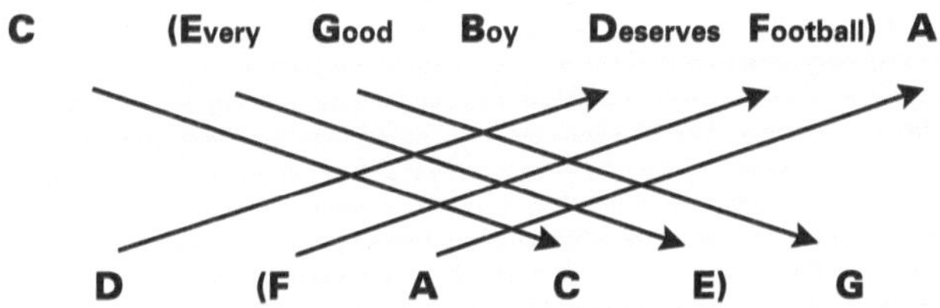

**These notes reappear further up the stave**

**Each of these pairs of notes contain an octave**

# Finding C–A On Your Instrument

When the space notes and line notes are put together, they form a continuous scale on the white notes leading up from middle C to the second A above middle C. To play them on your instrument, first find middle C, then go up a step at a time keeping to the notes of the C major scale.

Make sure you are aware of the difference between notes with the same name in different octaves. For instance, compare how you would play the E on the bottom line of the stave and the E on the top space.

## Finding C–A on your instrument

**middle C D E F G A B C D E F G A**

## The same notes on a keyboard

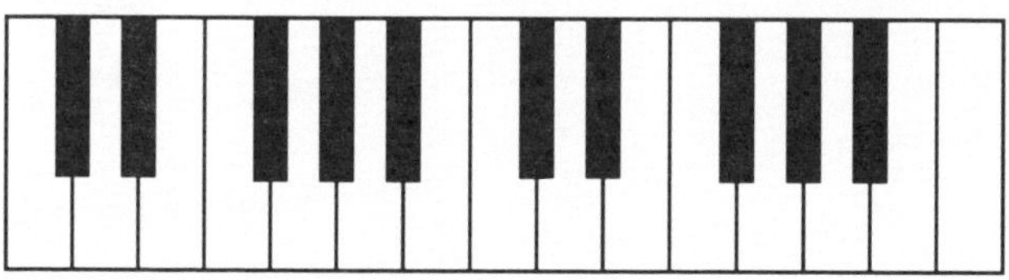

**middle C D E F G A B C D E F G A**

## The same notes on a guitar (standard tuning)

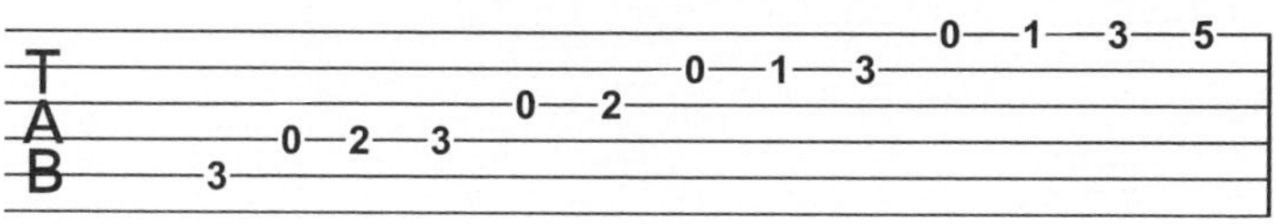


**middle C D E F G A B C D E F G A**

# Treble Clef: Exercises on C–G

These exercises use the notes C–G. For each exercise, first say all the notes names. Then say and play (or sing) each note in turn. Finally, play all the notes through without saying them.

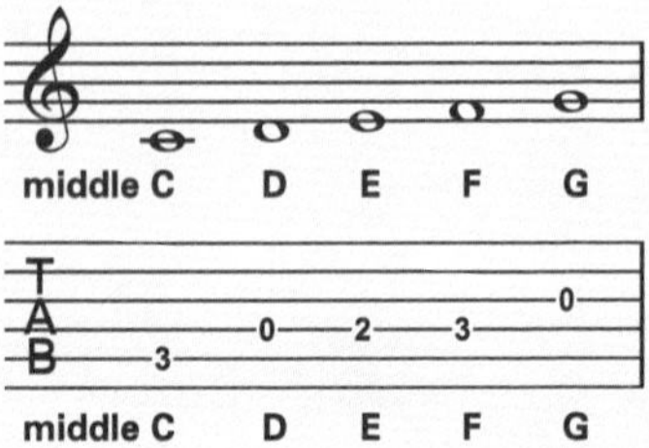


No. 1

No. 2

No. 3

No. 4

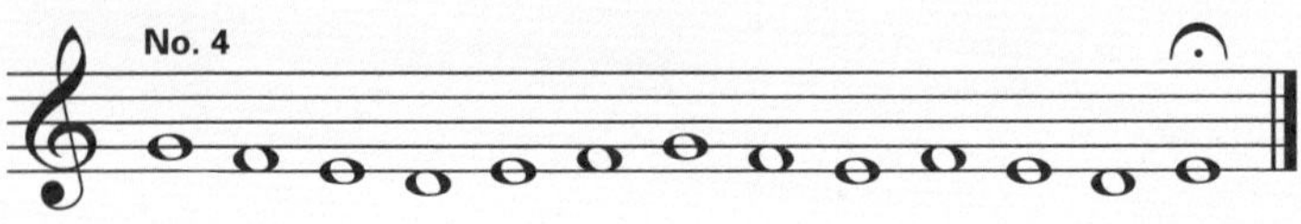

**No.5**

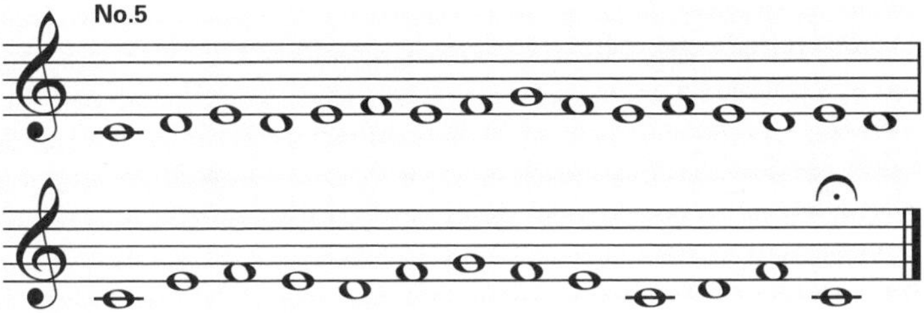

**No.6**

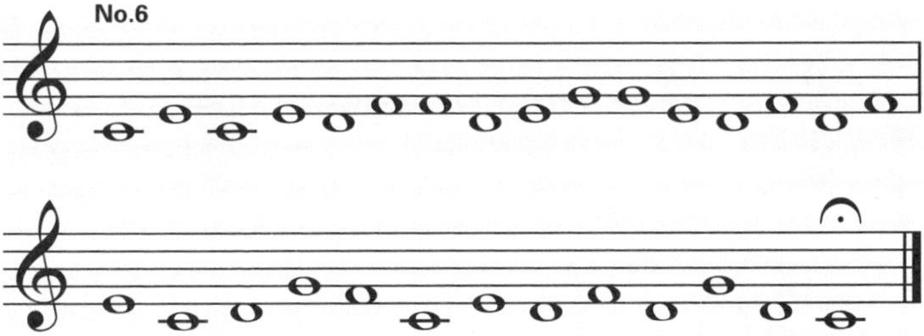

**No.7**

# Exercises on G–D

## These exercises use the notes G–D

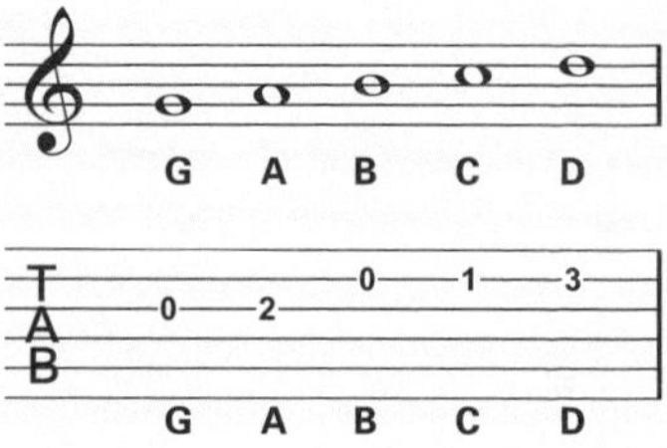


No. 1

No. 2

No. 3

No. 4

No. 5

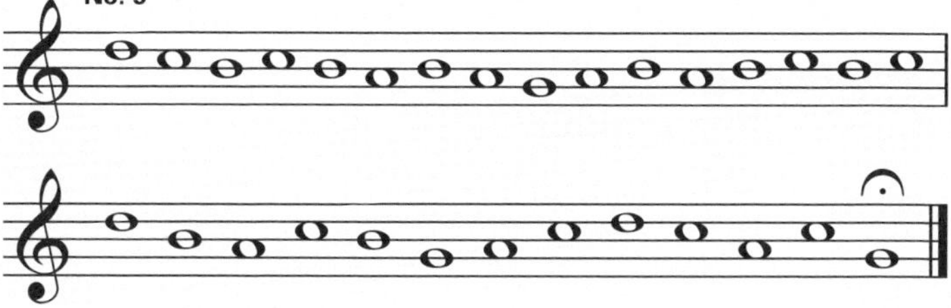

No. 6

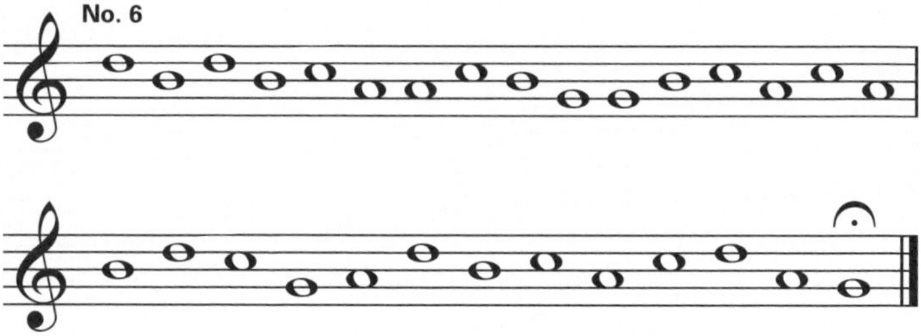

No. 7

# Exercises on D–A

**These exercises use the notes D–A**

No. 1

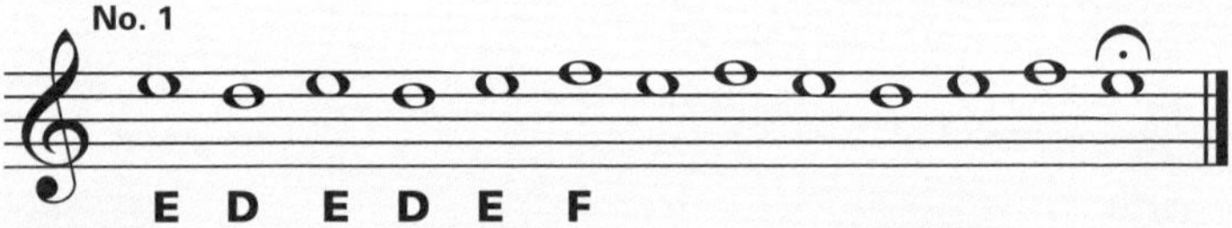


No. 2

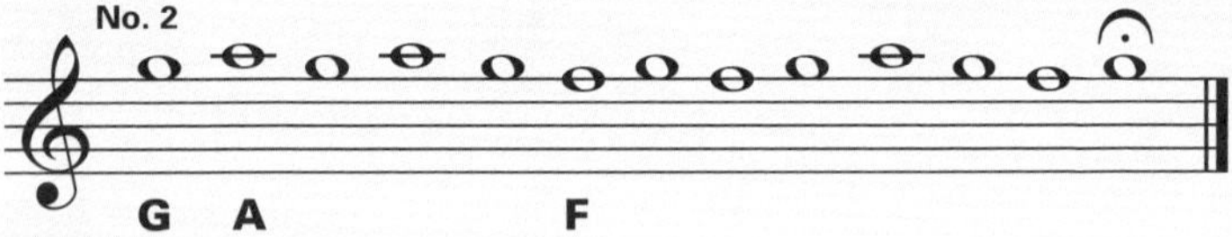


No. 3

No. 4

No. 5

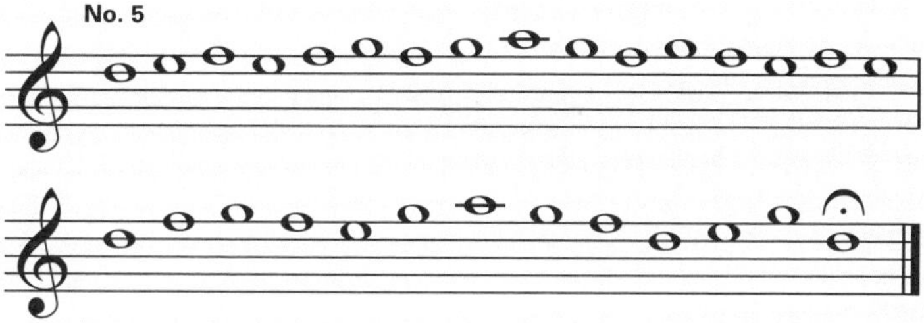

No. 6

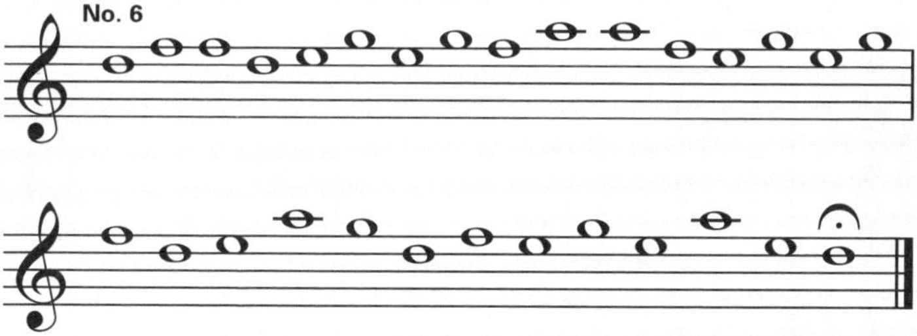

No. 7

# Exercises on C–C

**These exercises use the notes C–C**

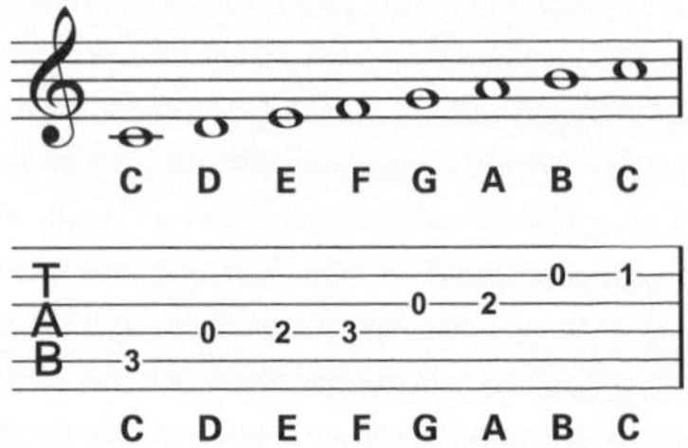


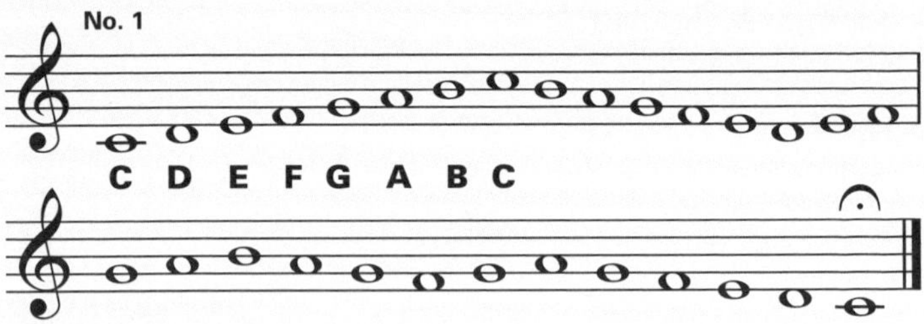

## Treble Clef

No. 3

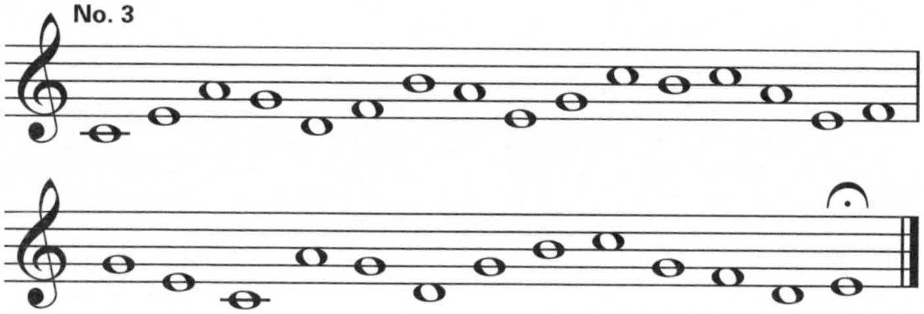

No. 4

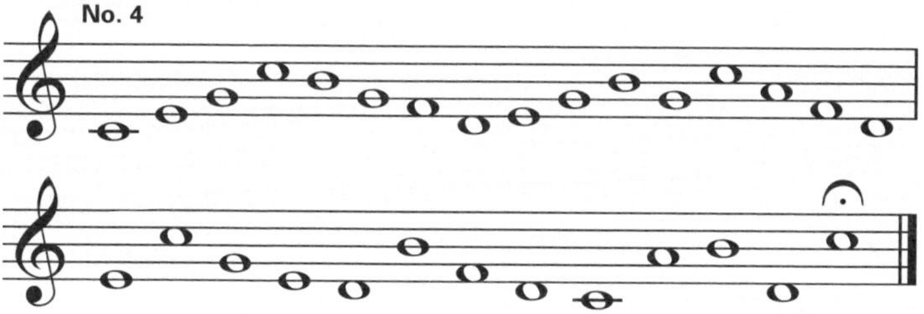

No. 5

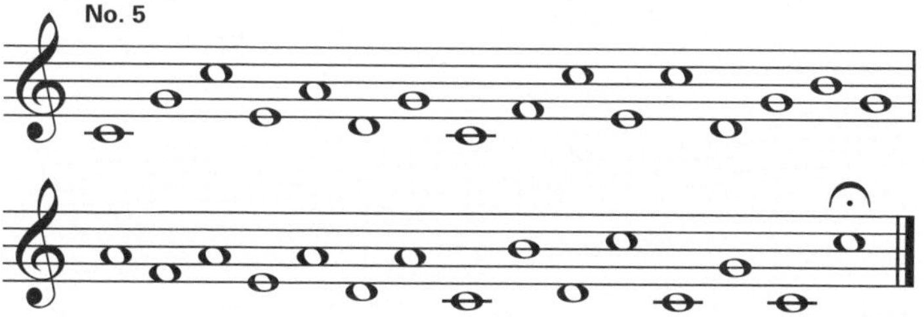

# Exercises on F–F

## These exercises use the notes F–F

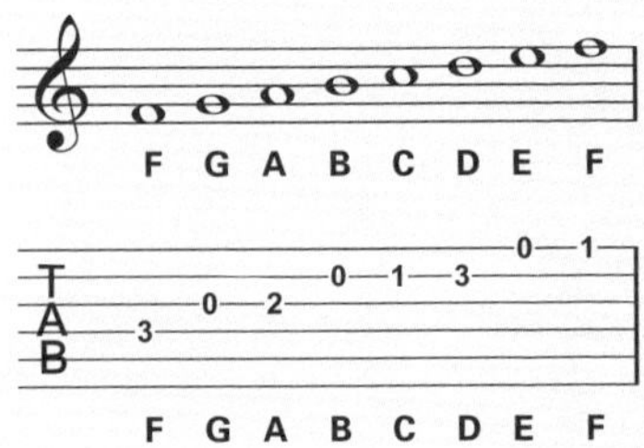


No. 1

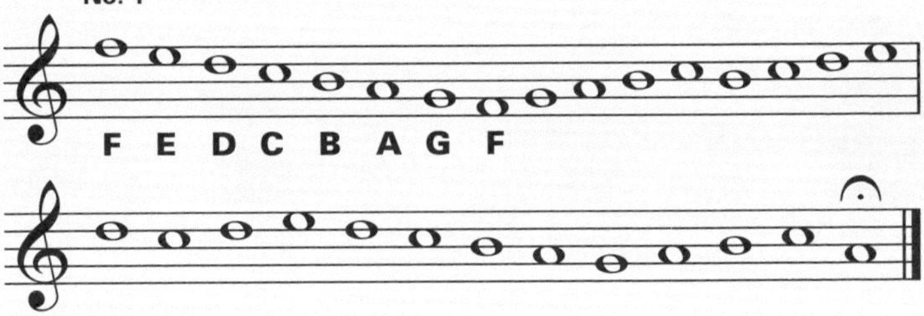


No. 2

No. 3

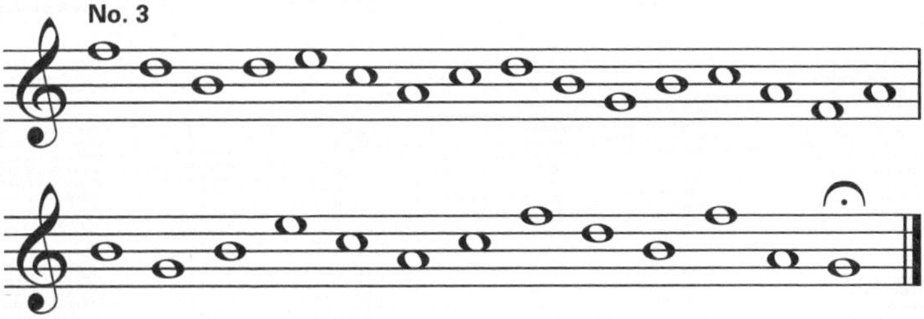

No. 4

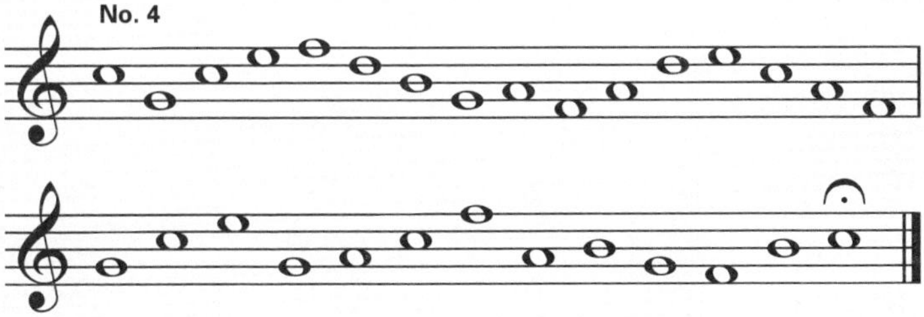

No. 5

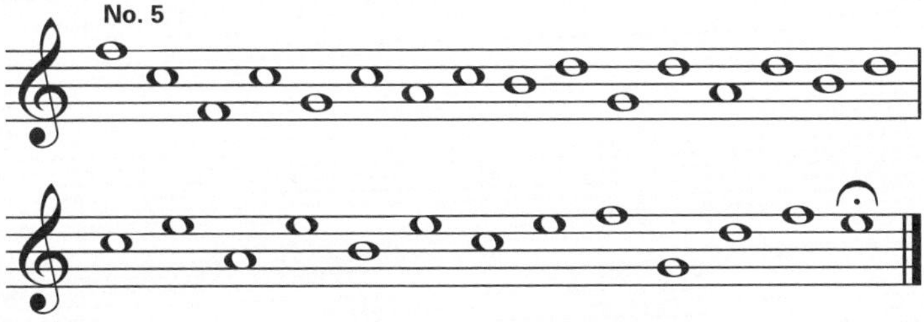

# Exercises on A–A

**These exercises use the notes A–A**

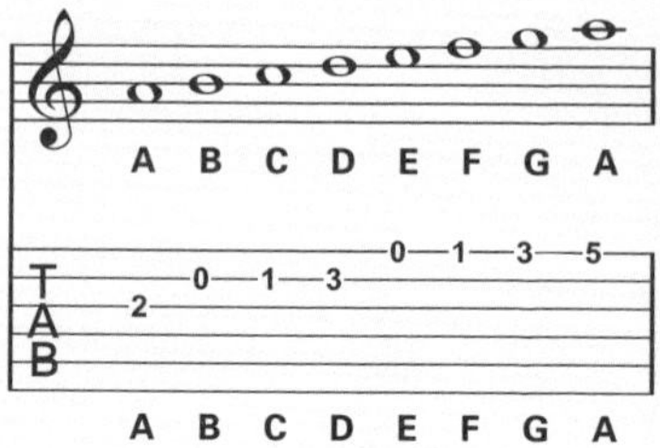


No. 1

No. 2

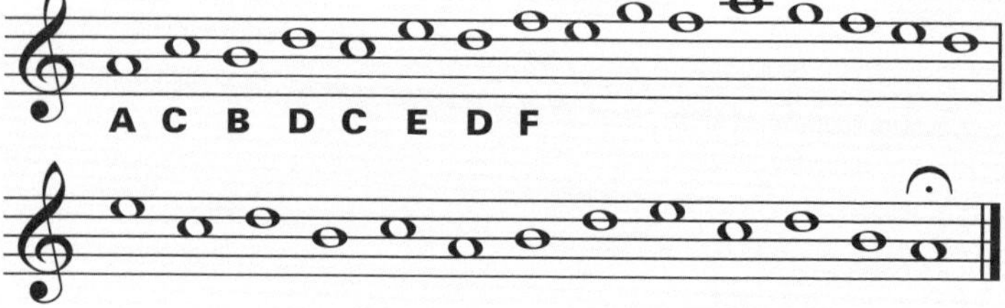

No. 3

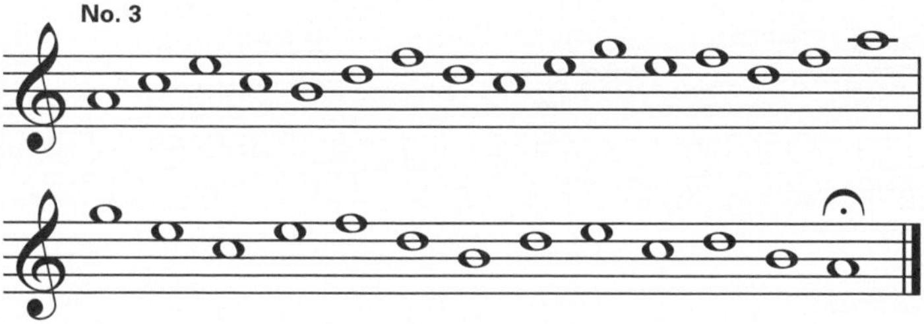

No. 4

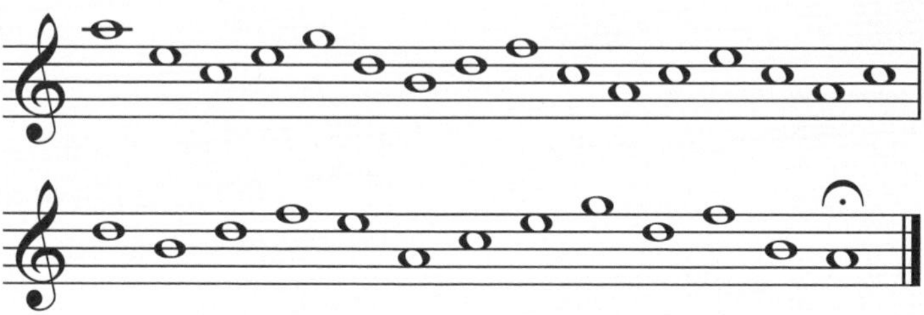

No. 5

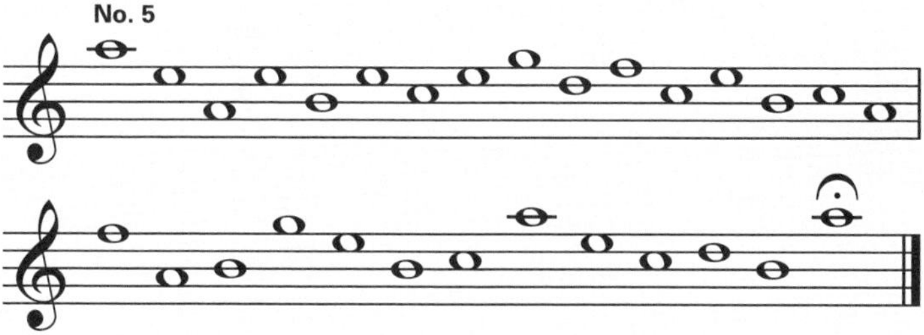

# Exercises on C–A

**These exercises use the notes C–A**

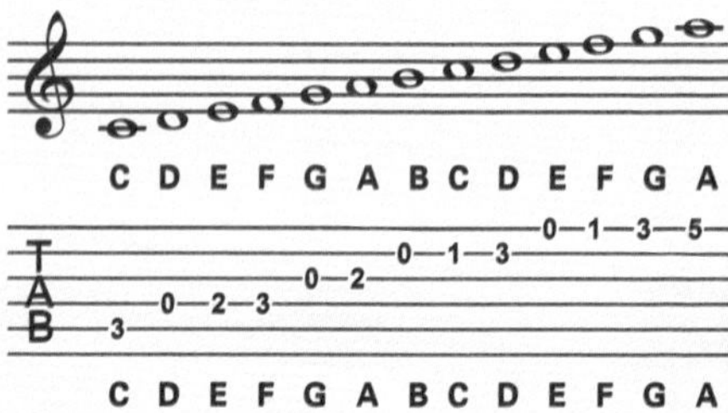


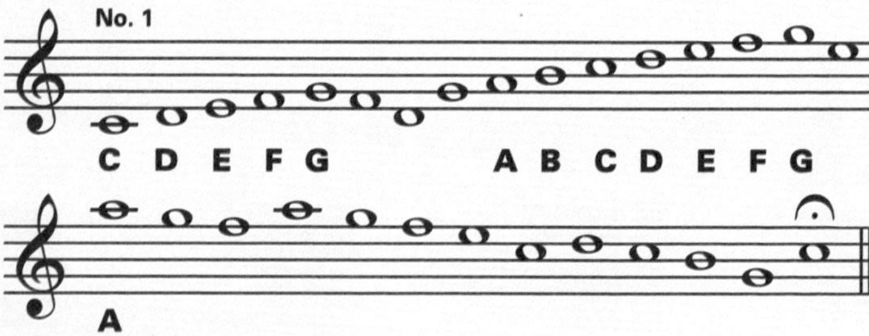


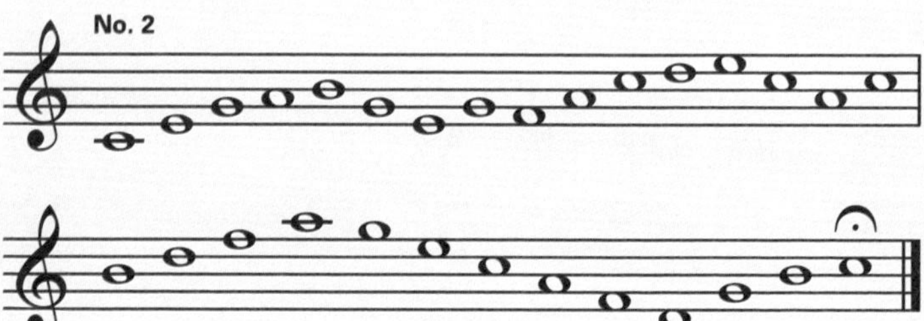

## Treble Clef

No. 3

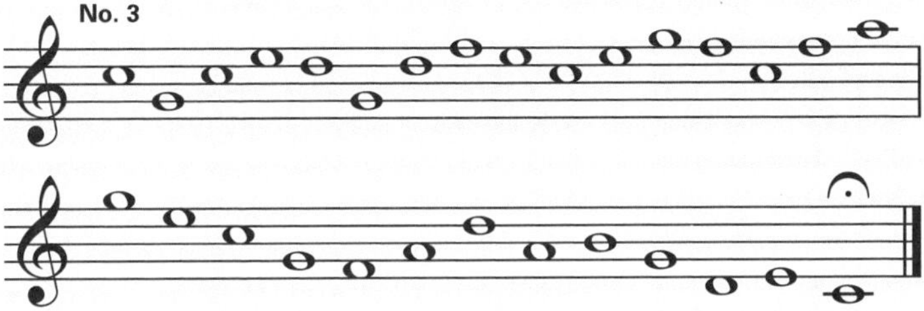

No. 4

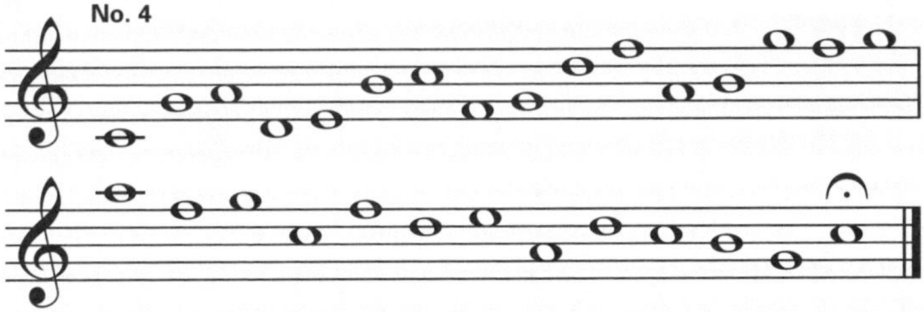

No. 5

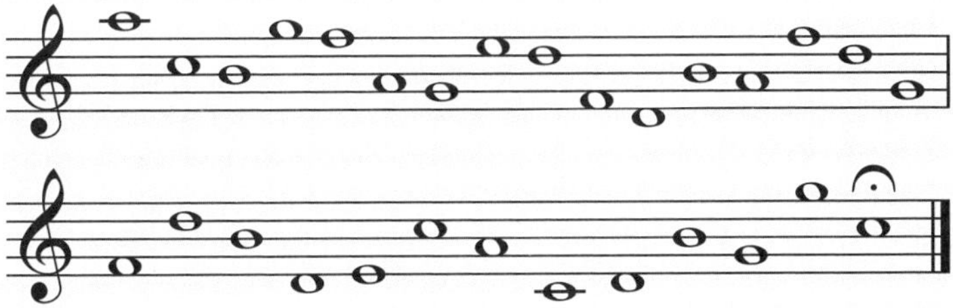

# Notesquare

To pull together what you have learned so far, have a go at this notesquare. This is like a wordsquare, but with the letters written out as notes on the treble clef. Find each word written underneath the grid spelt in musical letters in the notesquare grid.

Words are written horizontally, vertically, backwards, upside down and diagonally.

**Hint**: to make this a little easier, write the names of the notes in the boxes opposite and then continue as you would with a conventional wordsquare.

## Treble Clef

**Example**

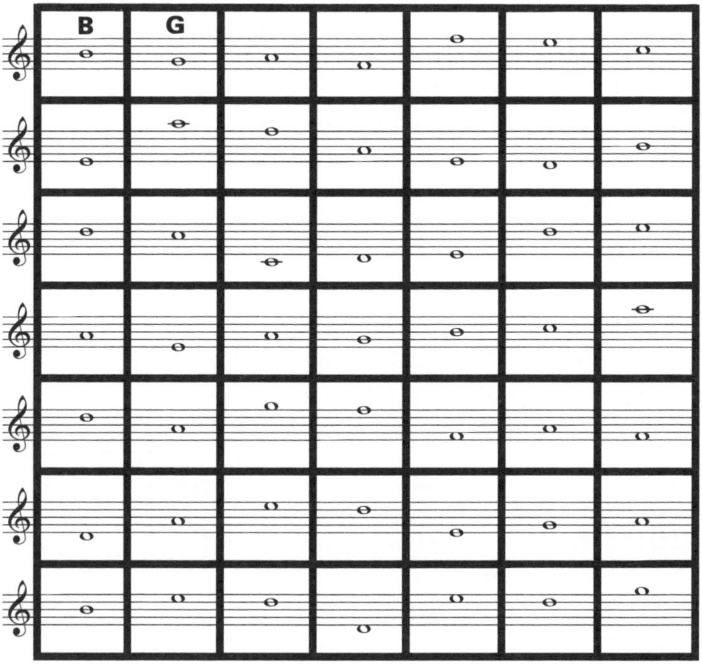


| | | | |
|---|---|---|---|
| **ACE** | **BEDDED** | **DAD** | **FACED** |
| **ADD** | **BEEF** | **DEAD** | **FAD** |
| **AGE** | **CAB** | **DEAF** | **FAFF** |
| **BED** | **CAFE** | **DEFACE** | **FEE** |
| **BAGGED** | **CAGED** | **EDGED** | **GAFFE** |

# E–B Below The Stave

## Notes below the treble clef

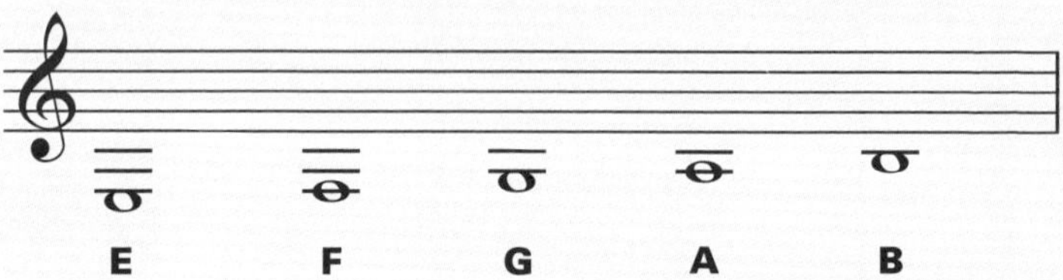


## Finding these notes on your instrument

| First find middle C | Then find: | | | | |
|---|---|---|---|---|---|
| | the first B below middle C | the first A below middle C | the first G below middle C | the first F below middle C | the first E below middle C |

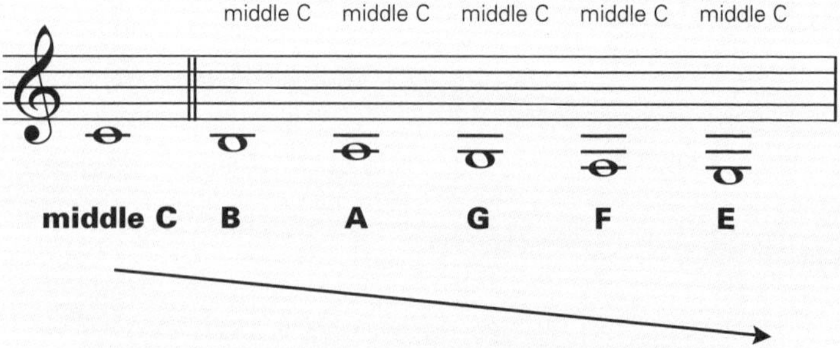


**Each note is lower than the previous one**

# E–B on a keyboard

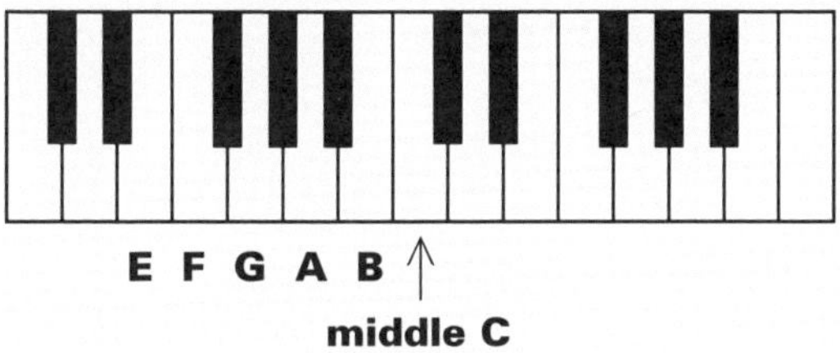


# E–B on a guitar (standard tuning)

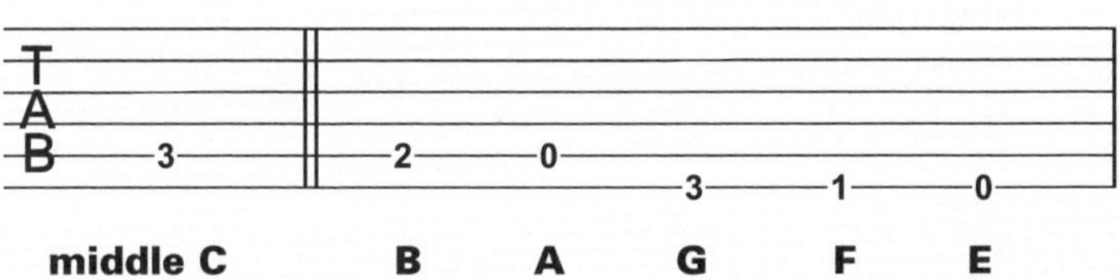

# Exercises on G–D Below The Stave

**These exercises use the notes G–D below the stave**

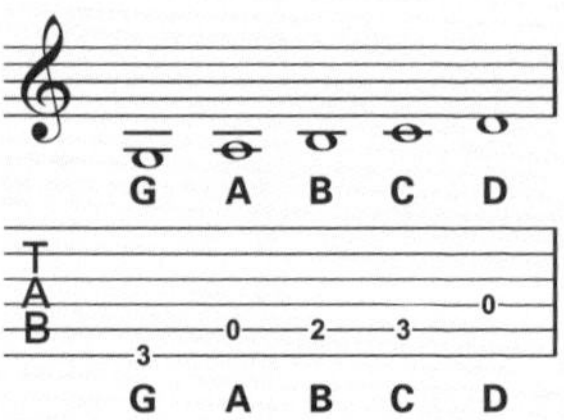


No. 1

No. 2

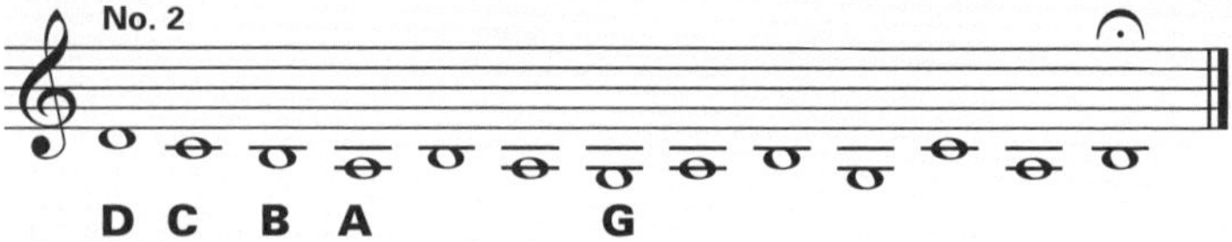


No. 3

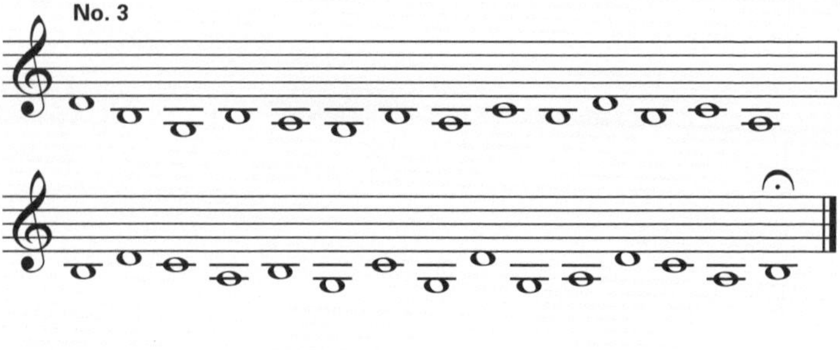

# Exercises on E–B Below The Stave

## These exercises use the notes E–B

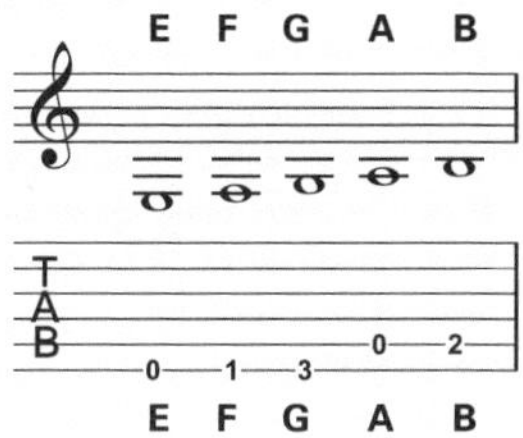


**No. 1**

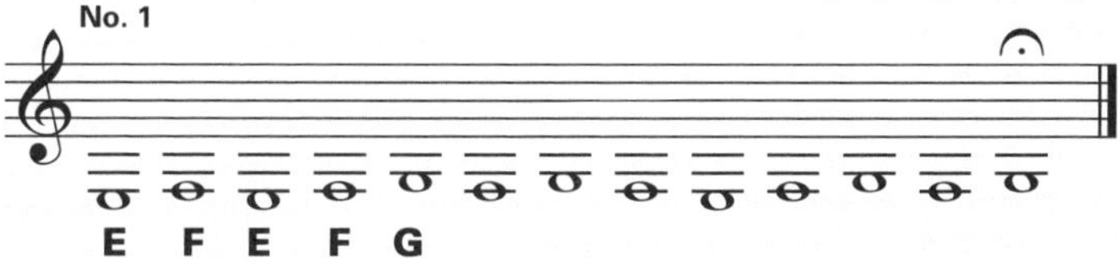


**No. 2**

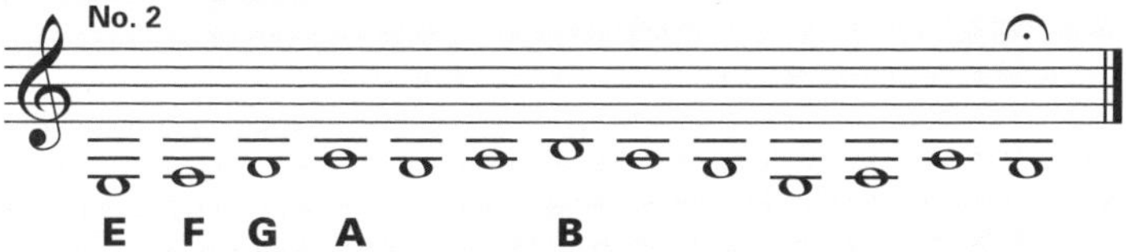


**No. 3**

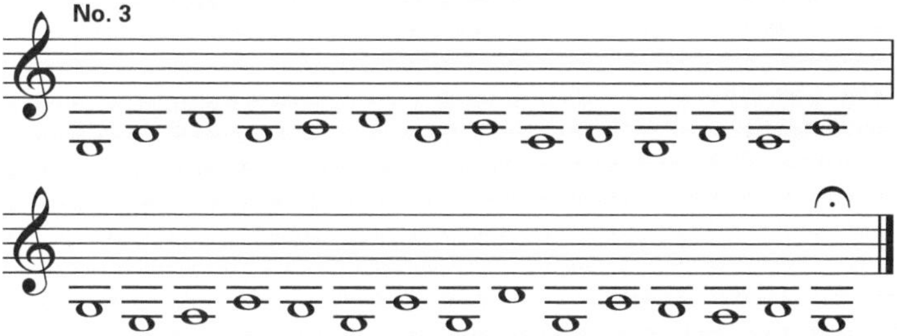

# B–F Above The Stave

## Notes above the treble clef

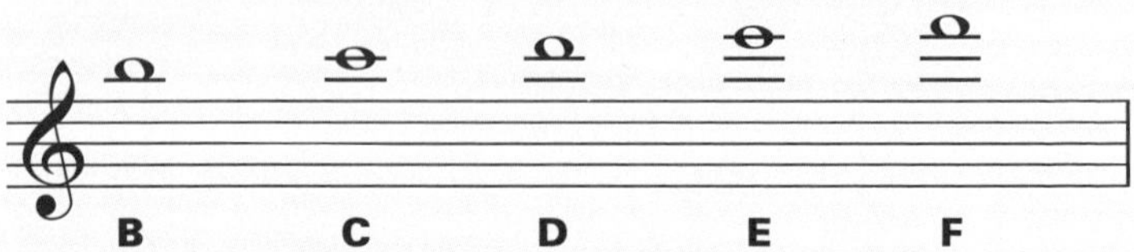


## Finding these notes on your instrument

| **First find middle C** | **Then find:** | | | | |
|---|---|---|---|---|---|
| | the second B above middle C | the second C above middle C | the third D above middle C | the third E above middle C | the third F above middle C |

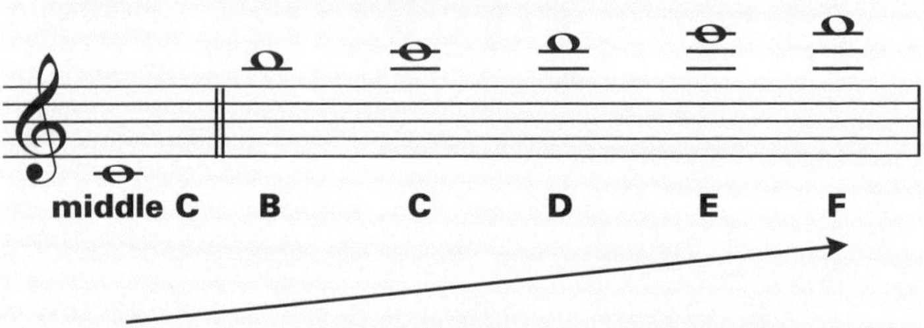


**Each note is higher than the previous one**

## B–F on a keyboard

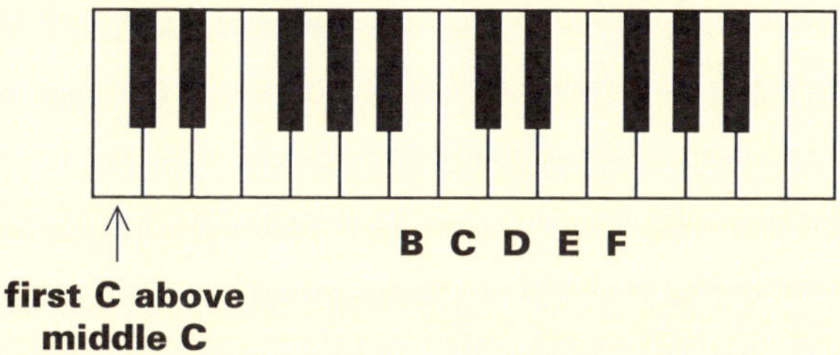


## B–F on a guitar (standard tuning)

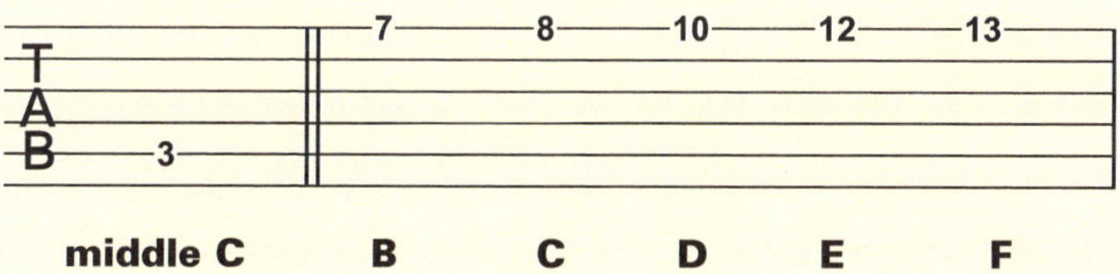


Pitch
Treble Clef
Bass Clef
Rhythm
Play Along 1
ACC Accidentals
Key Sign
Scales
Chords
Other Chords
Play Along 2
Comp

# Exercises on G–D Above The Stave

## These exercises use the notes G–D

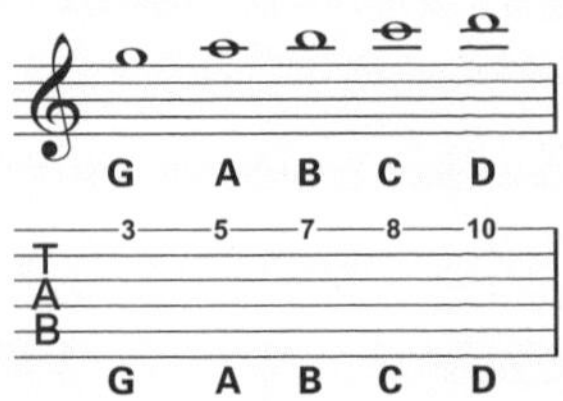


No. 1

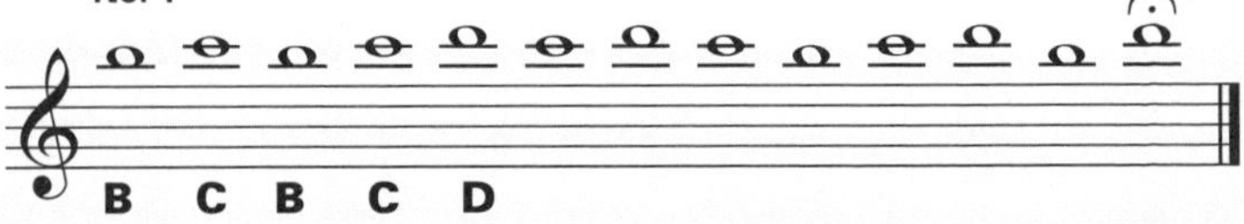


No. 2

No. 3

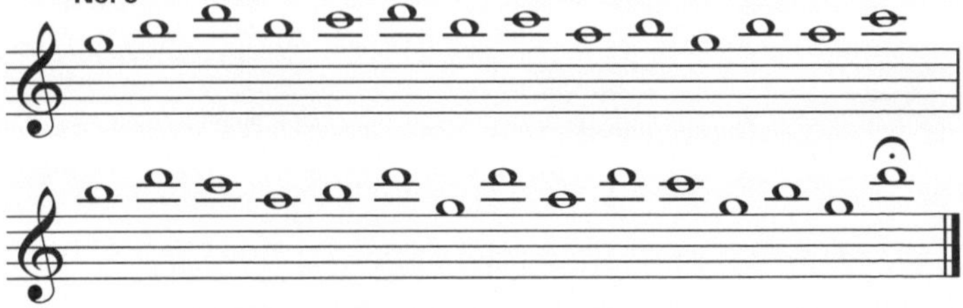

# Exercises on B–F Above The Stave

**These exercises use the notes B–F**

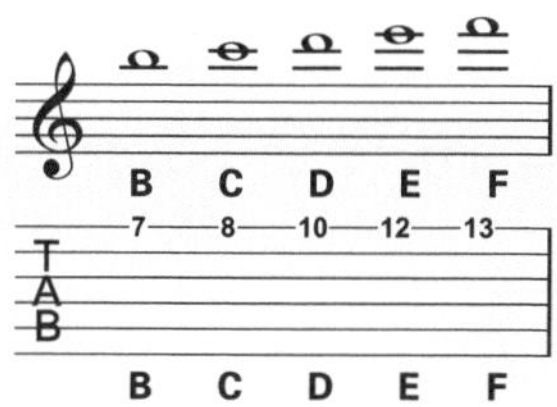


No. 1

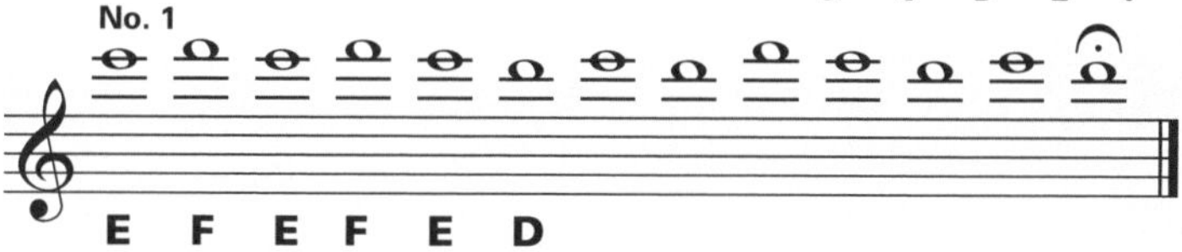


No. 2

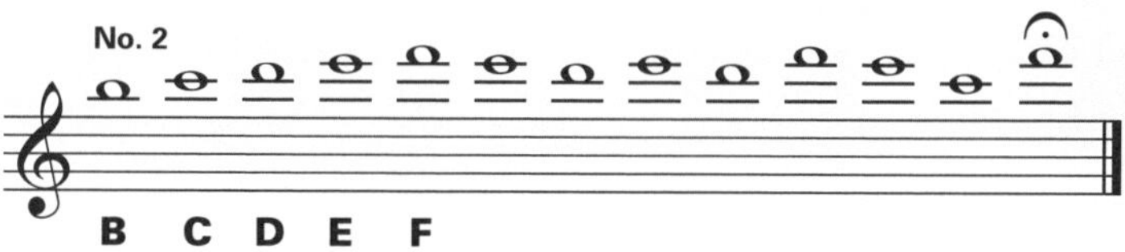


No. 3

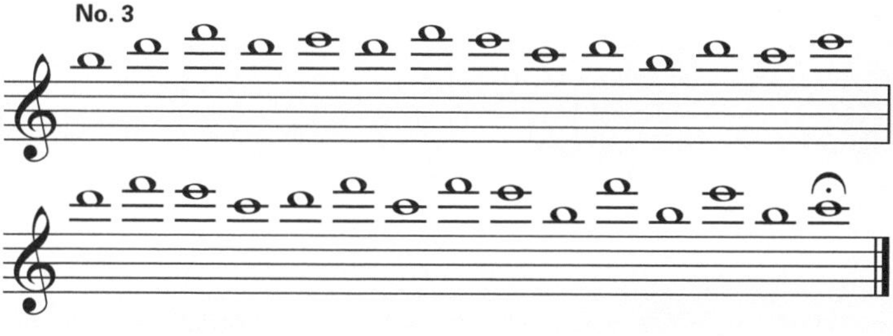

# The Notes of The Bass Clef

Learning the bass clef is very similar to learning the treble clef, so this section is in a similar format as the previous one. It starts by introducing two to five new notes at a time, showing you how to find them on your instrument and testing you on them through word games based on the note names you have learnt.

The bass clef has two mnemonics of its own: '**A**ll **C**ows **E**at **G**rass' for the space notes and '**G**ood **B**oys **D**eserve **F**ootball **A**lways'. As with the treble clef, learn these by heart and use them to help jog your memory.

Once you have learnt the note names, there is a series of short melodies in different areas of the clef, building up from three to eight notes. As with the treble clef, some of the notes covered here may be too low or high for your instrument, so choose only the exercises that apply to you.

Finally, there are exercises based on ledger line notes below and above the stave. Again, these may be too low or high for your instrument, so just pick the exercises relevant to you.

# The Space Notes (ACEG)

## The space notes of the bass clef

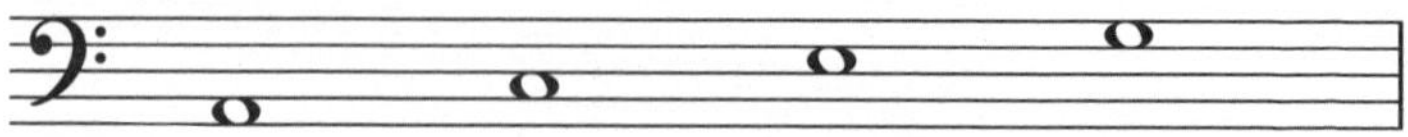

| **All** | **Cows** | **Eat** | **Grass** |
|---|---|---|---|
| (bottom space) | (second space) | (third space) | (top space) |

## Finding ACEG on your instrument

**First find middle C**

**Then find:**

| the first G below middle C | the first E below middle C | the first C below middle C | the second A below middle C |
|---|---|---|---|

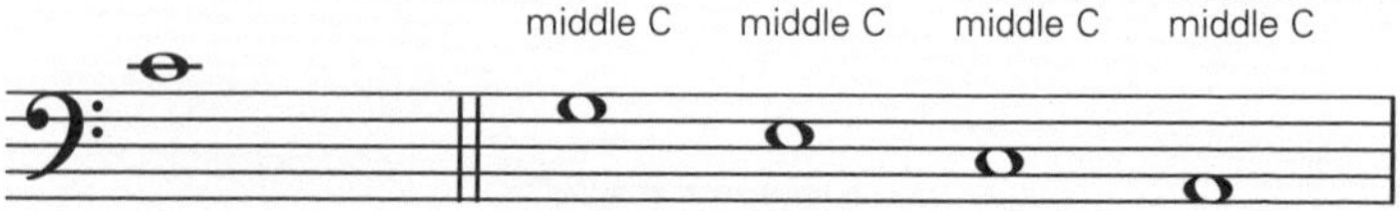

**middle C** — **Grass** **Eat** **Cows** **All**

**Each note is lower than the previous one**

# ACEG on a keyboard

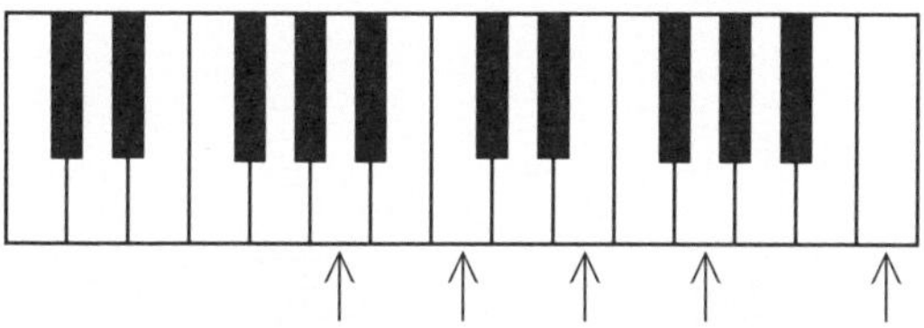

**A** **C** **E** **G** **middle C**

# ACEG on a bass guitar (standard tuning)

**First find middle C** **Then find:**

the first G below middle C | the first E below middle C | the first C below middle C | the second A below middle C

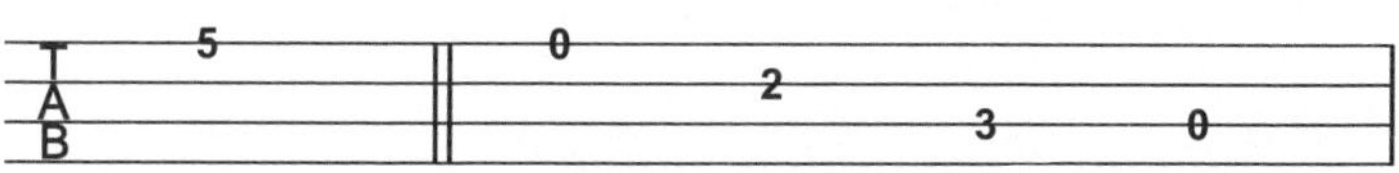


**middle C** **G**rass **E**at **C**ows **A**ll

# Space Notes (ACEG):
## EXERCISE 1

### Fill in the missing letters using the given notes

Example

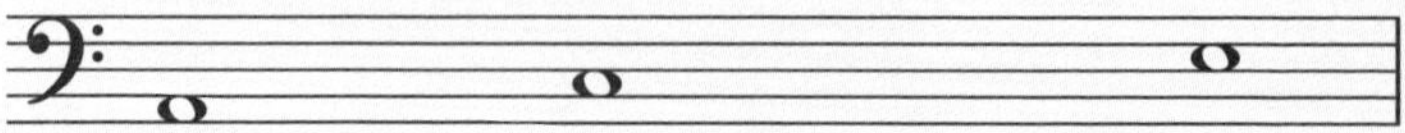

A R C H I E

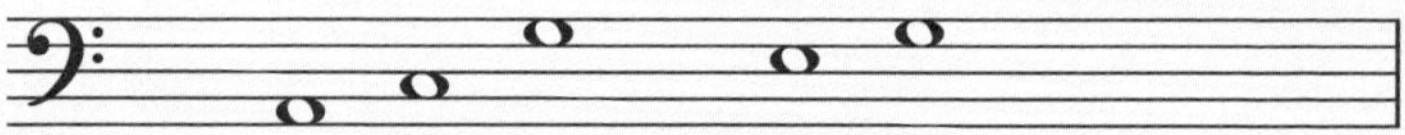

M _ _ _ R _ _ O R'S

_ O N _ _ _ L _ D

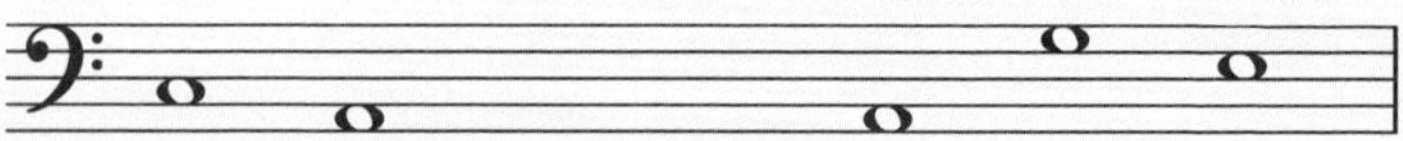

_ _ B B _ _ _

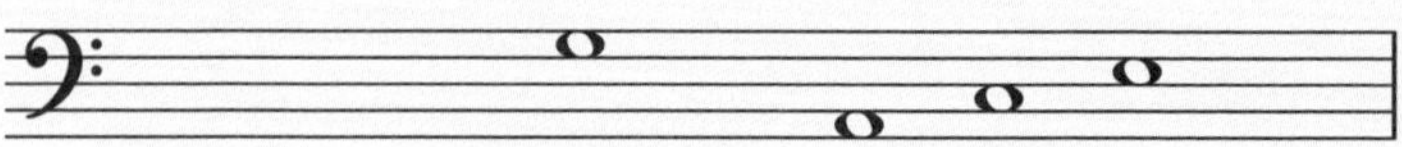

D I S _ R _ _ _ D

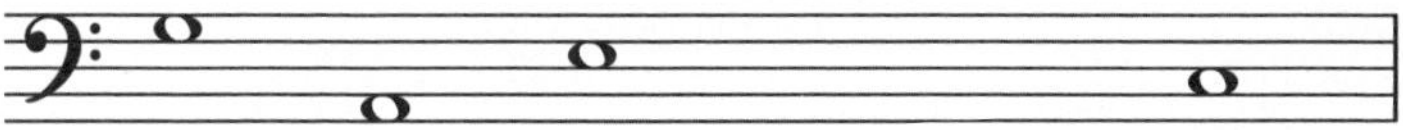

_ _ _ L I C

_ _ T _ R I N _

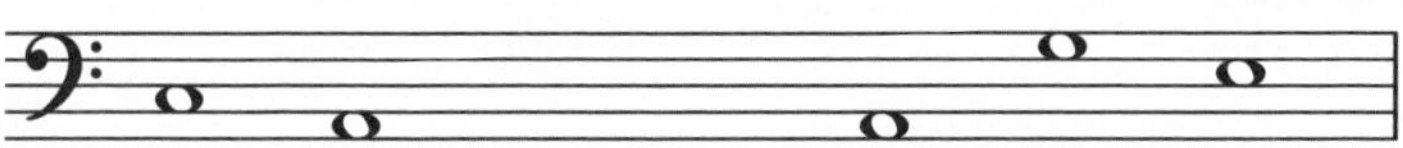

_ _ R N _ _ _

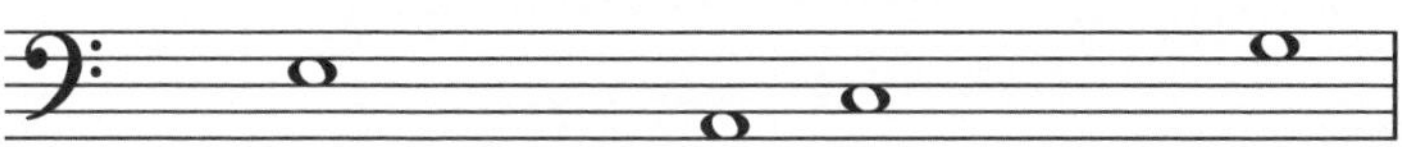

R _ P L _ _ I N _

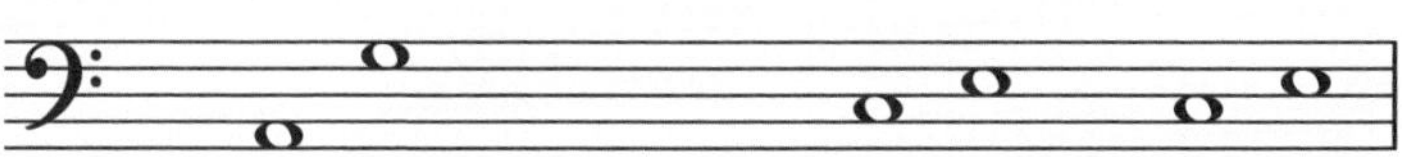

M _ _ N I F I _ _ N _ _

# Space Notes (ACEG): EXERCISE 2

## Write the boxed letters as space notes on the staves

Example

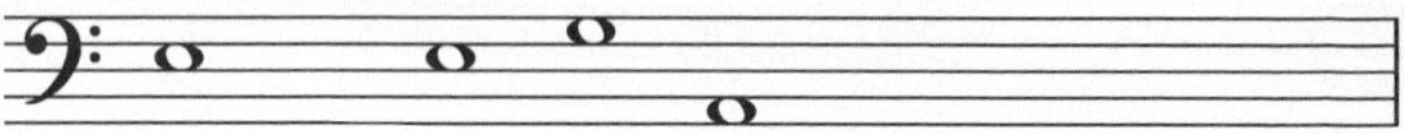

E L E G A N T L Y

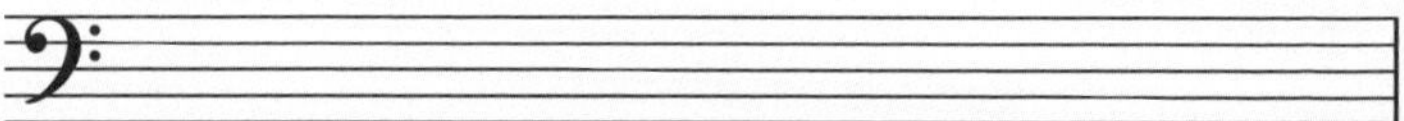

C O N C E A L I N G

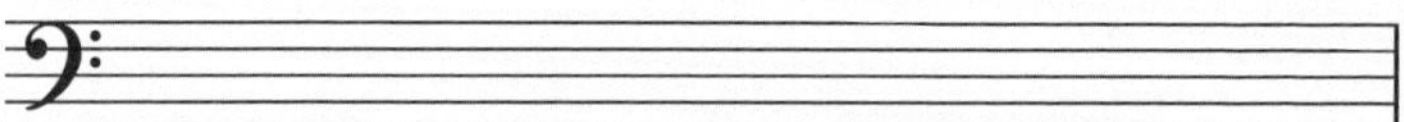

A N G E L A ' S

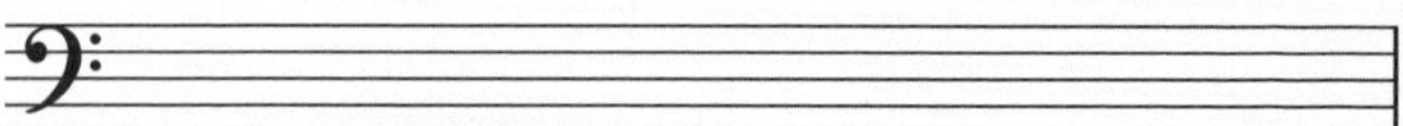

C I G A R E T T E

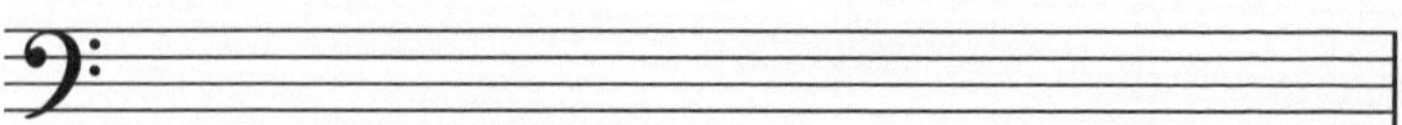

P A C K A G E

C L A I R E

A D V A N C E D

A N G E L I C A L L Y

E S C A P I N G

U N C H A L L E N G E D

# F Below and B Above The Stave

## F below the bass clef and B above the bass clef

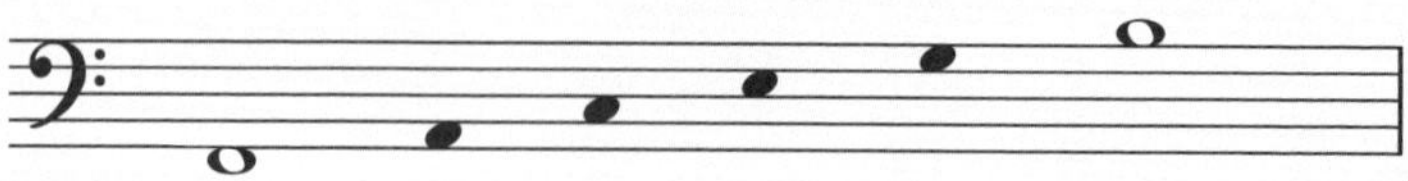

**F (All Cows Eat Grass) B**

## Finding the same F and B on your instrument

**First find middle C**

**Then find:**

the first B below middle C

the ACEG notes in reverse order

the second F below middle C

**middle C B (Grass Eat Cows All) F**

**Each note is lower than the previous one**

# F and B on a keyboard

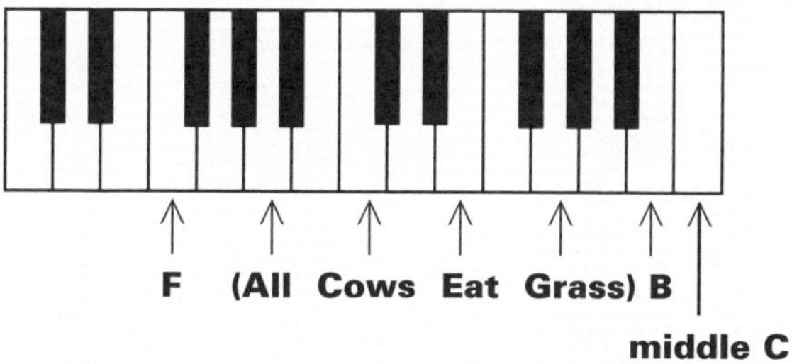


# Finding the same F and B on your instrument

**First find middle C**

**Then find:**

the first B below middle C

the ACEG notes in reverse order

the second F below middle C

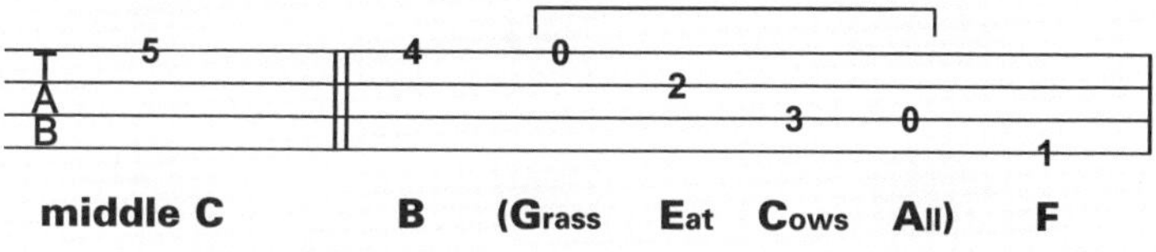

# F Below and B Above The Stave: EXERCISE 1

## Fill in the missing letters using the given notes

Example

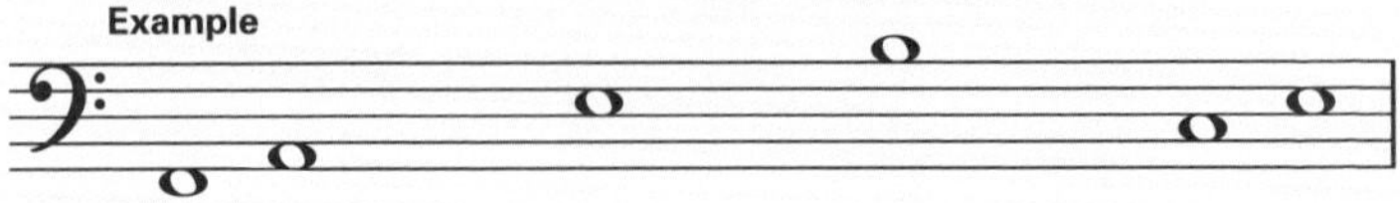

F A T H E R B R U C E

_ _ _ R I _ N D _ D _ N

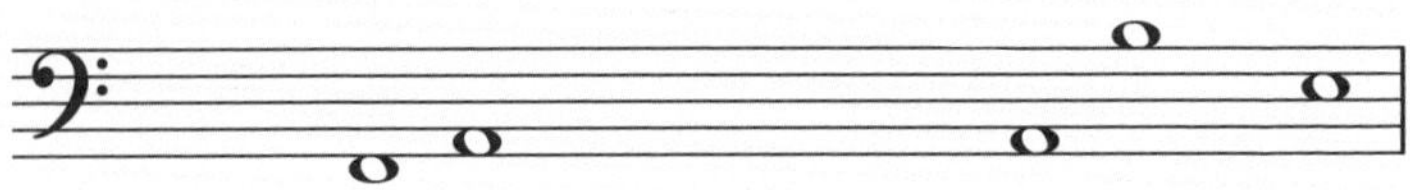

U N _ _ S H I O N _ _ L _

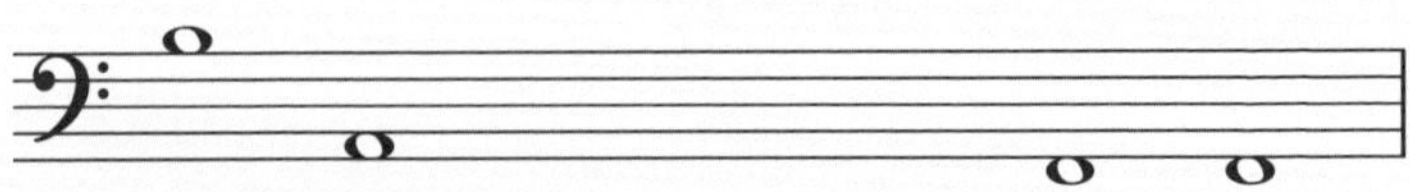

_ _ I L I _ _

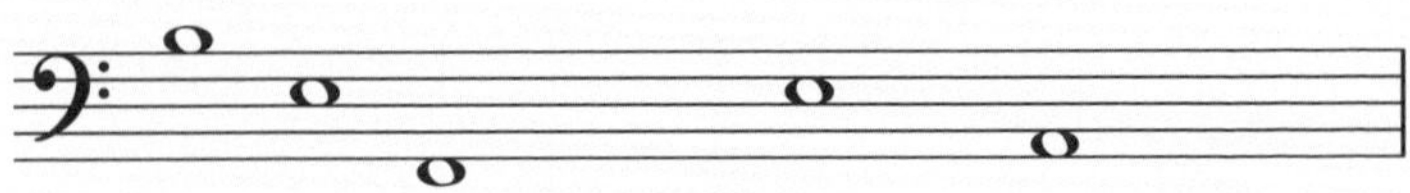

_ _ _ O R _ H _ N D,

U N _ O R _ _ T T _ _ L Y

_ _ _ R I _ _ T I N _

_ _ R _ _ _ _ _ D

_ _ L I _ _ S I N T H _

_ I R _ _ R I _ _ D _

# F Below and B Above The Staves: EXERCISE 2

## Write the boxed letters as notes on the staves

Example

[F] [E] [E] [B] L [E]

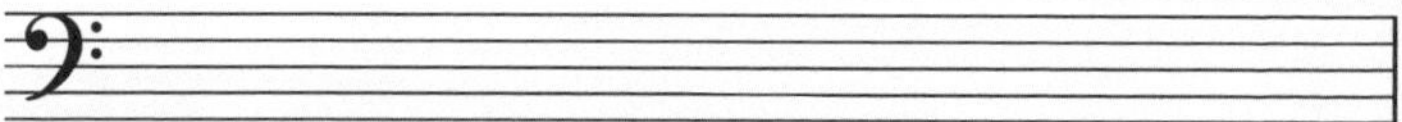

[F] R [A] N [C] [E] S [C] [A]’ S

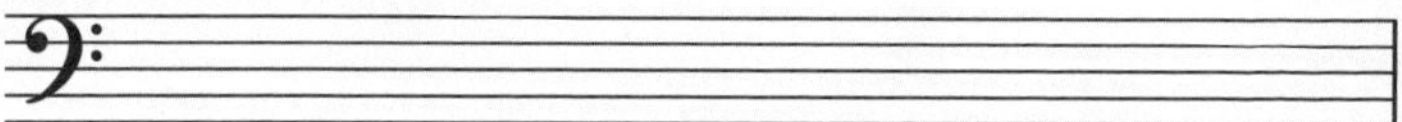

U N [C] O M [F] O R T [A] [B] L [E]

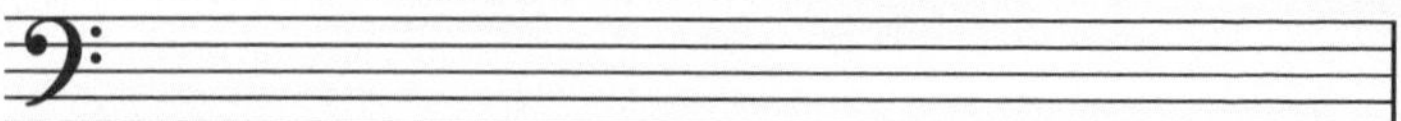

[B] [A] L L [E] T I [C]

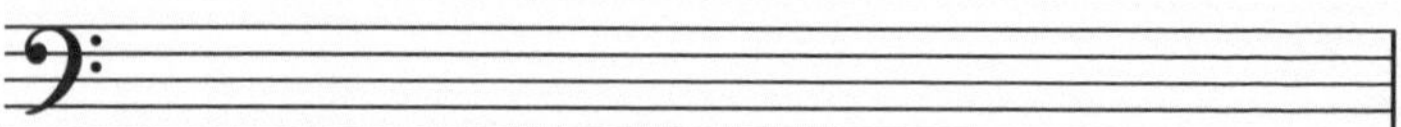

D [E] [F] [E] N D I N [G]

## Bass Clef

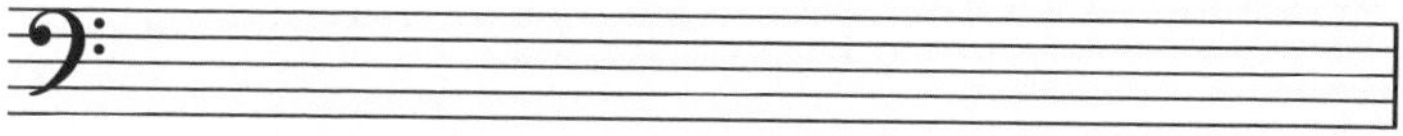

B A C K F I R E D

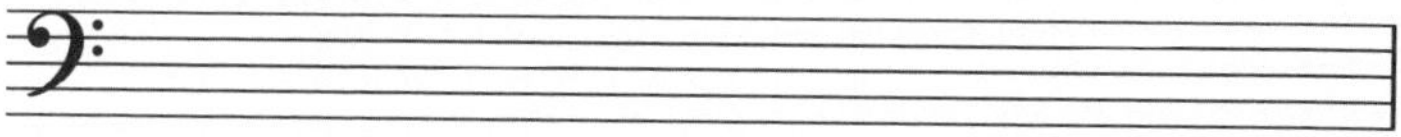

B E C A U S E O F H E R

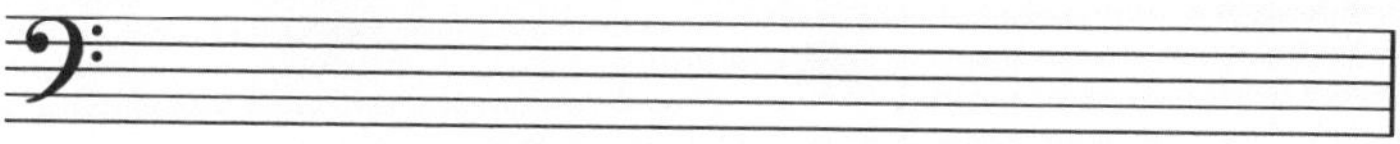

F O R G E T T A B L E

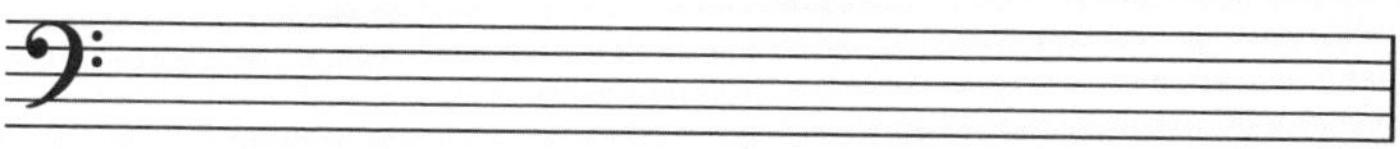

F O O T B A L L I N G

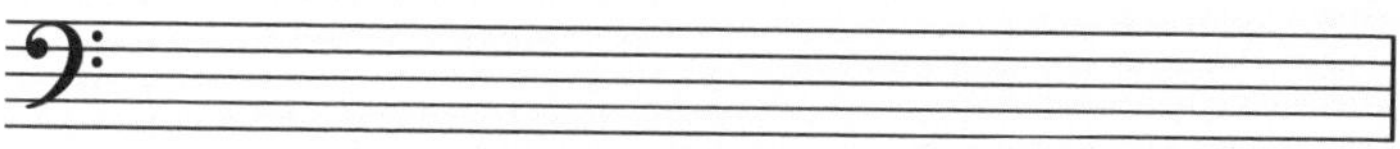

B A C K G R O U N D

# The Line Notes (GBDFA)

## The line notes of the bass clef

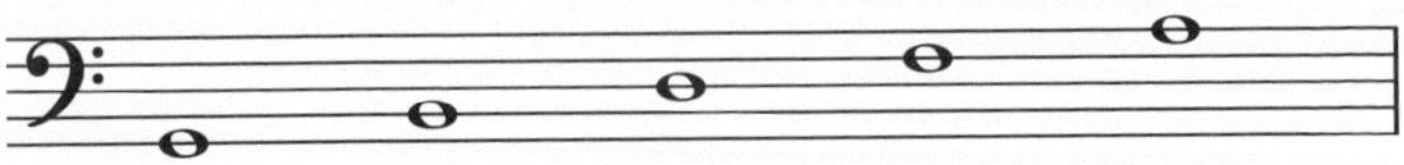

| Good (bottom line) | Boys (second line) | Deserve (third line) | Football (fourth line) | Always (top line) |
|---|---|---|---|---|

## Finding GBDFA on your instrument:

**First find middle C**

**Then find:**

the first A below middle C | the first F below middle C | the first D below middle C | the second B below middle C | the second G below middle C

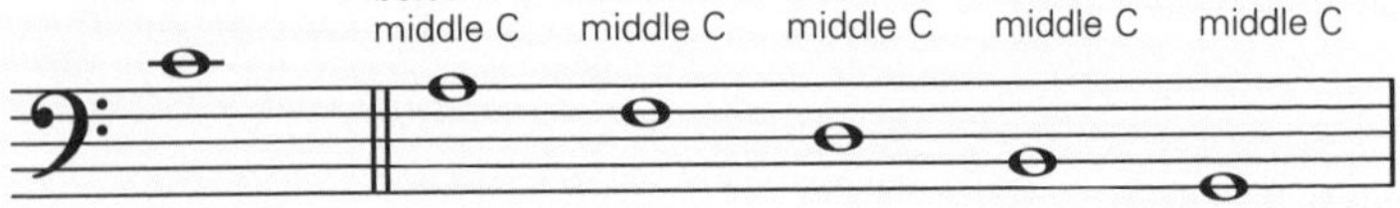

**middle C** | **Always** | **Football** | **Deserve** | **Boys** | **Good**

**Each note is lower than the previous one**

## GBDFA on a keyboard

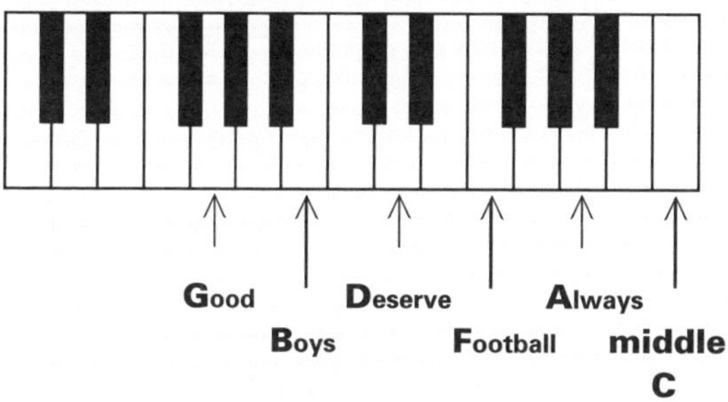


## GBDFA on a bass guitar (standard tuning)

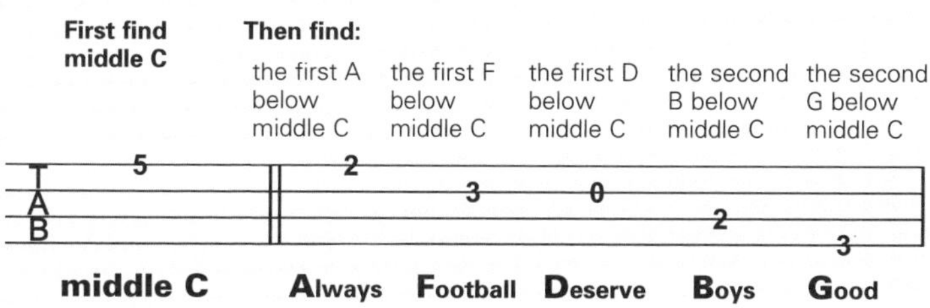

# Line Notes (GBDFA):

## EXERCISE 1

### Fill in the missing letters using the given notes

**Example**

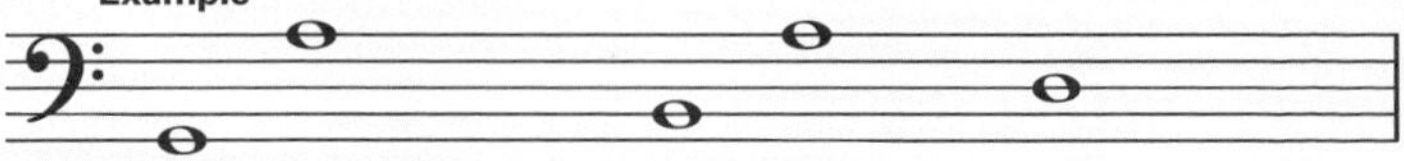

G A R I B A L D I ’ S

_ E _ L _ T _ _ L E

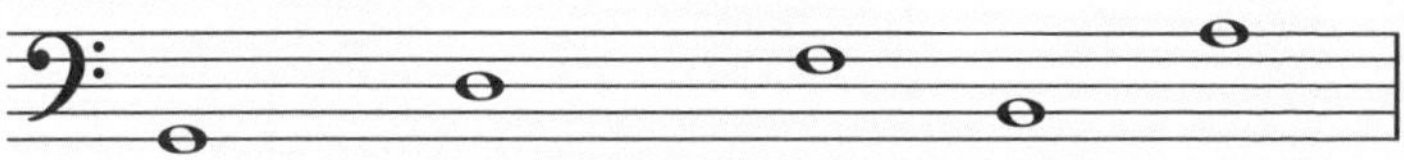

_ O L _ L I _ E _ O _ T

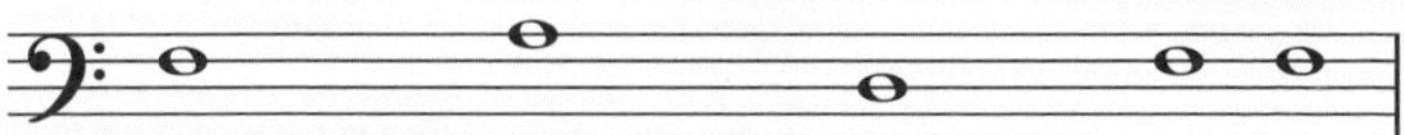

_ L O _ T E _ O _ _

_ M I _ S T _ _ R I _ H T

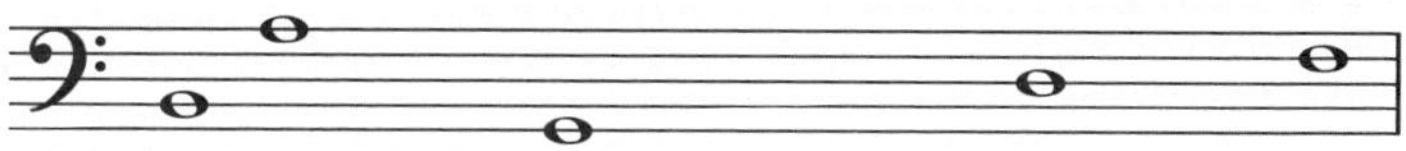

_ _ C K _ R O U N _ O _

_ I O _ E _ R _ _ _ _ L E

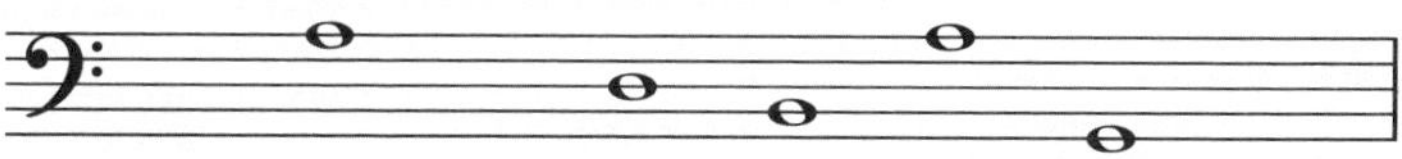

H _ N _ _ _ _ S

_ N _ _ _ _ _ L E _

_ _ _ Y _ I R _ _ _ E S

Pitch
Treble Clef
Bass Clef
Rhythm
Play Along 1
ACC Accidentals
Key Sign
Scales
Chords
Other Chords
Play Along 2
Comp

# Line Notes (GBDFA):
## EXERCISE 2

### Write the boxed letters as line notes on the staves

Example

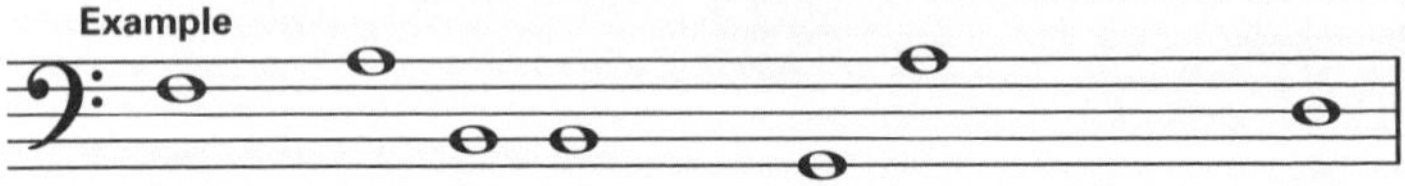

**F** L **A** **B** **B** E R **G** **A** S T E **D**

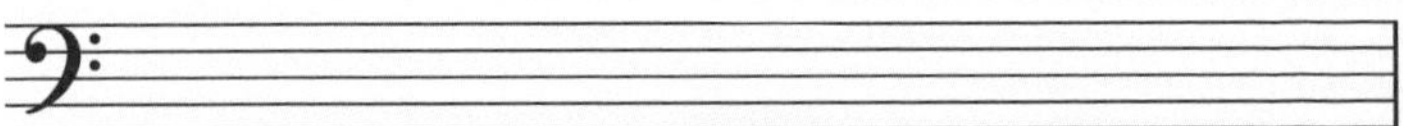

**D** **A** **F** **F** Y **D** **D** **G** **A** **B** **B** L E **D**

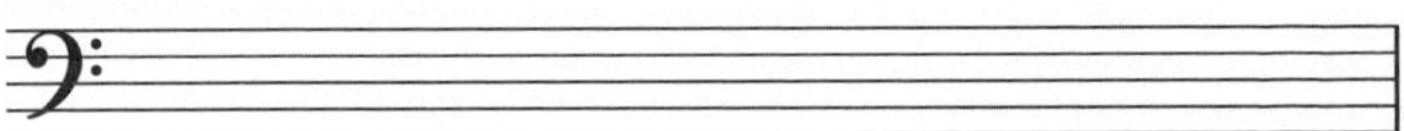

**D** E **A** **F** I N I N **G** L Y

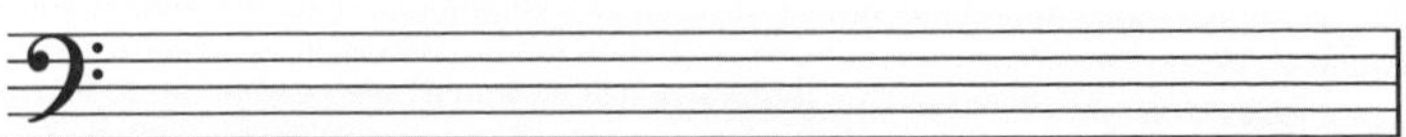

**A** **B** O U T **F** U **D** **G** E

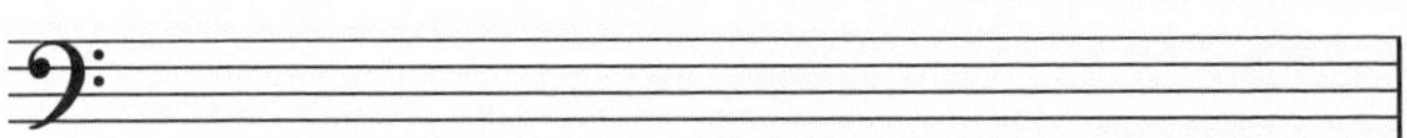

**A** N **D** **F** I **B** **B** E **D**

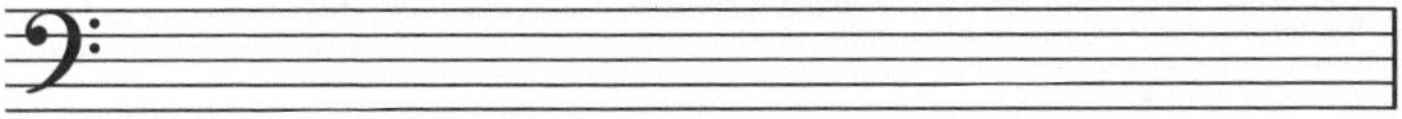

T H A T A B I G A I L

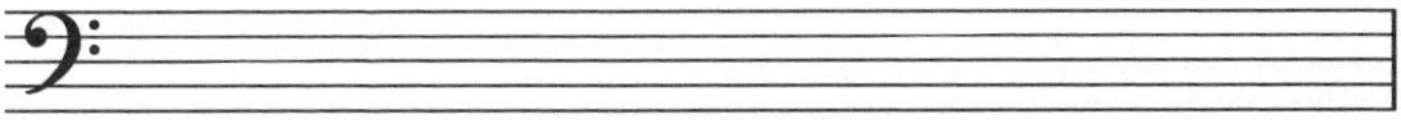

H A D G O B B L E D

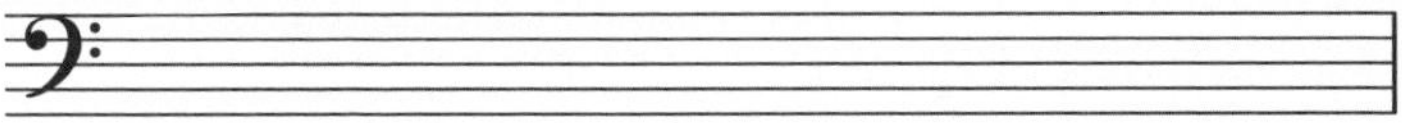

F O U R B A G S ,

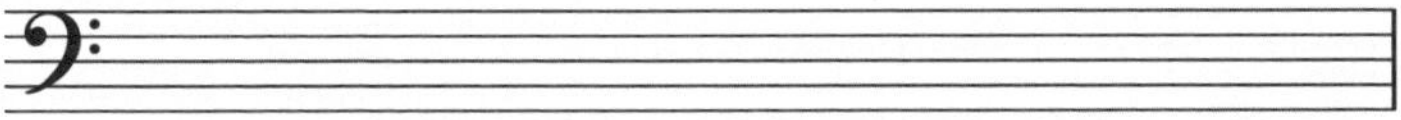

A D A F T B R A G

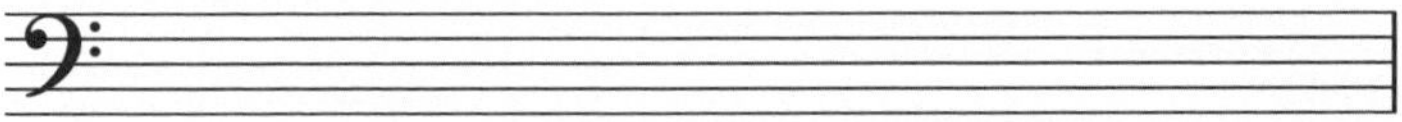

T H A T B A C K F I R E D

Pitch
Treble Clef
Bass Clef
Rhythm
Play Along 1
ACC Accidentals
Key Sign
Scales
Chords
Other Chords
Play Along 2
Comp

# E Below and C Above The Stave

## E below the bass clef and C above the bass clef

**E (Good Boys Deserve Football Always C**

## Finding the same E and C on your instrument

**First find middle C** **Then find:**

the GBDFA notes in reverse order

the second E below middle C

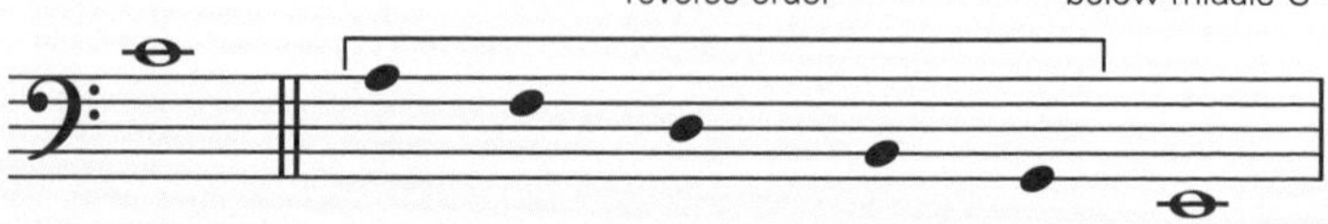

**middle C (Always Football Deserve Boys Good) E**

**Each note is lower than the previous one**

# E and C on a keyboard

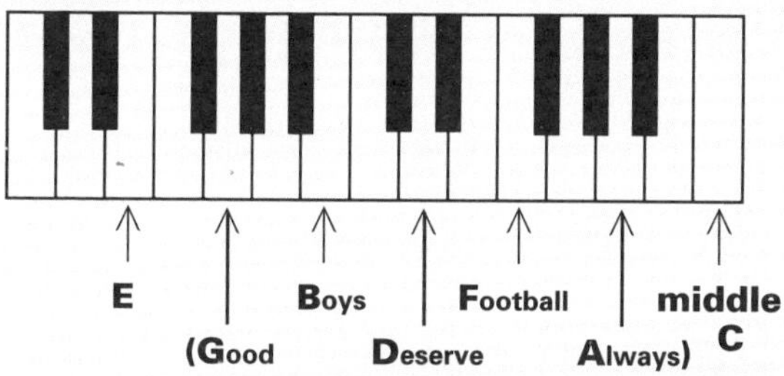


# E and C on a bass guitar (standard tuning)

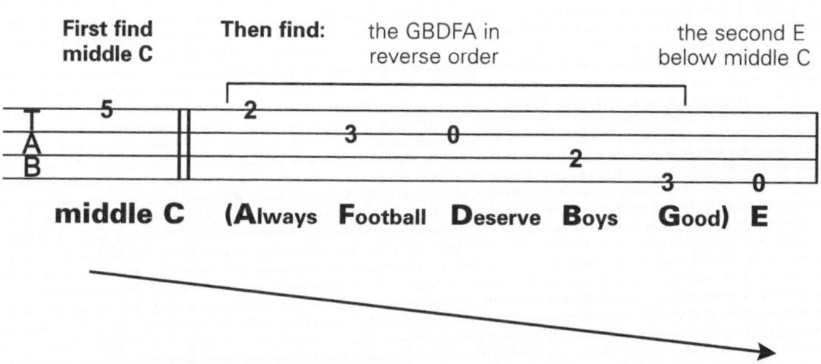

# E Below and C Above The Stave: EXERCISE 1

## Fill in the missing letters using the given notes

### MODES OF TRANSPORT

Example

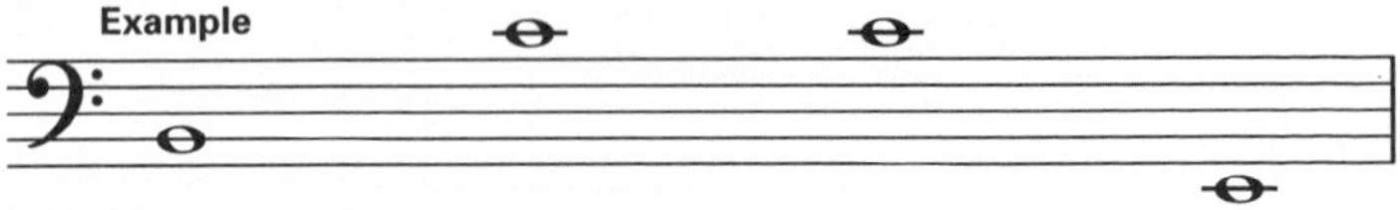

B I C Y C L E

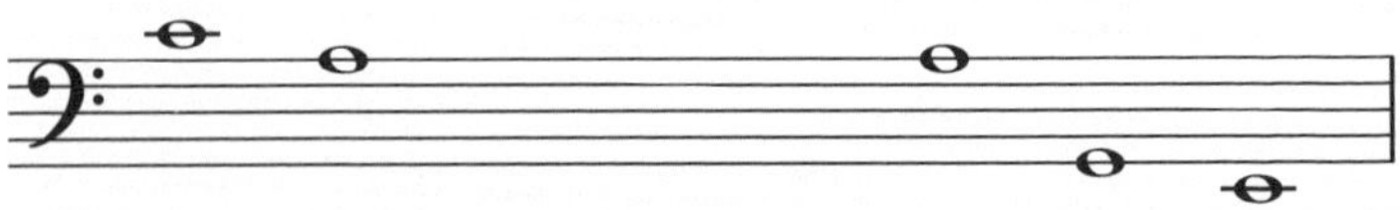

_ _ R R I _ _ _

_ I R _ R _ _ T _ _ R R I _ R

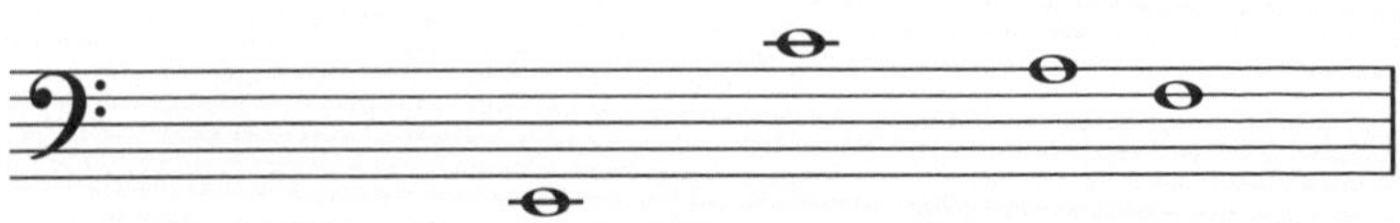

H O V _ R _ R _ _ T

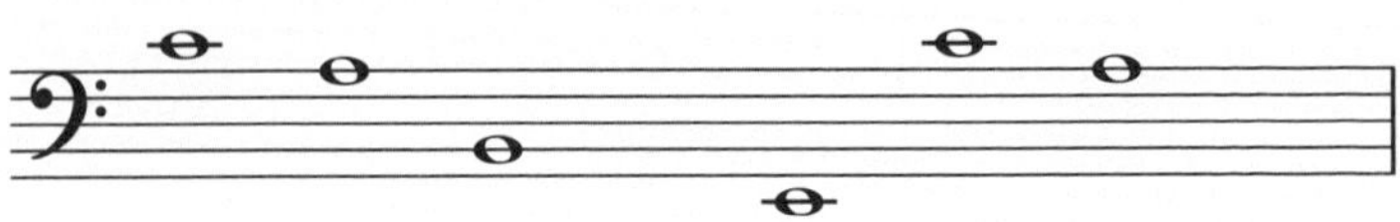

_ _ _ L _ _ _ R

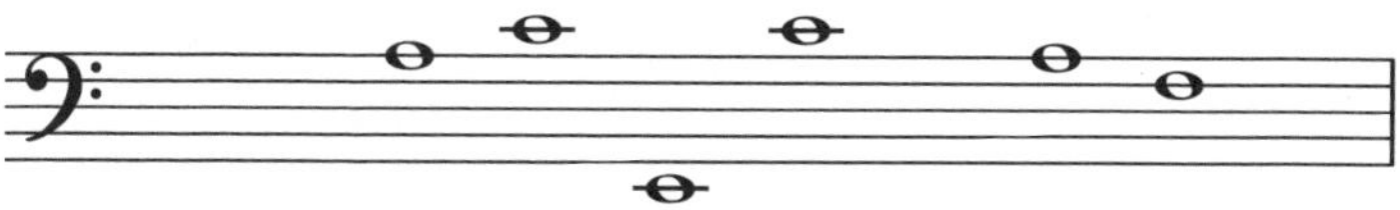

S P _ _ _ _ R _ _ T

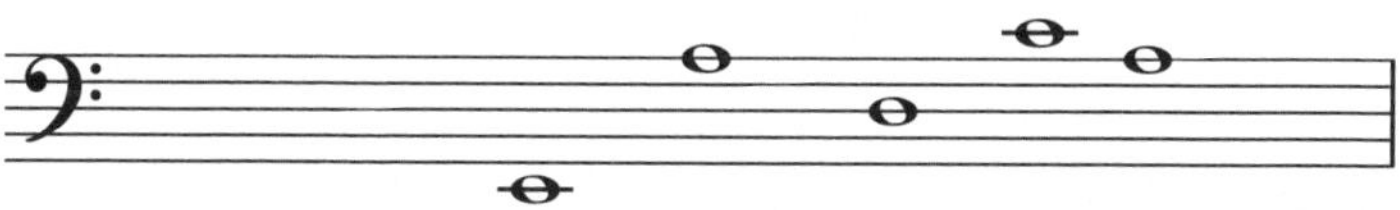

H O R S _ _ N _ _ _ R T

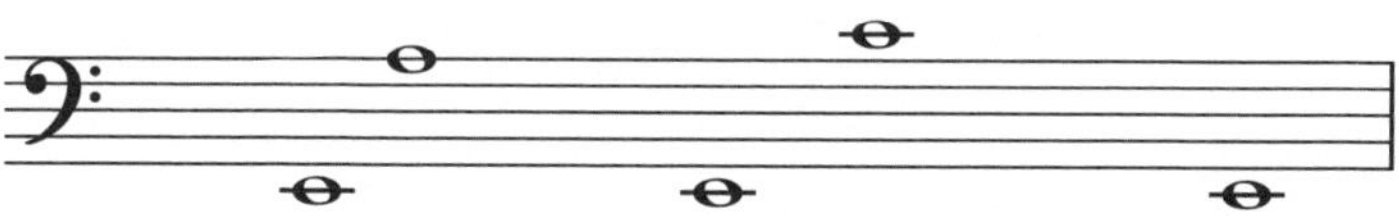

P L _ _ S U R _ _ R U I S _ R

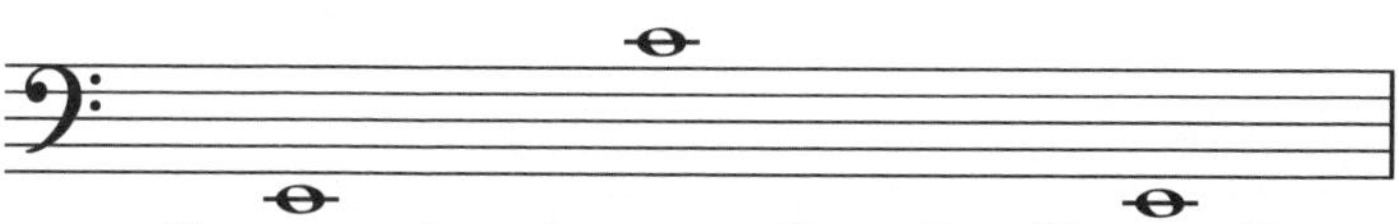

H _ L I _ O P T _ R

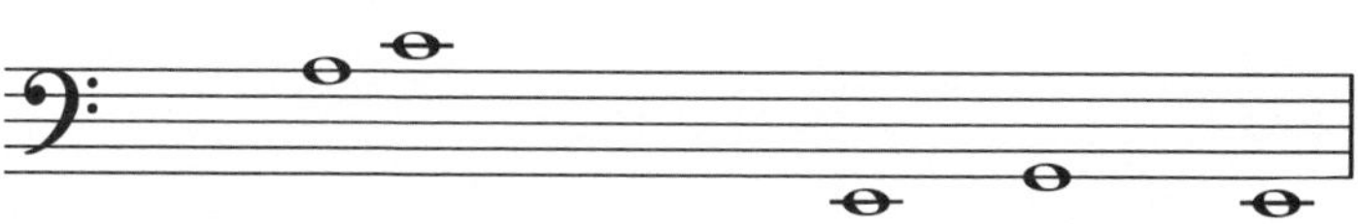

T R _ _ T I O N _ N _ I N _

# E Below and C Above The Stave: EXERCISE 2

## Write the boxed letters as line notes on the staves

### FOOTBALL CLUBS

Example

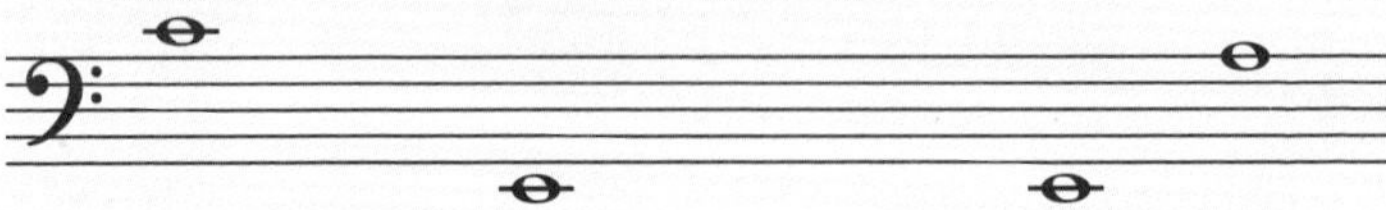

**C** H **E** L S **E** **A**

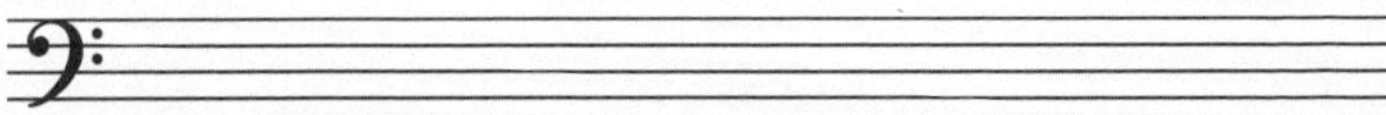

N **E** W **C** **A** S T L **E** U N I T **E** **D**

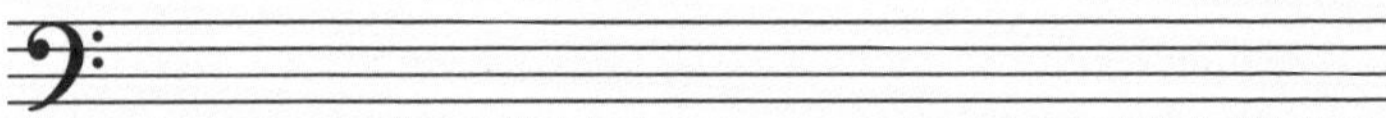

M **A** N **C** H **E** S T **E** R U N I T **E** **D**

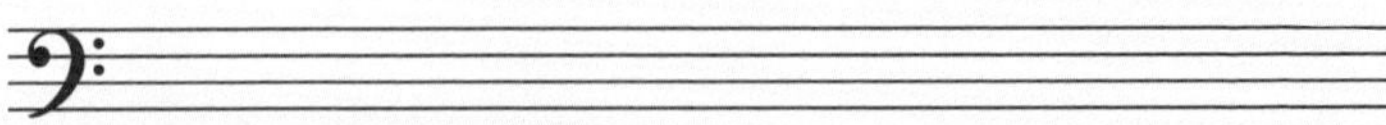

**B** L **A** **C** K **B** U R N R O V **E** R S

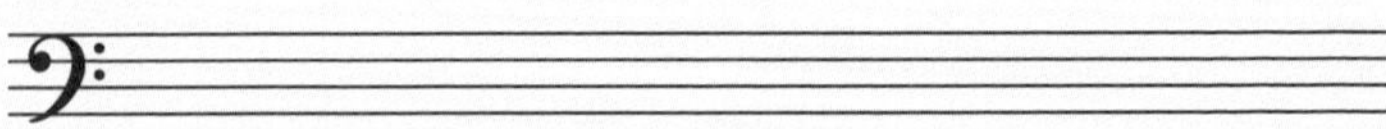

**D** **E** R **B** Y **C** O U N T Y

CHARLTON ATHLETIC

CRYSTAL PALACE

DONCASTER ROVERS

MACCLESFIELD

WYCOMBE WANDERERS

# Putting Space and Line Notes Together

As with the treble clef, the space notes and line notes interlock to give the notes of the C major scale: the note names C, D, E, F, G, A and B without any accidentals. These are again the same notes as the white notes of a piano or keyboard.

# How line notes and space notes fit together

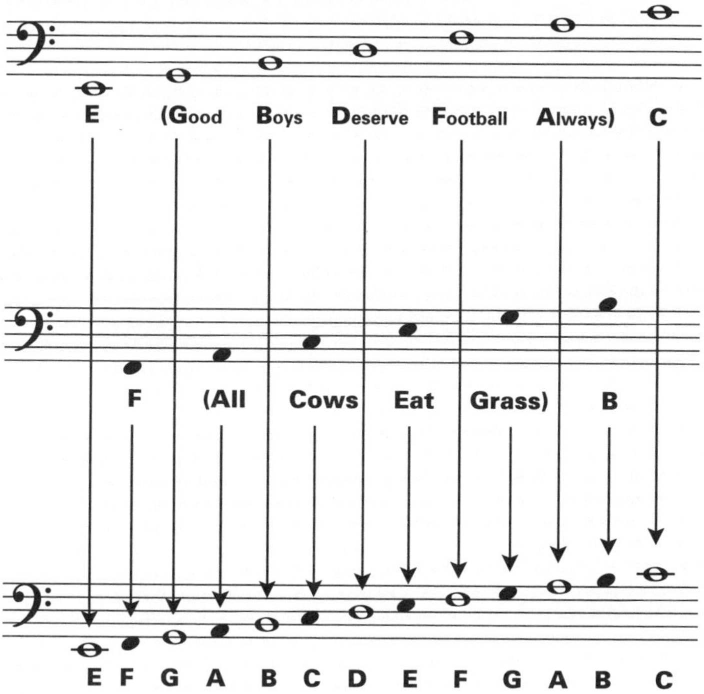

# Octaves

Just as in the treble clef, octaves appear in the bass clef; after every seven notes of the C major scale, the same note sequence is repeated. If you have learned the treble clef as well, by now you will have come across four or five different Es.

Make sure you can distinguish between the lower and higher notes of the same name on your instrument by going through each pair of notes in turn and making a mental note of how they differ.

# Octaves

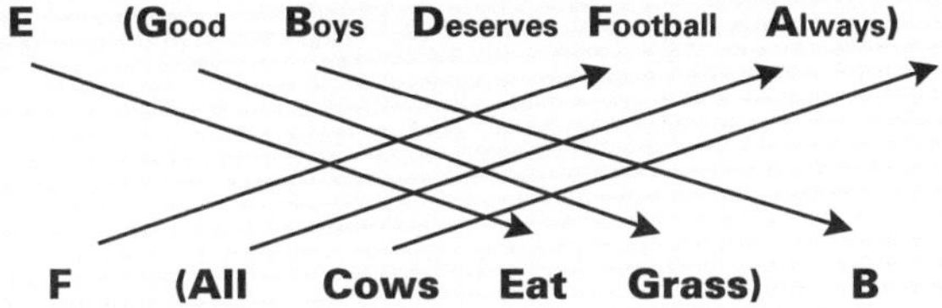
E (Good Boys Deserves Football Always) C
F (All Cows Eat Grass) B

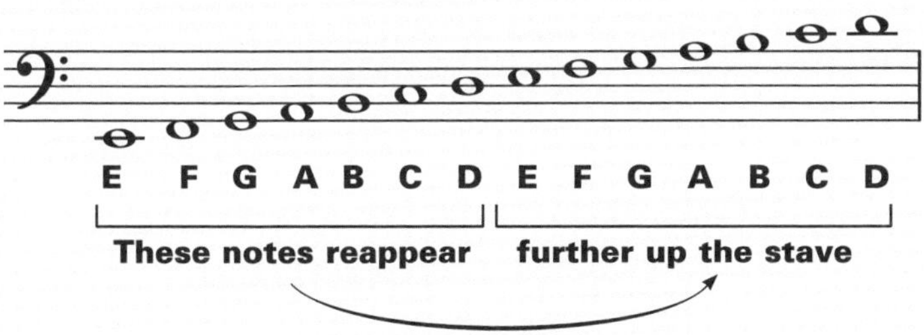
E F G A B C D E F G A B C D
These notes reappear further up the stave

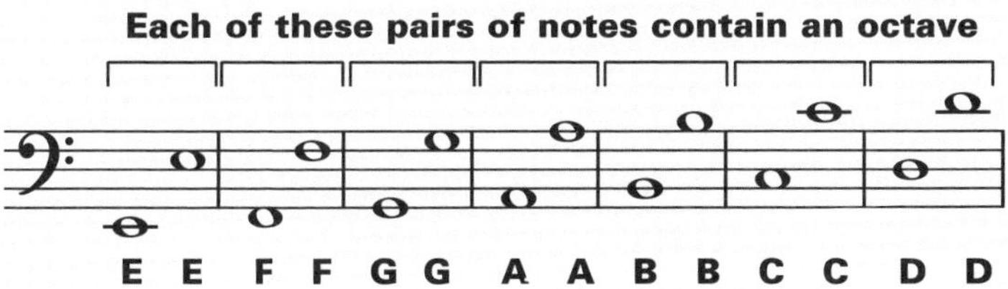
Each of these pairs of notes contain an octave
E E F F G G A A B B C C D D

# Finding E–C On An Instrument

Finding these notes on your instrument is most easily achieved by finding middle C and then working downwards through the notes of the C major scale until you reach the second E below middle C.

## Finding E–C on your instrument

middle C B A G F E D C B A G F E

## The same notes on a keyboard

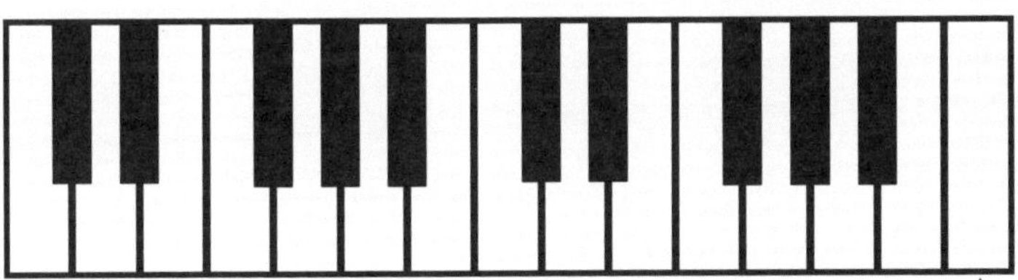

E F G A B C D E F G A B ↑ middle C

## The same notes on bass guitar (standard tuning)

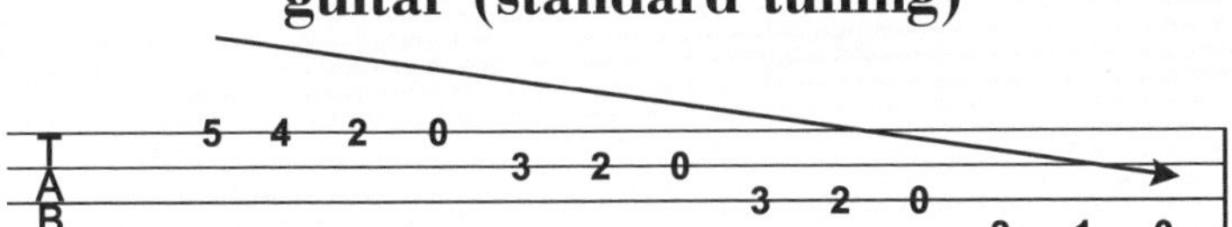


middle C B A G F E D C B A G F E

Pitch
Treble Clef
Bass Clef
Rhythm
Play Along 1
ACC Accidentals
Key Sign
Scales
Chords
Other Chords
Play Along 2
Comp

# Notes E–C: EXERCISE 1

## Fill in the missing letters using the given notes

### DANCES

Example

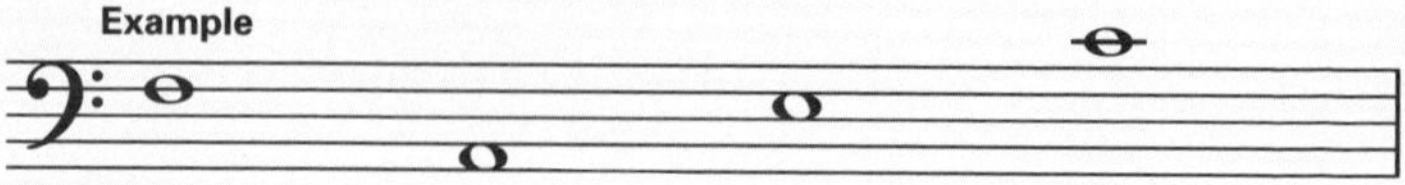

F L A M E N C O

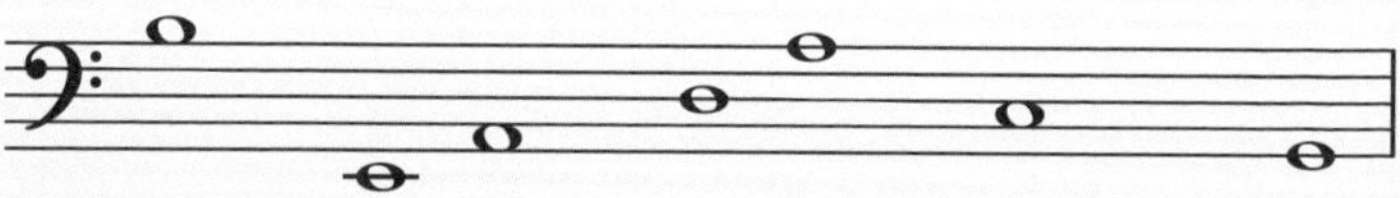

_ R _ _ K _ _ N _ I N _

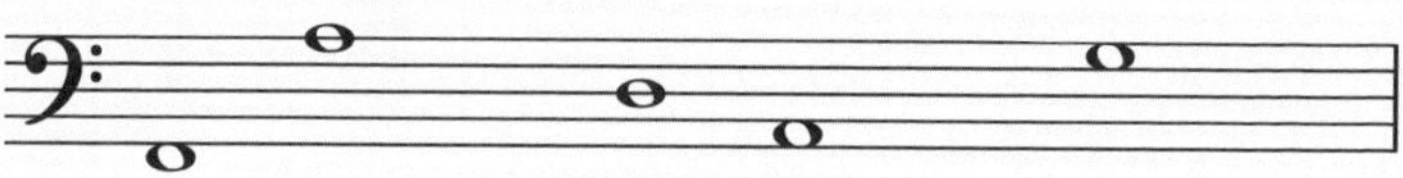

_ _ N _ _ N _ O

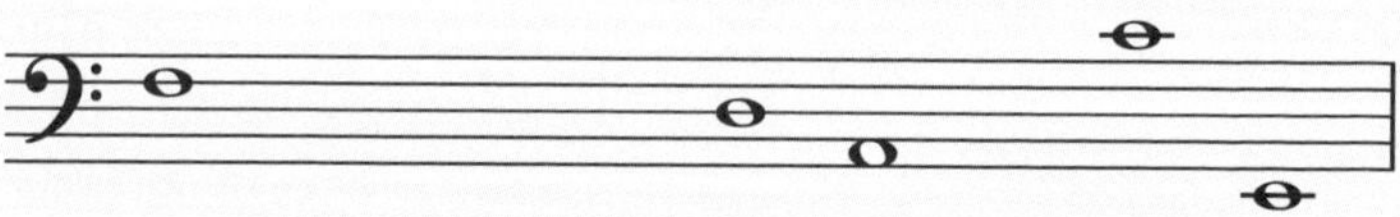

_ O L K _ _ N C _

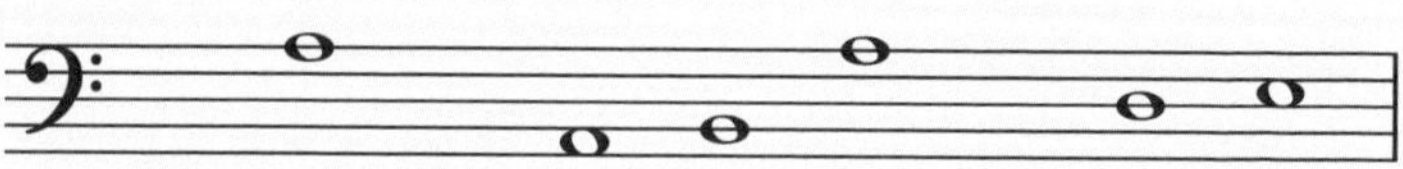

S _ R _ _ _ N _ _

# EXERCISE 2

## FILMS

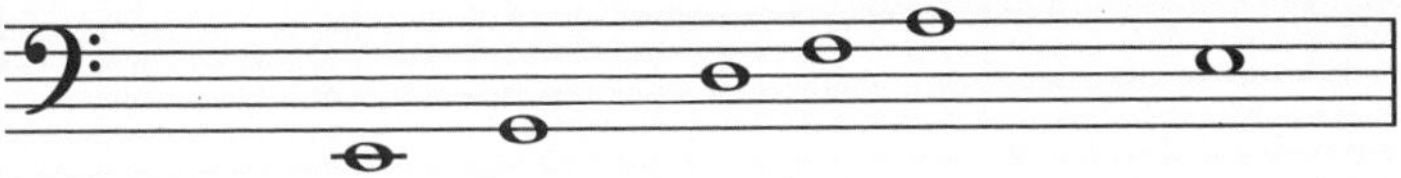

T H _ _ O _ _ _ T H _ R

_ _ S _ _ L _ N C _

T H _ _ R _ _ K F _ S T _ L U _

_ I _ L _ O _ _ R _ _ M S

T H _ _ R _ _ T _ S C _ P _

# Notes E–C: EXERCISE 3

## BRITISH BIRDS

C A N A D A G O O S E

R _ _ - _ R _ _ S T _ _ M _ R _ _ N S _ R

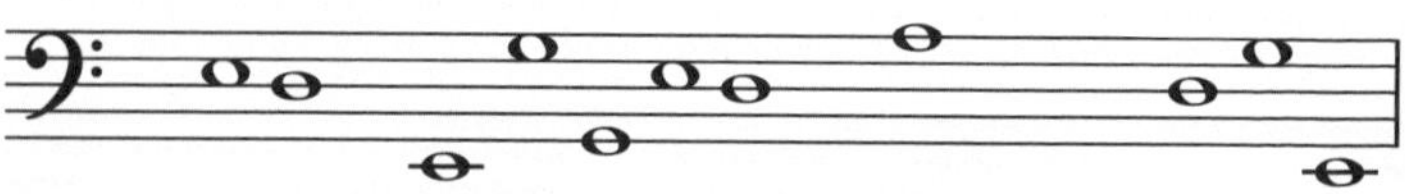

R _ _ - L _ _ _ _ _ _ P _ R T R I _ _ _

_ R _ _ T _ R _ S T _ _ _ R _ _ _

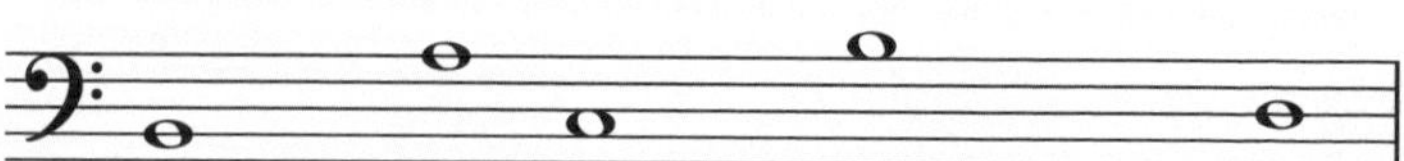

_ L _ _ K _ I R _

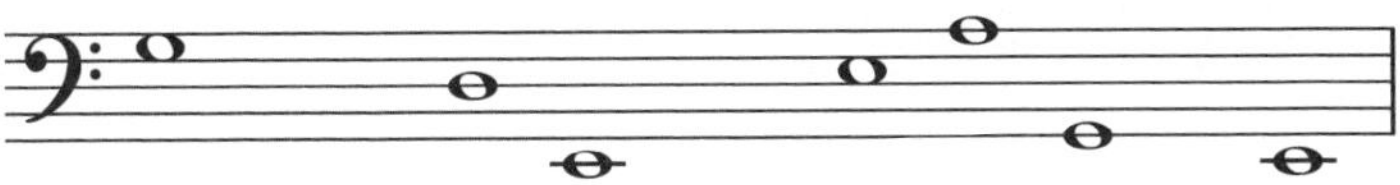

_ O L _ _ N _ _ _ L _

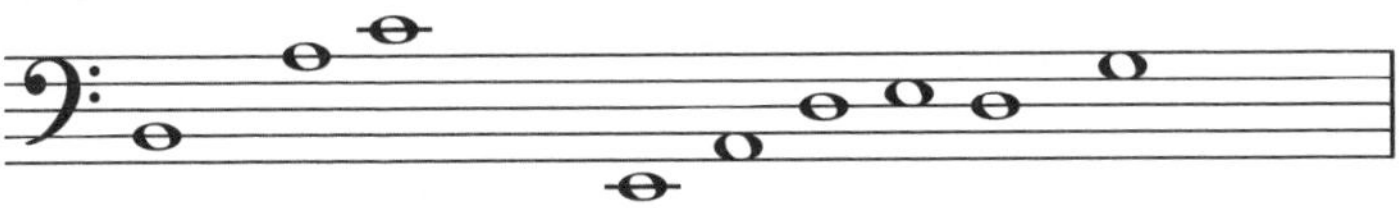

_ L _ _ K H _ _ _ _ _ _ U L L

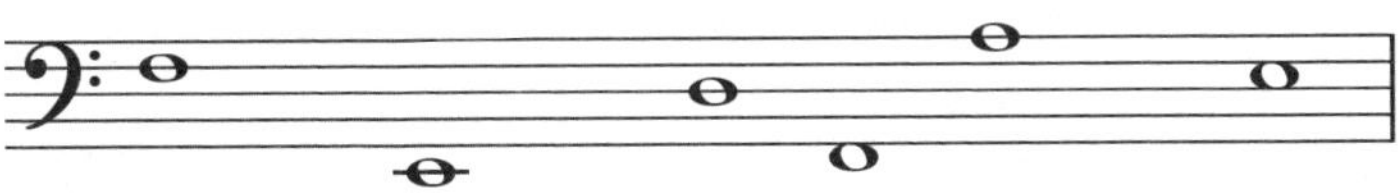

_ I _ L _ _ _ R _

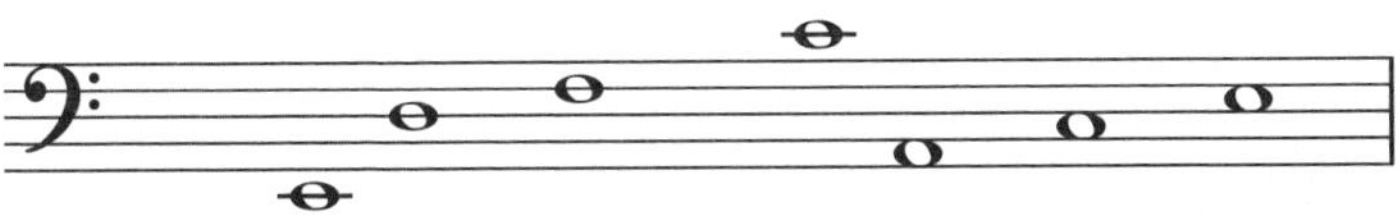

P I _ _ _ L Y _ _ T _ H _ R

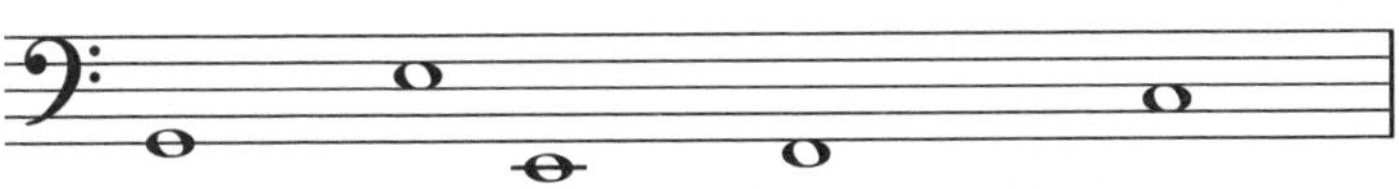

_ R _ _ N _ I N _ H

# Bass Clef: Exercises on E–B

**These exercises use the notes E–B. For each exercise, first say the note names. Then say and play (or sing) each note in turn. Finally, play all the notes through without saying them.**

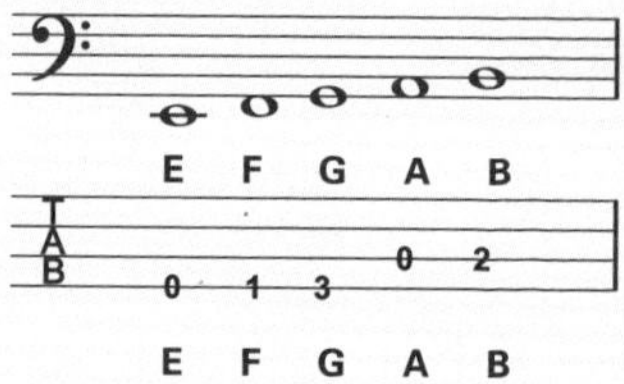


No. 1

No. 2

No. 3

No. 4

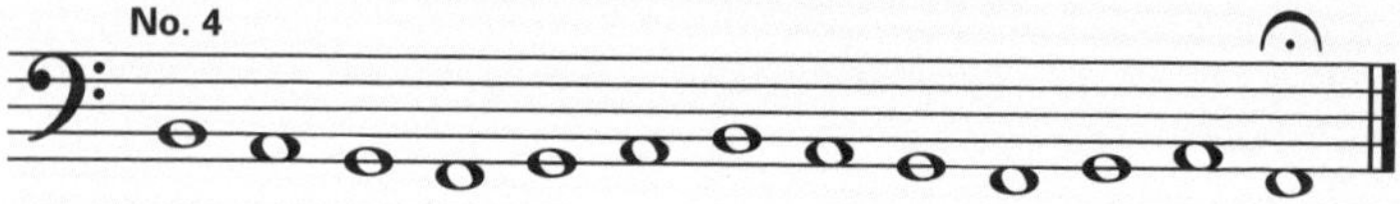

No. 5

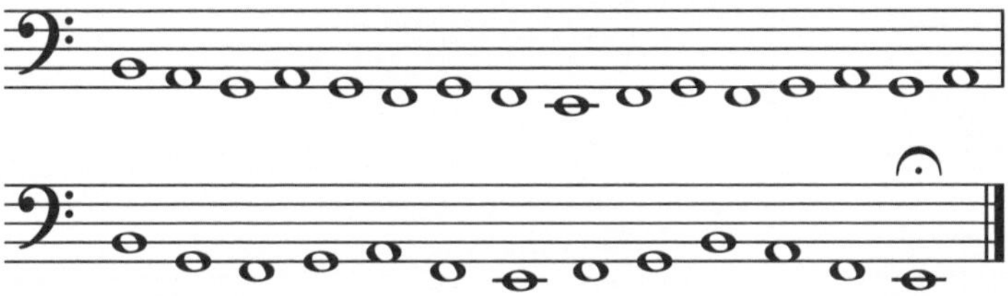

No. 6

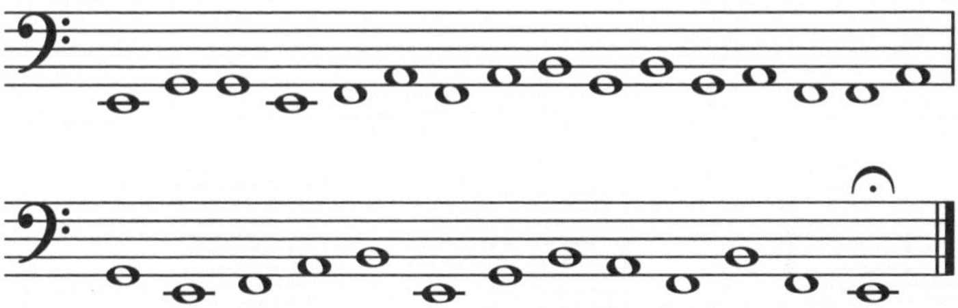

No. 7

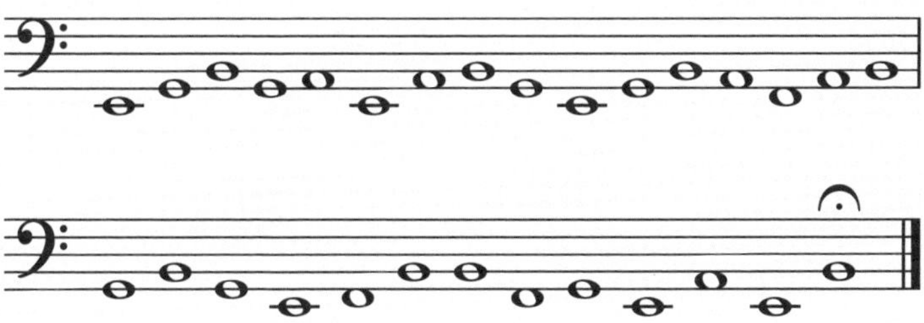

# Exercises on C–G

## These exercises use the notes C–G

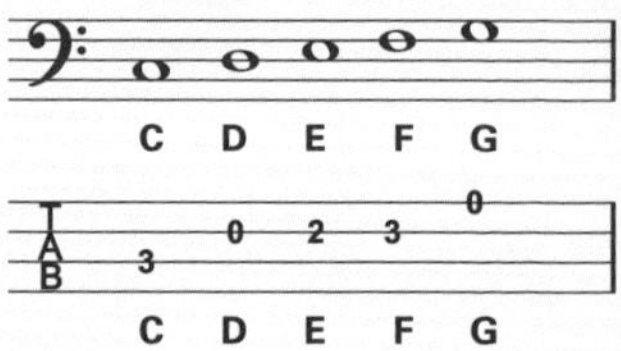


No. 1

No. 2

No. 3

No. 4

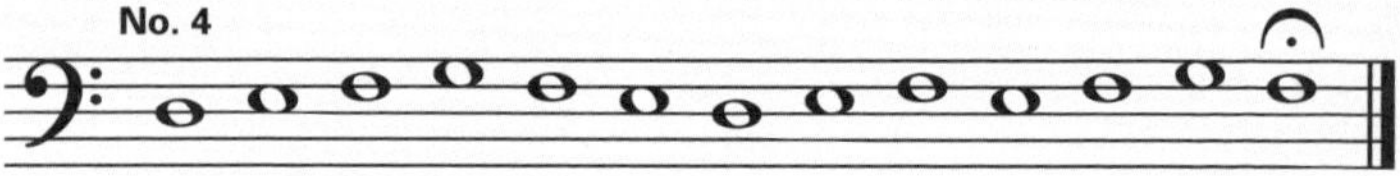

No. 5

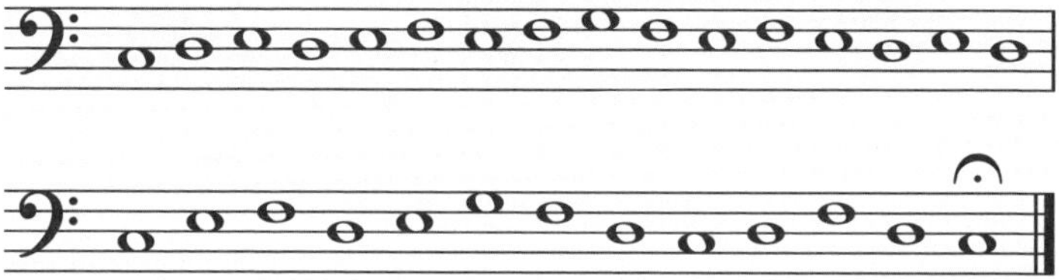

No. 6

No. 7

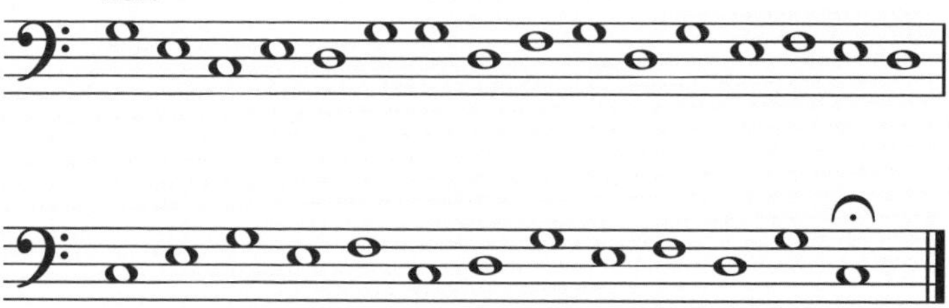

# Exercises on F–C

## These exercises use the notes F–C

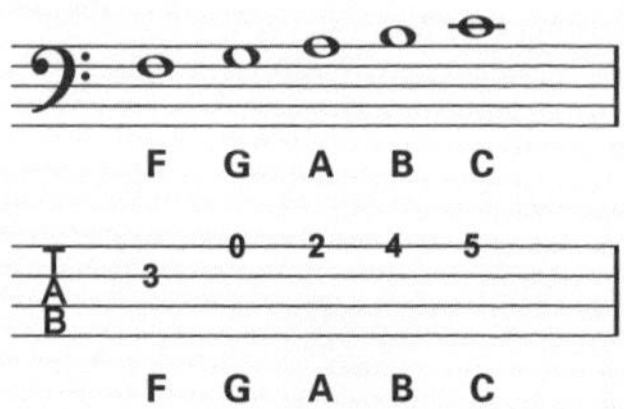


No. 1

No. 2

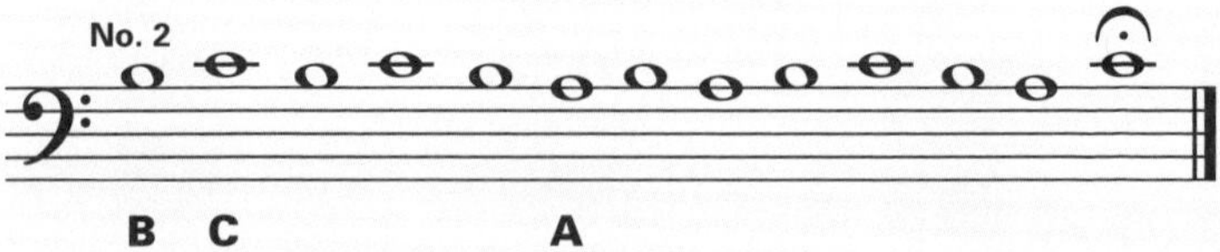


No. 3

No. 4

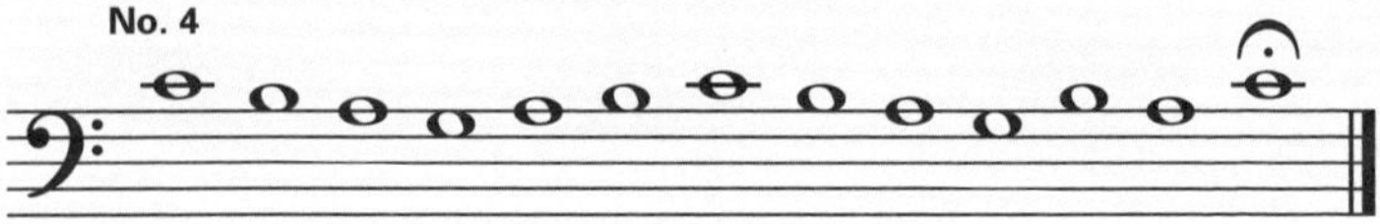

**No. 5**

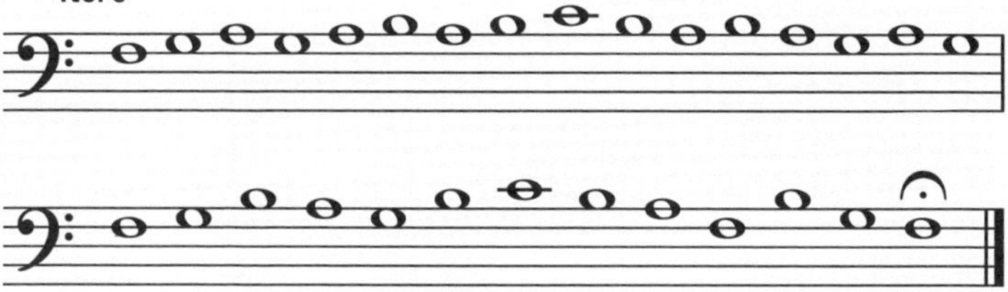

**No. 6**

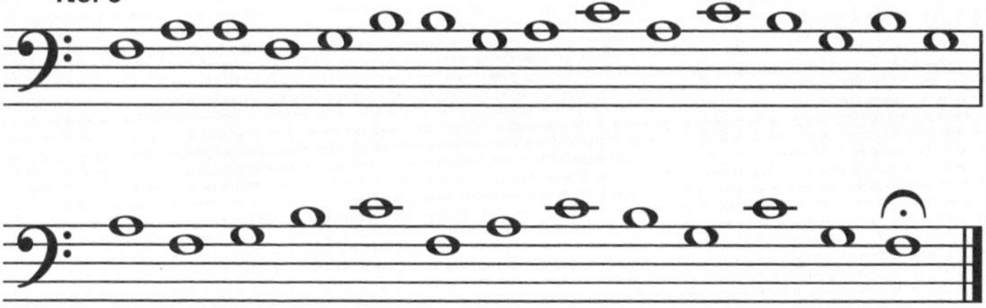

**No. 7**

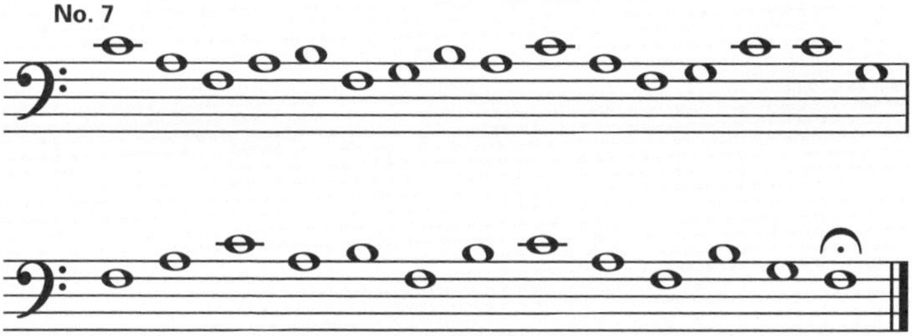

# Exercises on E–E

## These exercises use the notes E–E

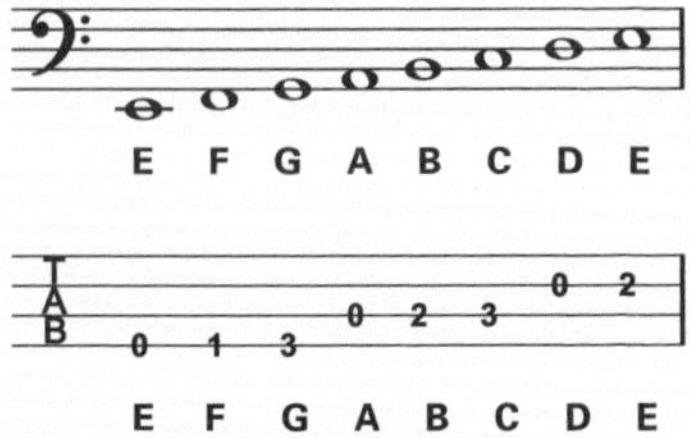


**No. 1**

**No. 2**

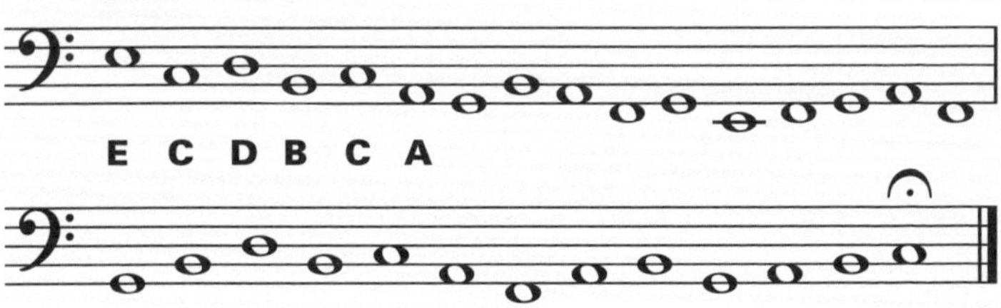

No. 3

No. 4

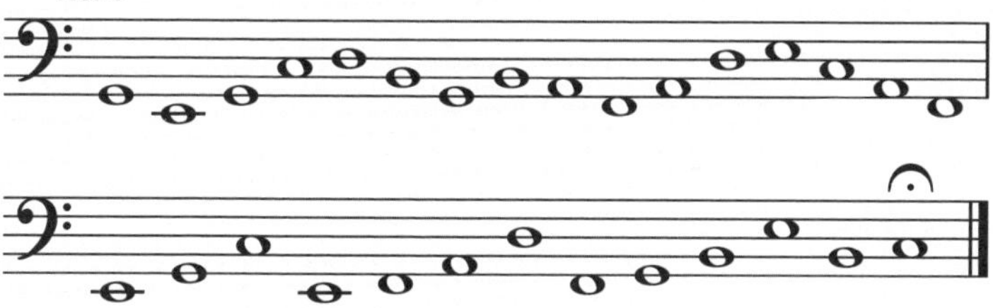

No. 5

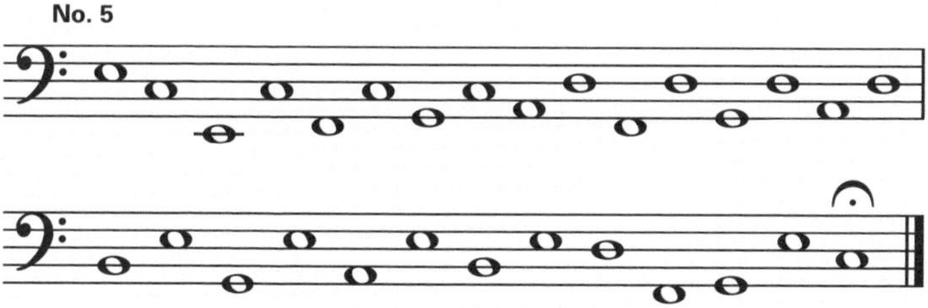

# Exercises on A–A

## These exercises use the notes A–A

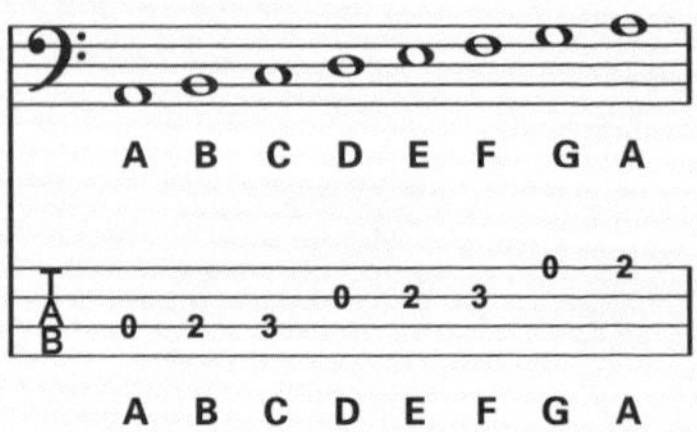


No. 1

No. 2

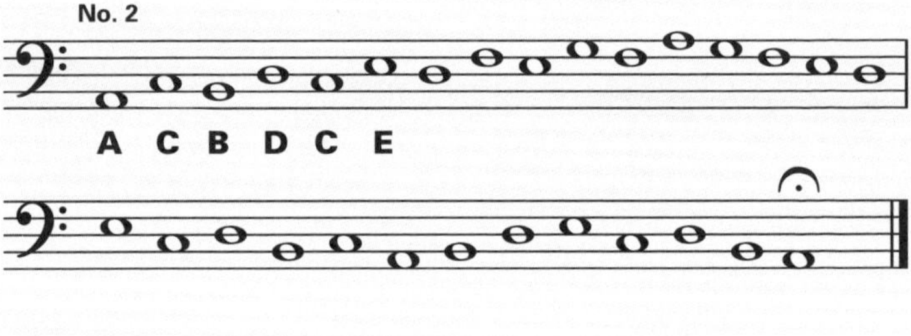

**No. 3**

**No. 4**

**No. 5**

# Exercises on C–C

**These exercises use the notes C–C**

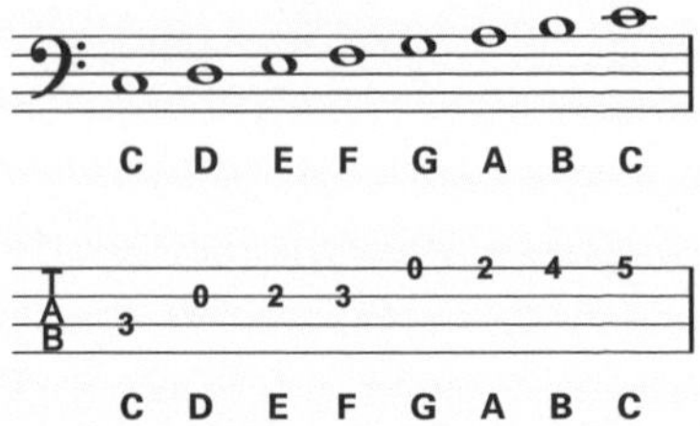


No. 1

No. 2

No. 3

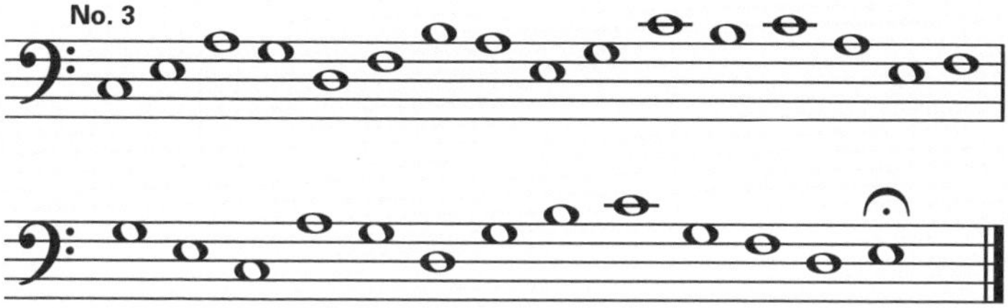

No. 4

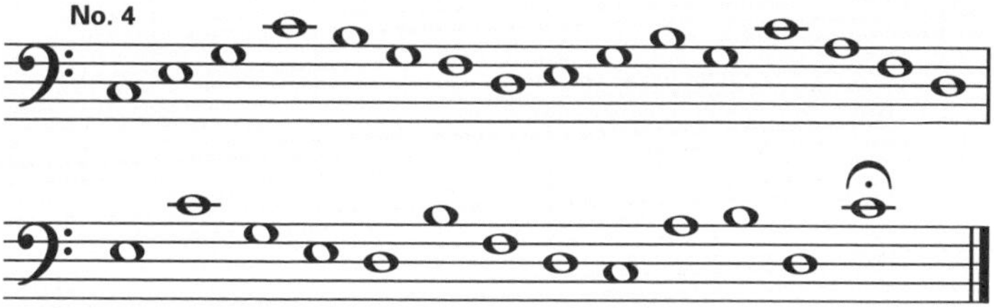

No. 5

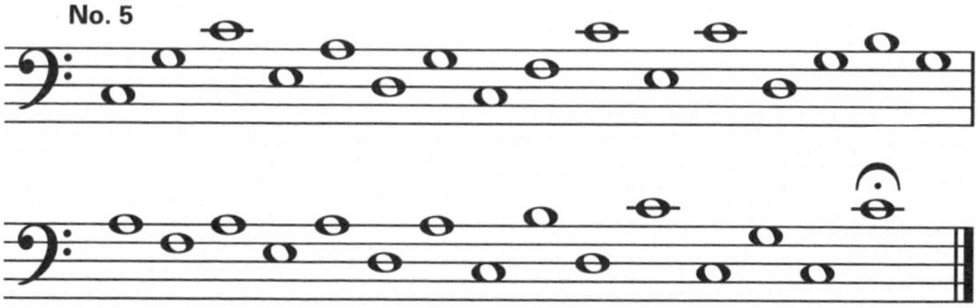

Pitch
Treble Clef
Bass Clef
Rhythm
Play Along 1
ACC Accidentals
Key Sign
Scales
Chords
Other Chords
Play Along 2
Comp

# Exercises on E–C

## These exercises use the notes E–C

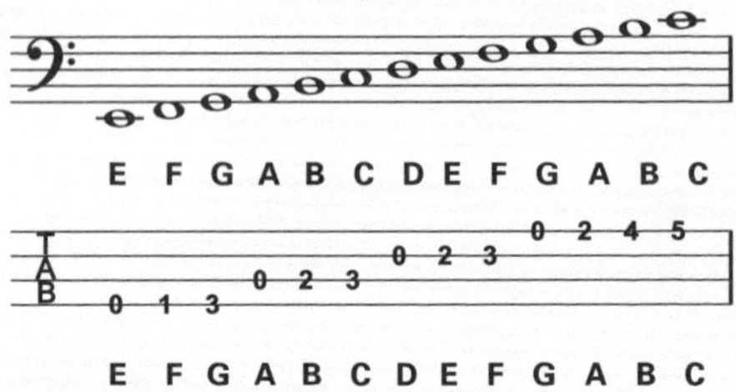


No. 1

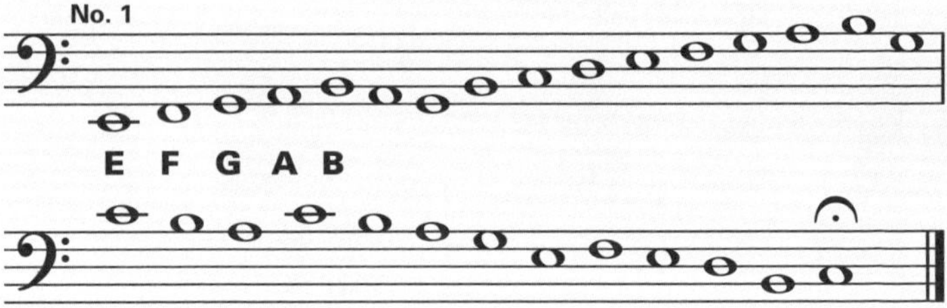


No. 2

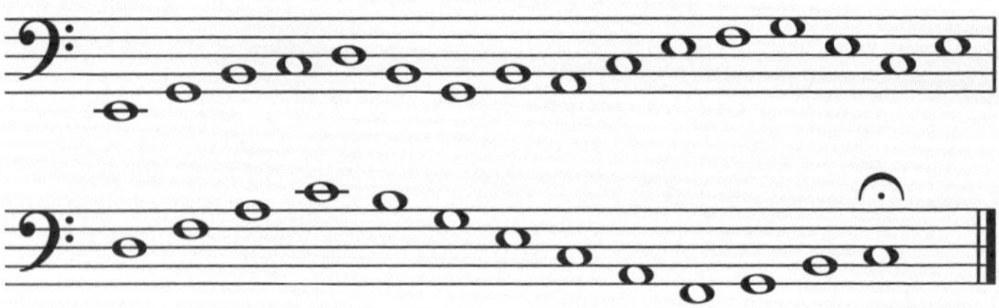

No. 3

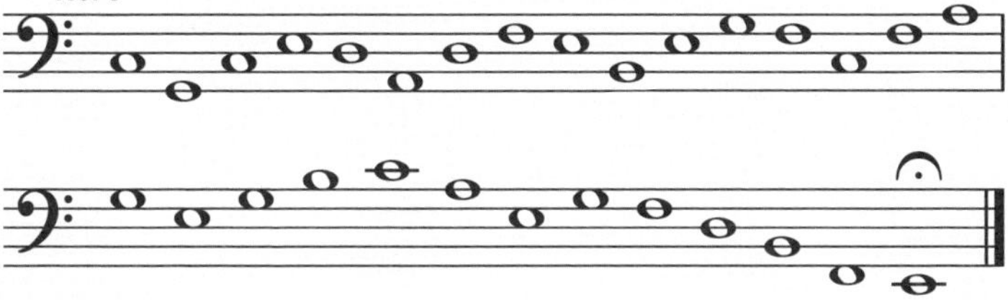

No. 4

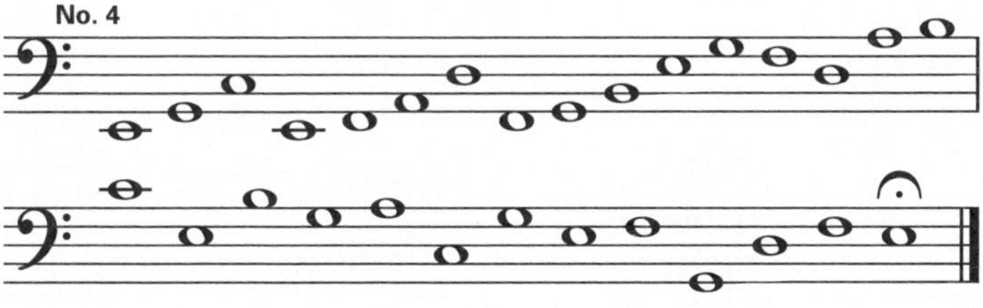

No. 5

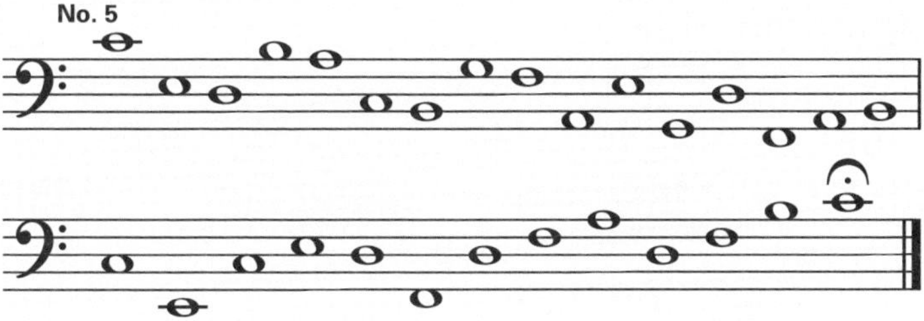

Pitch
Treble Clef
Bass Clef
Rhythm
Play Along 1
ACC Accidentals
Key Sign
Scales
Chords
Other Chords
Play Along 2
Comp

# A–D Below The Stave

## Notes below the bass clef

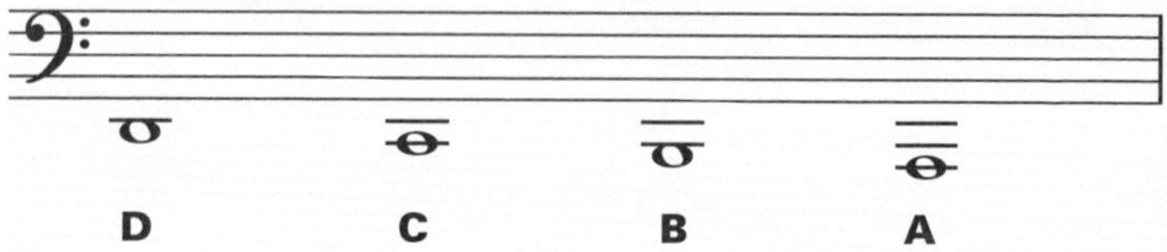


## Finding these notes on your instrument

**First find middle C**

**Then find:**

the second D below middle C

the second C below middle C

the third B below middle C

the third A below middle C

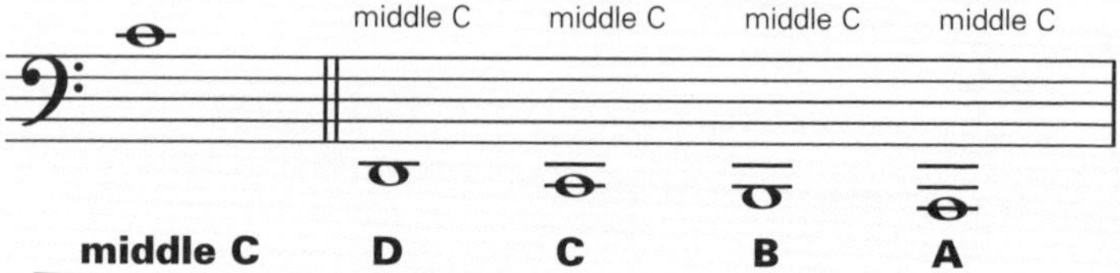


**Each note is lower than the previous one**

# D–A on a keyboard

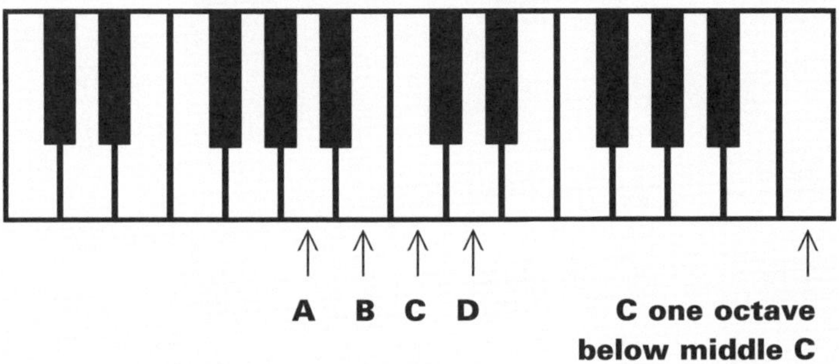


**These notes are out of range for a bass guitar set to standard tuning**

# Exercises on C–G Below The Stave

## These exercises use the notes C–G

No. 1

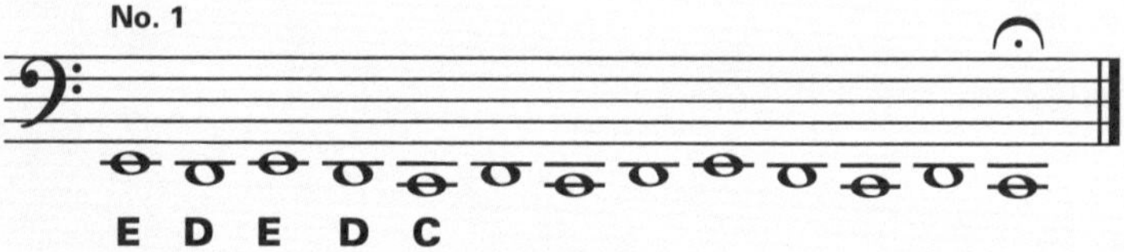


No. 2

No. 3

# Exercises on A–E Below The Stave

## These exercises use the notes A–E

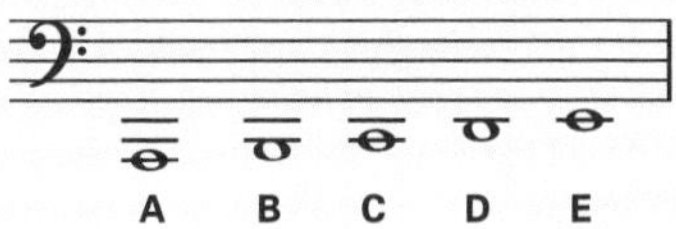


**No. 1**

**No. 2**

**No. 3**

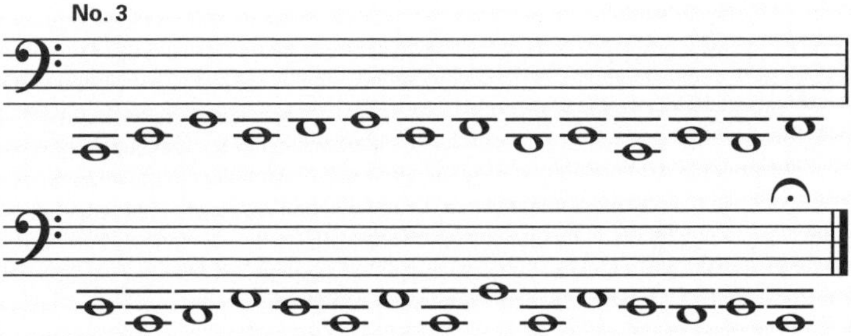

Pitch
Treble Clef
Bass Clef
Rhythm
Play Along 1
ACC Accidentals
Key Sign
Scales
Chords
Other Chords
Play Along 2
Comp

# D–G Above The Stave

## Notes above the bass clef

## Finding these notes on your instrument

**First find middle C**

**Then find:**

the first C above middle C

the first E above middle C

the first F above middle C

the first G above middle C

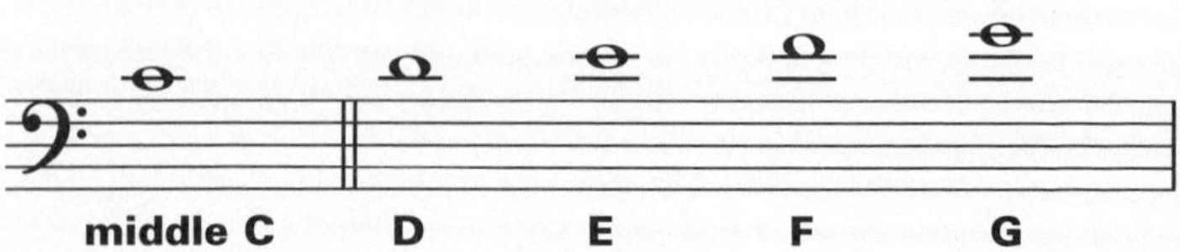


**Each note is higher than the previous one**

## D–G on a keyboard

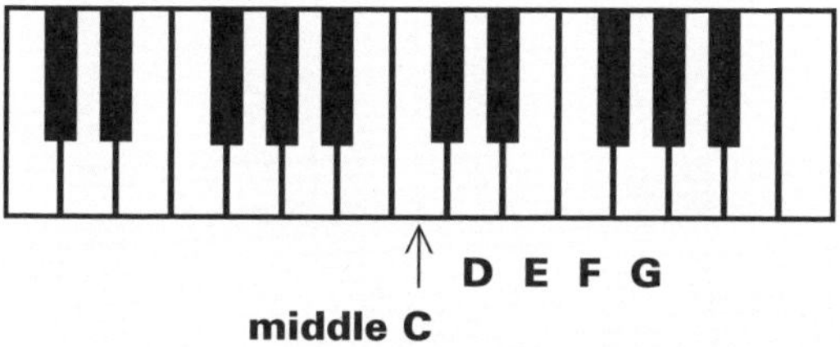


## D–G on bass guitar (standard tuning)

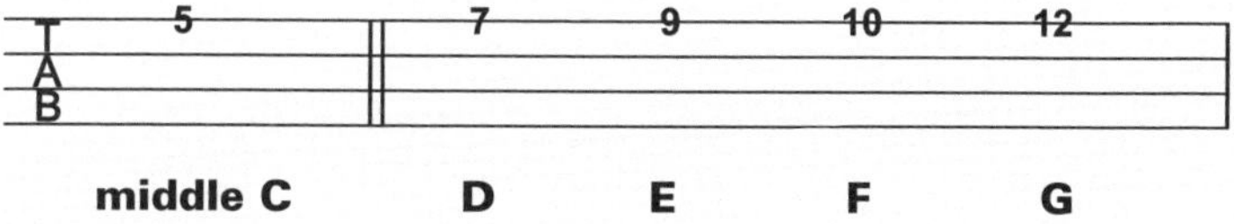


Pitch
Treble Clef
Bass Clef
Rhythm
Play Along 1
ACC Accidentals
Key Sign
Scales
Chords
Other Chords
Play Along 2
Comp

# Exercises on A–E Above The Stave

## These exercises use the notes A–E

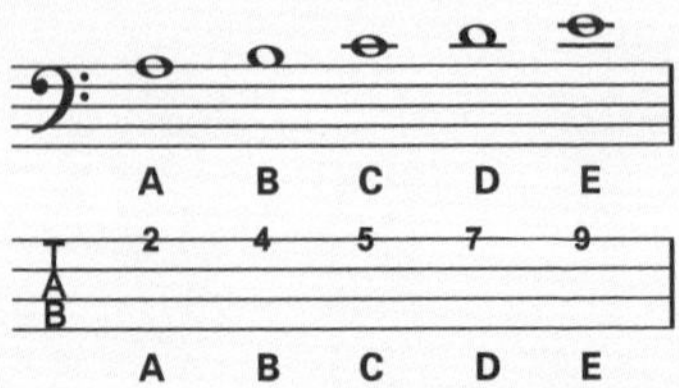


**No. 1**

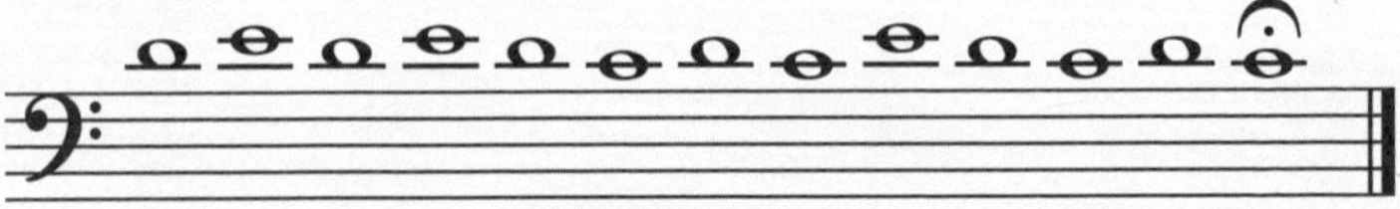

**D E D E D C**

**No. 2**

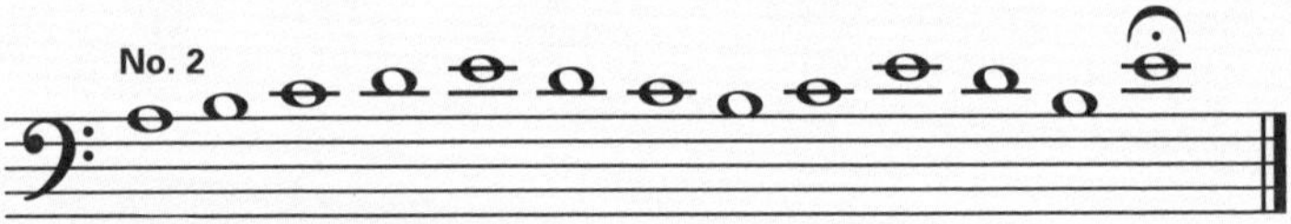

**A B C D E**

**No. 3**

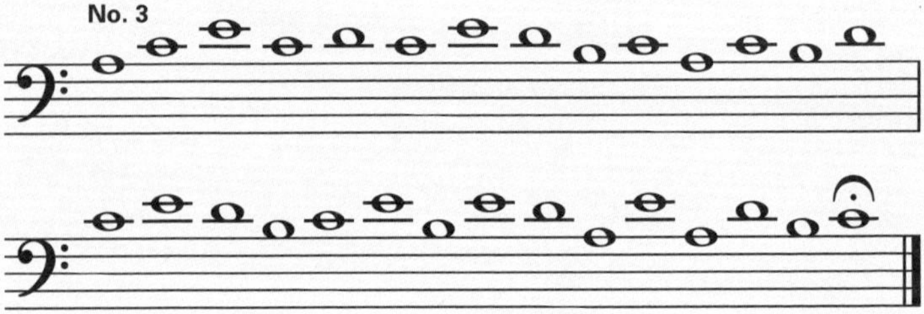

# Exercises on C–G Above The Stave

## These exercises use the notes C–G

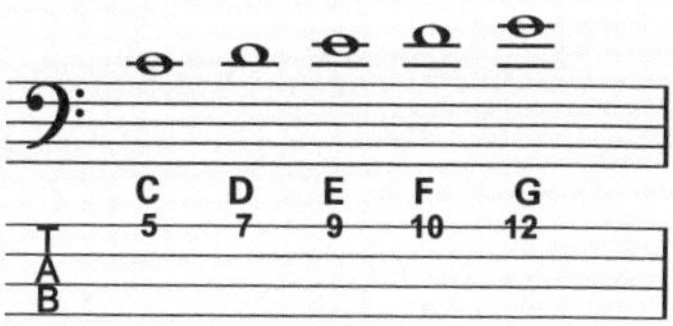


C D E F G

No. 1

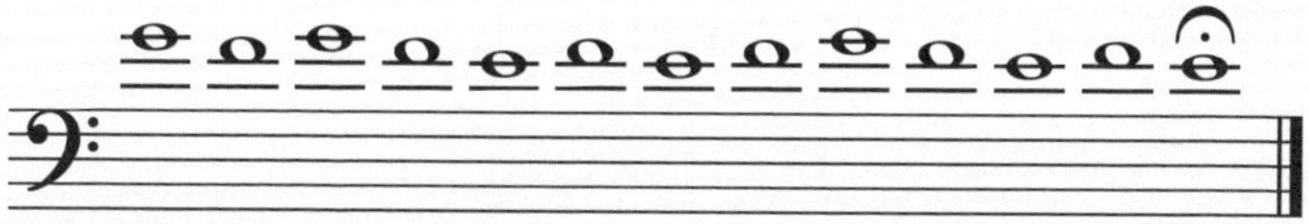

G F G F E

No. 2

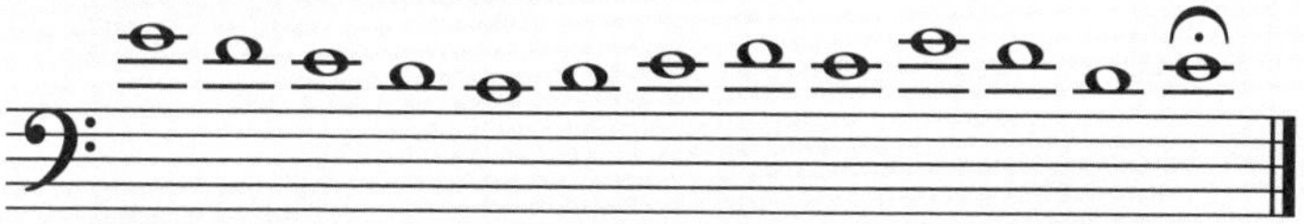

G F E D C

No. 3

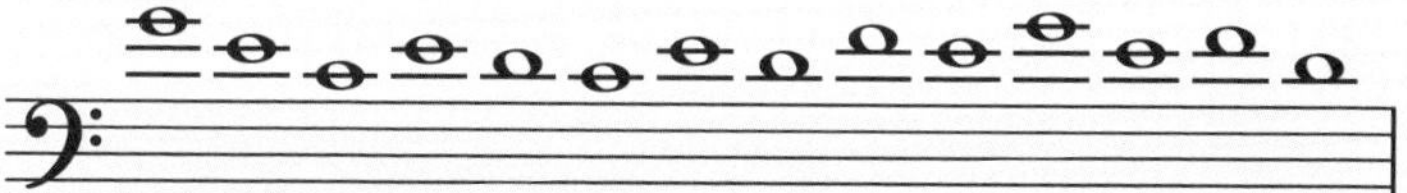

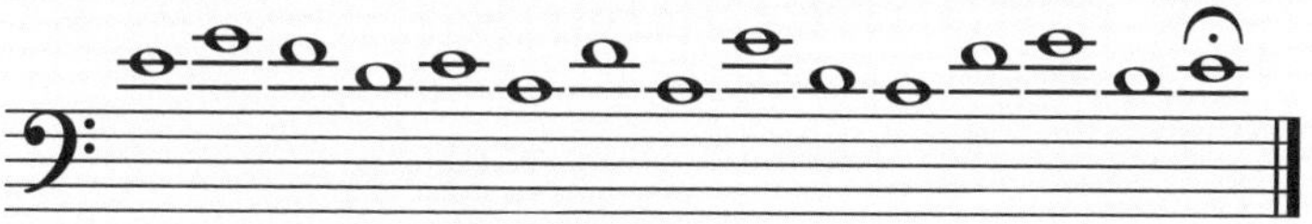

# Rhythm

Rhythm is the essential ingredient of all music. It is important in all styles of music, although it is more obvious in some types of music, such as African drumming, than others, such as plainsong.

What is rhythm? Basically, it includes all aspects of music to do with time. This can be split up into the following categories:

## Tempo

This is the speed of the music, which can be from very slow to very fast. It can also speed up or slow down.

## Metre

The metre of a piece of music is the number of beats in each bar and how they are grouped. Most rock and pop music, for instance, is in 4/4 or four beats to a bar, whereas waltzes are in 3/4 or three beats a bar.

## Rhythm

This is the actual sequence of note-values that make up the music: three short notes followed by one long one and then two short ones, for instance. Most of this section will concentrate on how to read note values.

# Keeping A Steady Pulse

The key to reading rhythm successfully is to be able to do it in time. To do this, you need to have a steady pulse beating in your head as you read and play the notes.

As practice, get hold of a clock or watch that makes a ticking noise every second. Clap your hands every time the clock ticks and keep going until you are exactly in time with the clock, clapping every second. You are clapping at 60 beats per minute (60b.p.m.)

Now clap twice for every tick of the clock, trying to make your claps as evenly-spaced as possible. You should be clapping twice a second, 120 times a minute, or 120 b.p.m.

Now clap four times for each tick of the clock, again aiming to make your claps as even and regular as possible. This speed is 240 b.p.m.

Next, try clapping along to the main beat of a recording of a piece of music. This may be easiest with a rock or pop song with a drum track, as the drum kit normally emphasizes the main beat very strongly.

When you try out the exercises on the following pages, always try to keep a similarly strong pulse. If possible, get hold of a metronome, a device which gives out a steady pulse for whichever tempo you select.

Learning the first few note values (quavers, crotchets, minims and semibreves) up to page 163 and their equivalent rests on page 183 will be enough to get you started. You can then return to the other note values from pages 164–181 as and when you need to learn them.

# Note Values

In the previous section on pitch, we only looked at the part of a note known as the notehead. This, together with several other parts that may or may not be found on a typical note, tells you how long the note lasts: what its note value is. The following parts of a note affect its note value:

- the notehead, which may be filled-in or hollow
- a dot, which might be found to the right of the notehead
- a stem, a vertical line leading up or down from the notehead
- a flag, which can be found at the end of the stem
- a beam, which can be found joining several note stems together.

Each different note value has its own particular combination of one or more of these features. To work out how long a particular note lasts, you need to identify which of the above features the note has. Most note values have one or more of these features, so the best way to learn them is to memorize what each note value looks like so that you can spot it quickly.

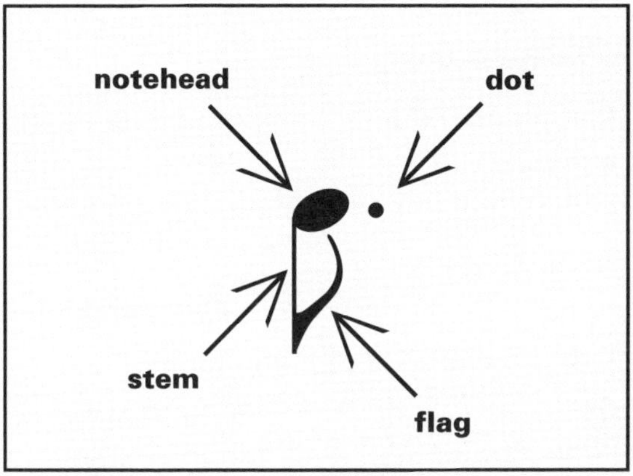
notehead
dot
stem
flag

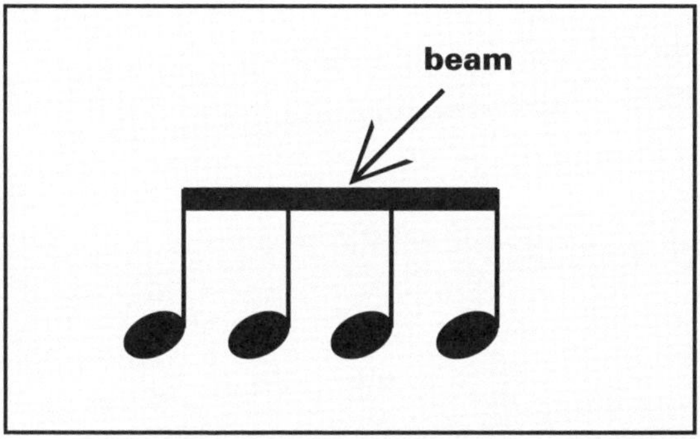
beam

# Quavers

The first note value we will look at is called the quaver, or eighth-note.

A quaver on its own has:

- a filled-in notehead
- a stem
- a single flag.

However, if there are two or more quavers next to each other, they can be joined together in groups by a single beam, which replaces any flags.

For quavers and all other notes with stems, the stem direction depends on where the note is on the stave. If the note is above the middle line, the stem goes down. If it is below the middle line, then the stem goes up. If the note is on the middle line, the stem can go either up or down. This rule applies to all notes with stems.

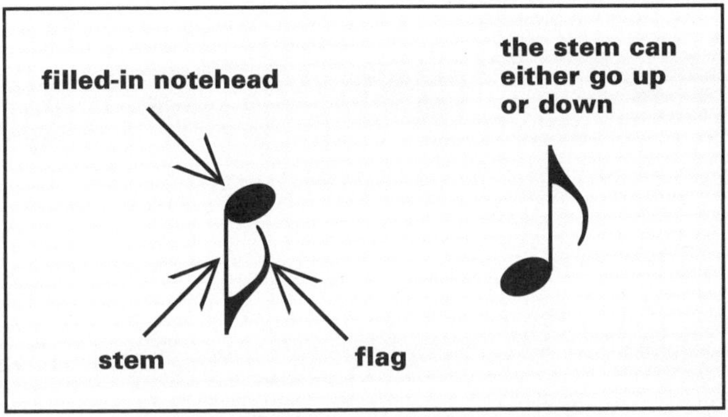
filled-in notehead
the stem can either go up or down
stem
flag

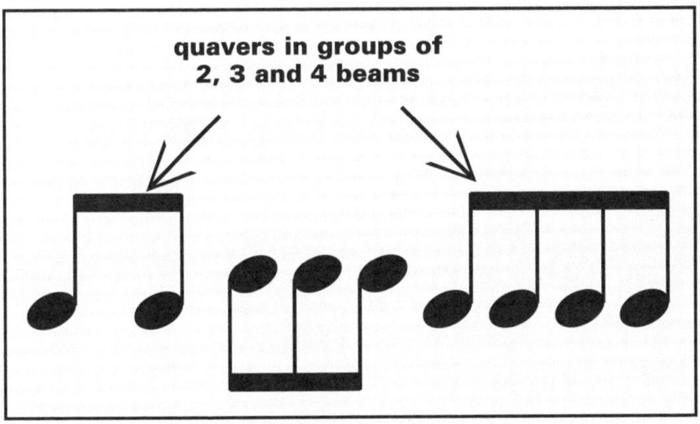
quavers in groups of 2, 3 and 4 beams

# Counting Quavers

When quavers appear in groups, it is important to be able to play them evenly.

Fitting each group of quavers to a regular pulse, such as the tick of a clock, practise saying the words to these patterns, putting a slight emphasis on the first syllable of each group.

Then clap the same groupings whilst saying the words, also putting a slight accent on the first note of each group.

Finally, clap the rhythms without the words, trying to stay in time and always emphasizing the first note of each group.

## quavers in groups of two

**1** 2 **1** 2 **1** 2 **1** 2 **1** 2 **1** 2 **1** 2 **1** 2

**pit**-ter **pat**-ter **pit**-ter **pat**-ter **pit**-ter **pat**-ter **pit**-ter **pat**-ter

## quavers in groups of three

**1** 2 3 **1** 2 3 **1** 2 3 **1** 2 3

**hig**-gle-dy **pig**-gle-dy **hig**-gle-dy **pig**-gle-dy

## quavers in groups of four

**1** 2 3 4 **1** 2 3 4 **1** 2 3 4 **1** 2 3 4

**cat**-er-pil-lar **cat**-er-pil-lar **cat**-er-pil-lar **cat**-er-pil-lar

## quavers in groups of six

**1** 2 3 4 5 6 **1** 2 3 4 5 6 **1** 2 3 4 5 6

one-and-two-and-three-and one-and-two-and-three-and one-and-two-and-three-and

Pitch
Treble Clef
Bass Clef
Rhythm
Play Along 1
ACC Accidentals
Key Sign
Scales
Chords
Other Chords
Play Along 2
Comp

Pitch
Treble Clef
Bass Clef
Rhythm
Play Along 1
ACC Accidentals
Key Sign
Scales
Chords
Other Chords
Play Along 2
Comp

# Crotchets

The second note value is the crotchet.

A crotchet has a filled-in notehead and a stem, but no flag or beam. Like quavers, a crotchet's stem can go either up or down (see page 140 for further explanation).

A crotchet lasts twice as long as a quaver. If you are counting in quavers, a crotchet will take up the same length of time as two quavers.

Practise clapping crotchets as you count quavers by counting '1 2 1 2 1 2...' and clapping every time you say '1'.

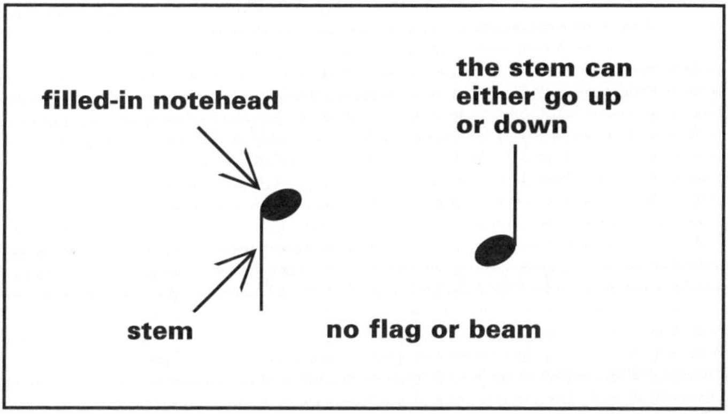
filled-in notehead
the stem can either go up or down
stem
no flag or beam

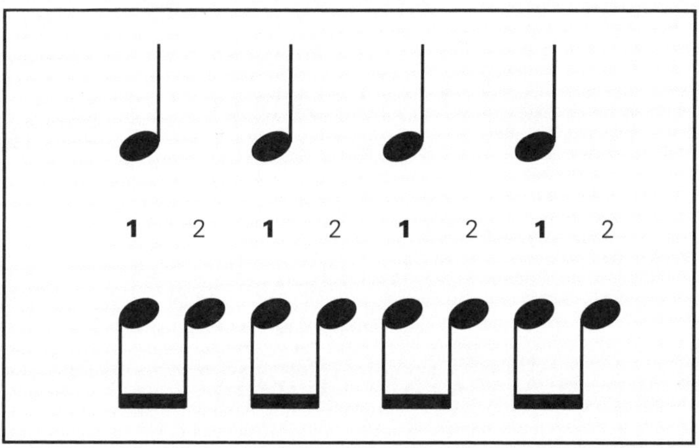
1 2 1 2 1 2 1 2

# Crotchet and Quaver Exercises

For the first half of each exercise, clap the rhythms in the boxes whilst counting out the numbers underneath, repeating this rhythm over and over again. Do not clap for numbers that are in brackets (or do a 'silent' clap). When ready, move on to the second half of each exercise, clapping the rhythms without the aid of the numbers written underneath.

**No. 1**

**No. 2**

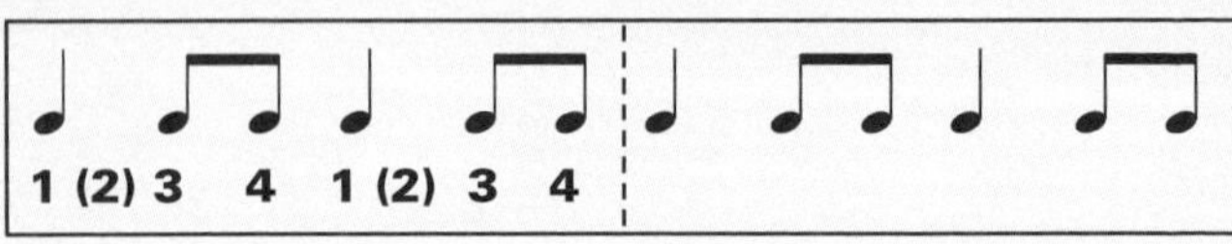


**No. 3**

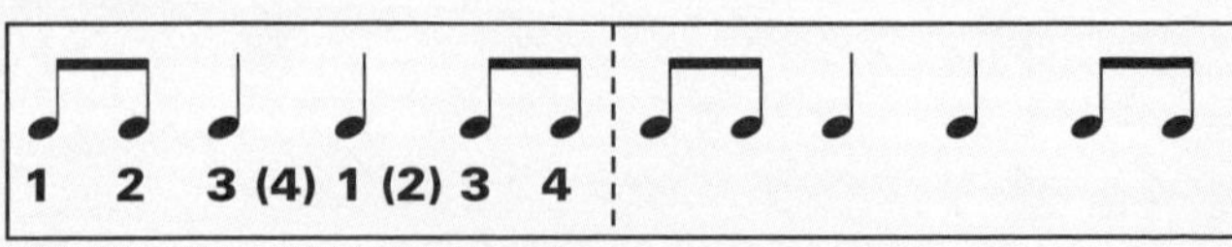


**No. 4**

No. 5

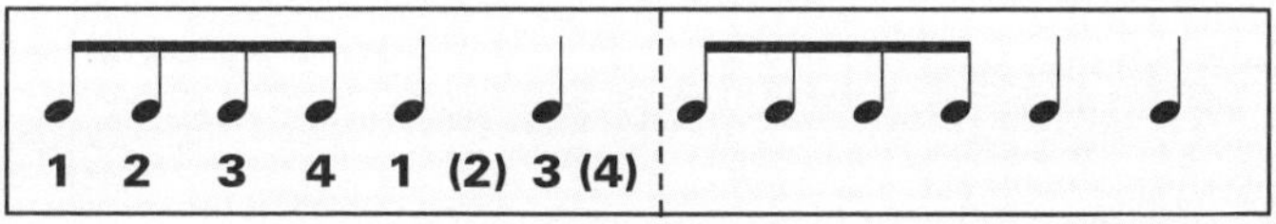


No. 6

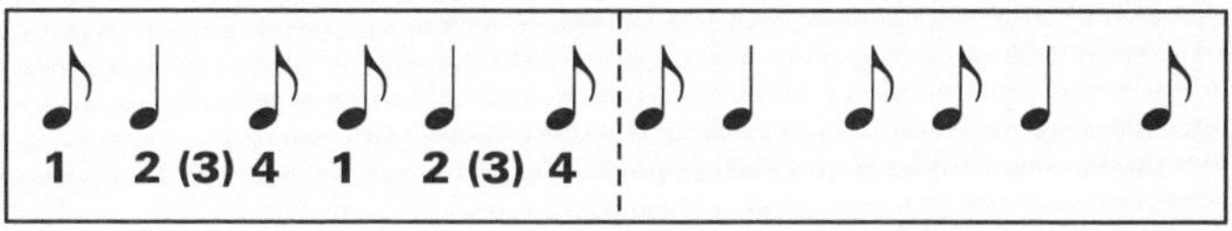


No. 7

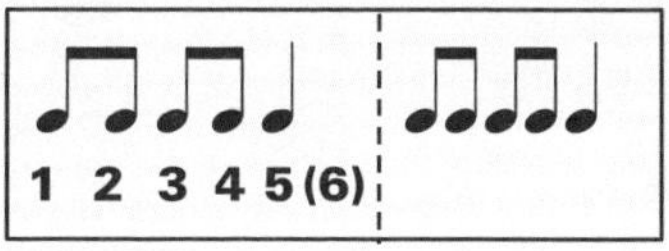


No. 8

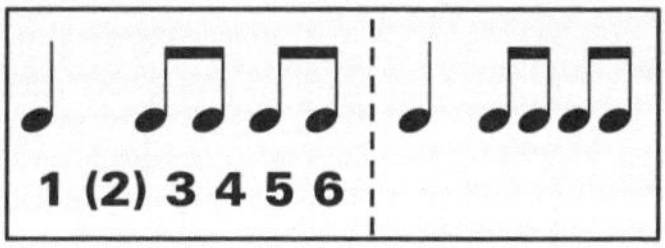


No. 9

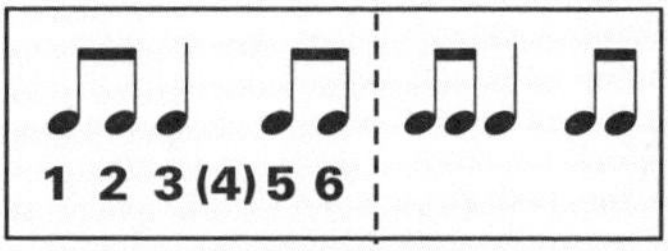


No. 10

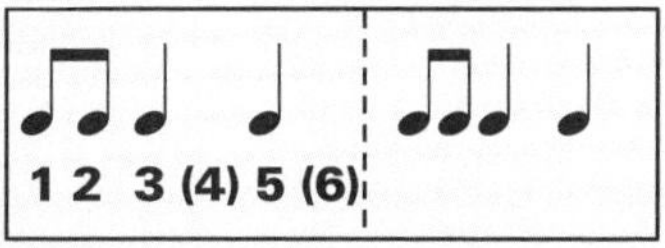


No. 11

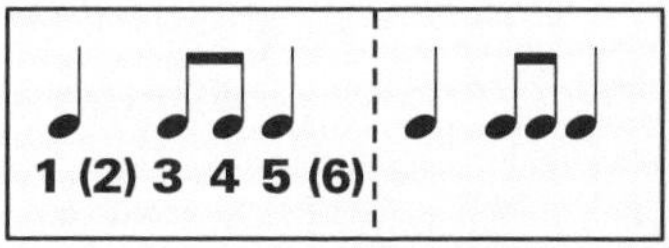


No. 12

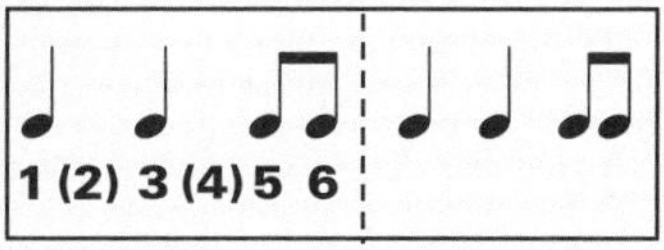

# Dotted Crotchets

A dotted crotchet is a crotchet with a dot written after it.

Unlike the crotchet, which is worth two quavers, a dotted crotchet is worth three quavers (a dot after a note means 'make the note longer by half of its value'). If you are counting in quavers, a crotchet will take up the same length of time as three quavers.

Practise clapping dotted crotchets as you count quavers by counting '1 2 3 1 2 3 1 2 3…' and clapping every time you say '1'.

Practise the rhythms on the following pages to familiarize yourself with this note value.

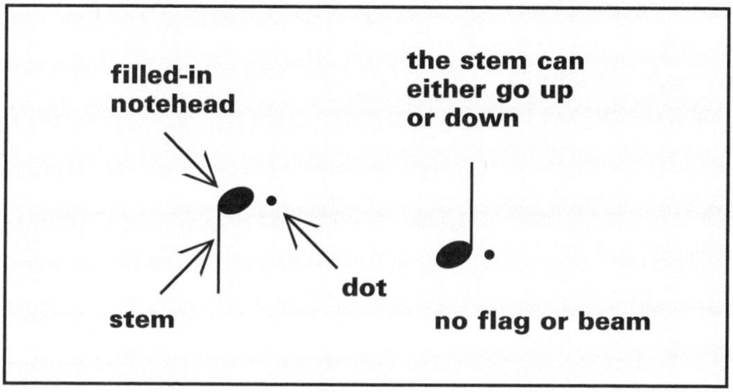
filled-in
notehead
the stem can
either go up
or down
dot
stem
no flag or beam

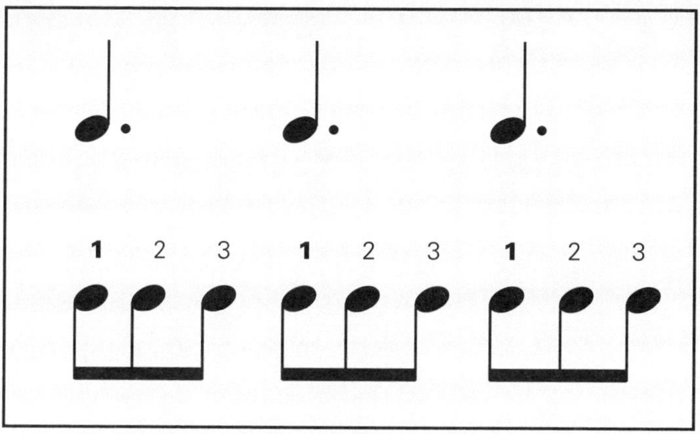
1 2 3 1 2 3 1 2 3

# Dotted Crotchet Exercises

For the first half of the exercise, clap the rhythms in the boxes whilst counting out the numbers underneath, repeating this rhythm over and over again. Do not clap for numbers that are in brackets (or do a 'silent' clap). When ready, move on to the second half of each exercise, clapping the rhythms without the aid of the numbers written underneath.

**No. 1**

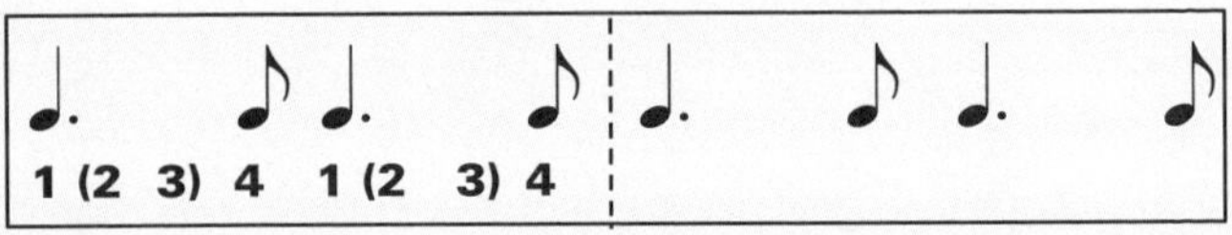


**No. 2**

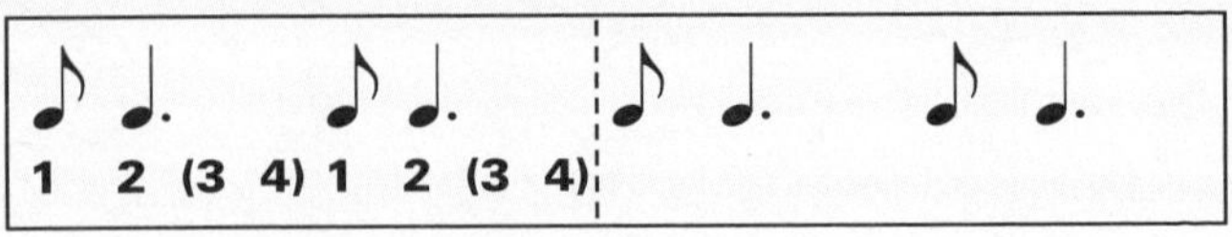


**No. 3**

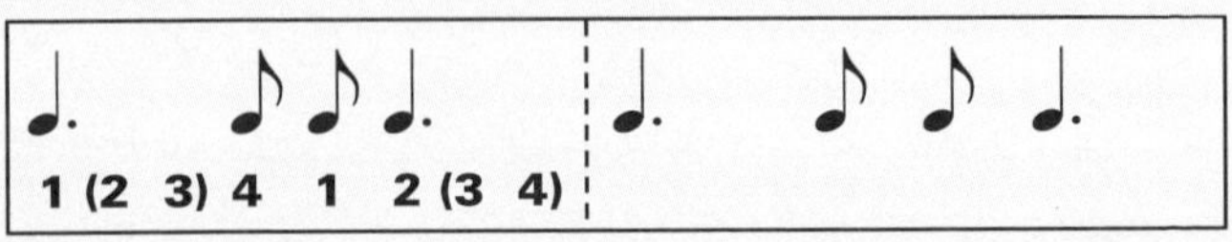


**No. 4**

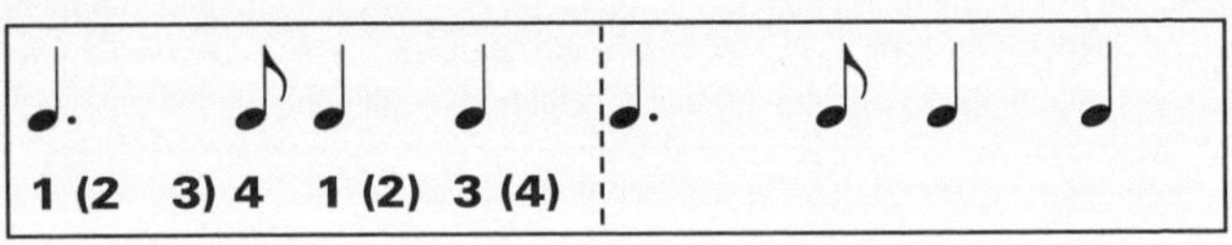

No. 5

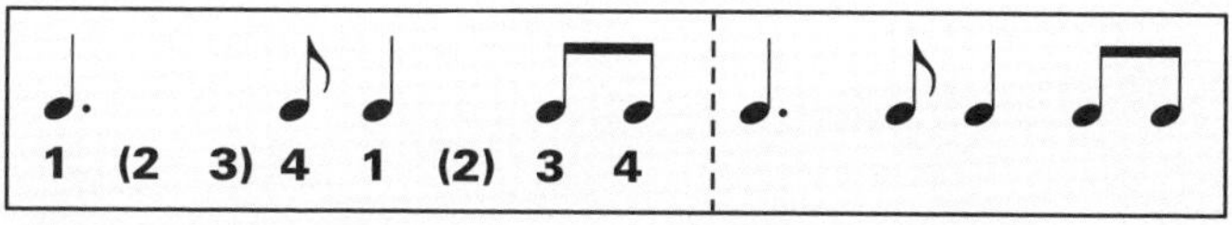


No. 6

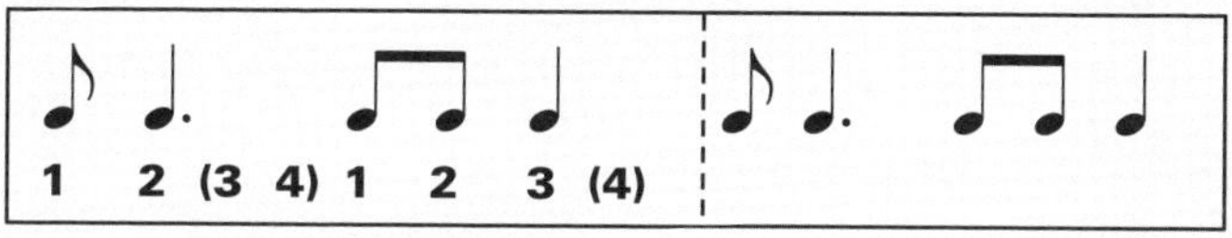


No. 7

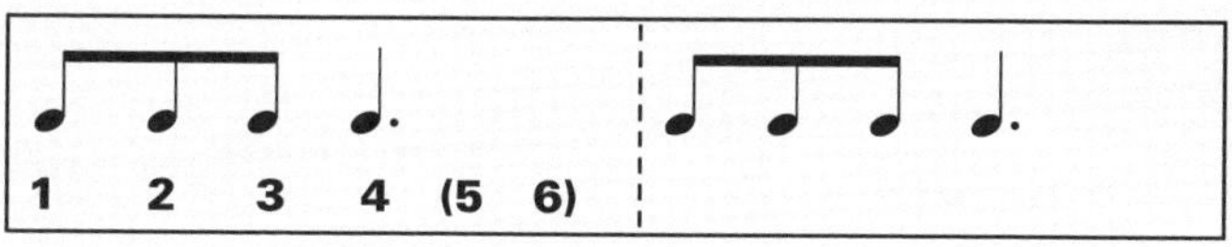


No. 8

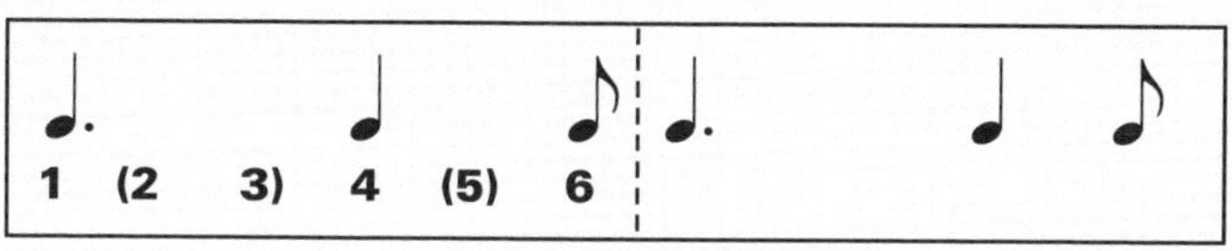


No. 9

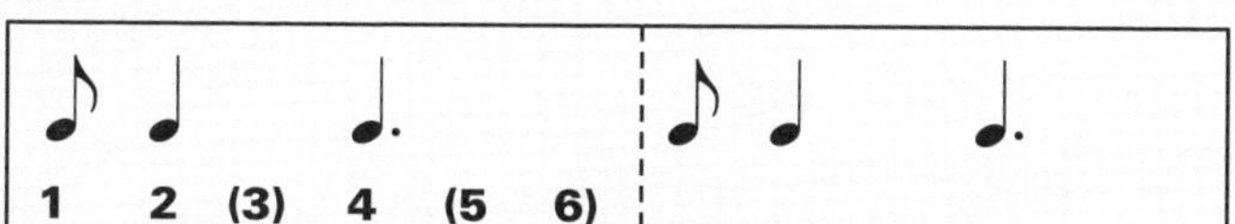

# Minims

A minim has a hollow notehead and a stem but no flag or beam.

A minim is worth four quavers or two crotchets. If you are counting in quavers, a minim will take up the same length of time as four quavers. If you are counting in crotchets, a minim lasts two crotchets.

Practise clapping minims in two ways. First, count quavers, clapping every four quavers: count '1 2 3 4 1 2 3 4...' and clap every time you say '1'.

Secondly, count in crotchets, clapping every two crotchets: count '1 2 1 2...' and clap each time you say '1'.

Practise the rhythms on the following pages to familiarize yourself with this note value.

hollow notehead
the stem can either go up or down
stem
no flag or beam

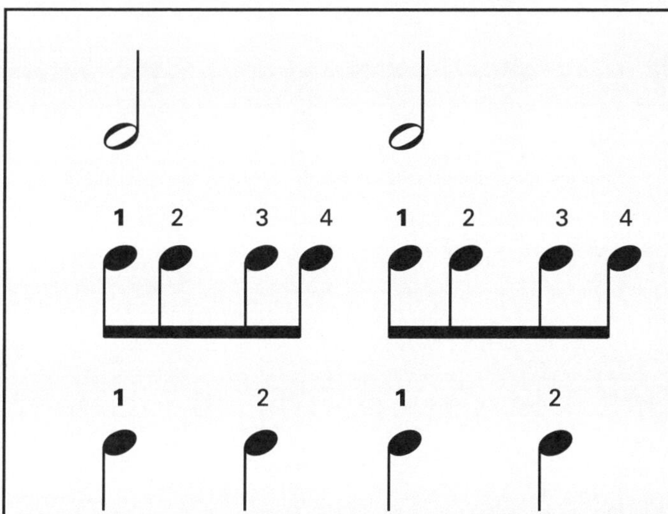
1 2 3 4 1 2 3 4
1 2 1 2

# Minim Exercises

For the first half of the exercise, clap the rhythms in the boxes whilst counting out the numbers underneath, repeating this rhythm over and over again. Do not clap for numbers that are in brackets (or do a 'silent' clap). When ready, move on to the second half of each exercise, clapping the rhythms without the aid of the numbers written underneath.

**No. 1**

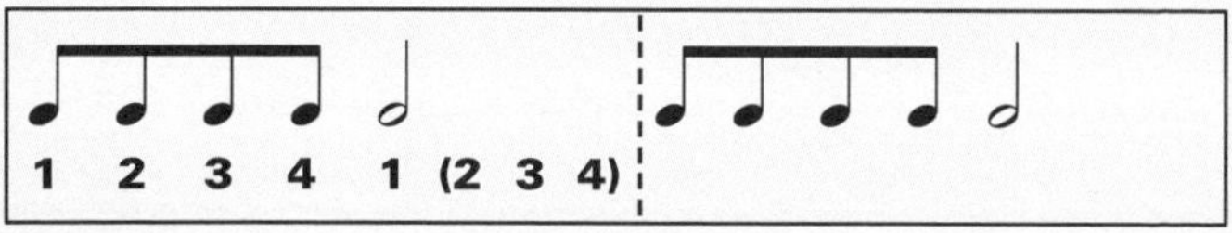


**No. 2**

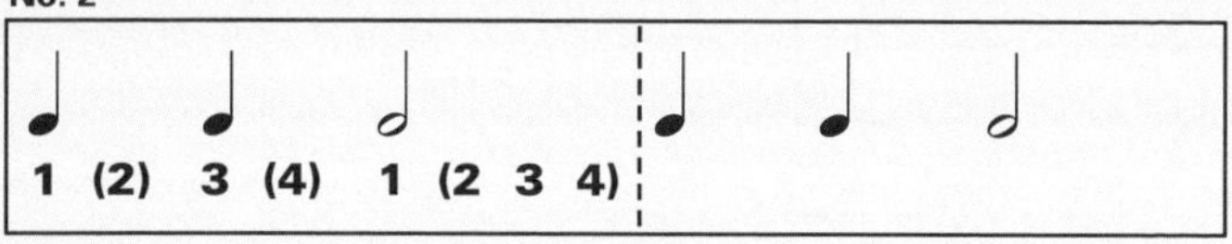


**No. 3**

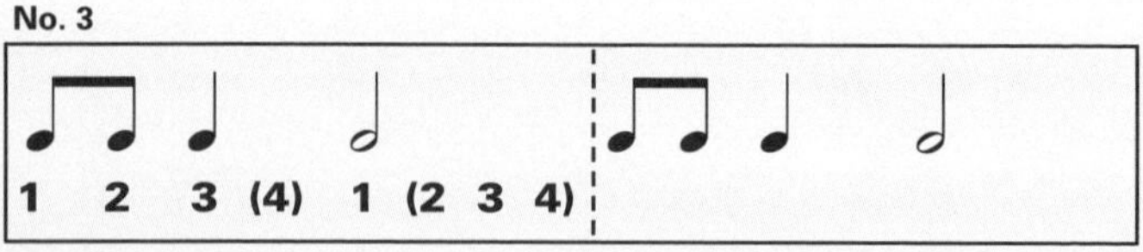


**No. 4**

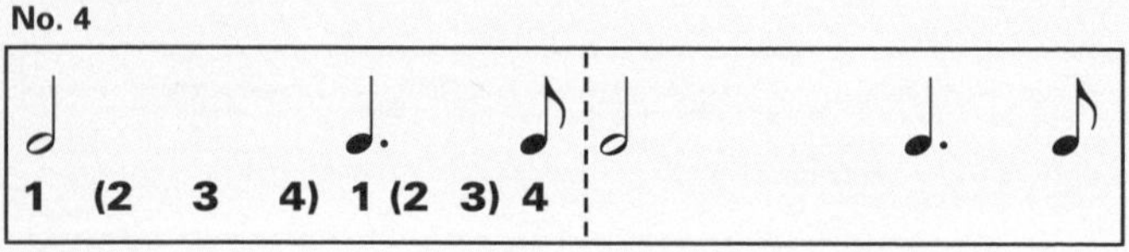

No. 5

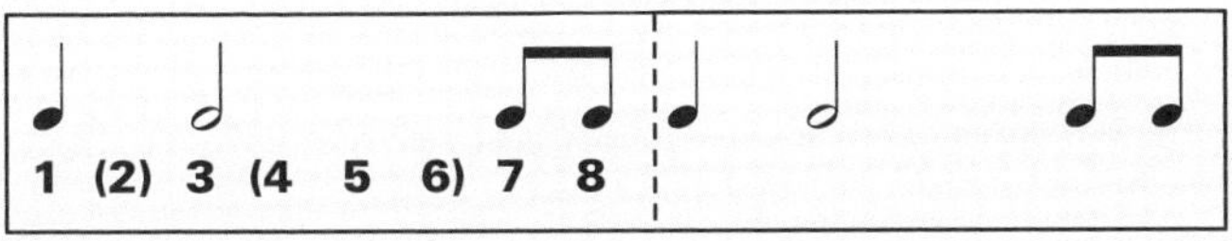


No. 6

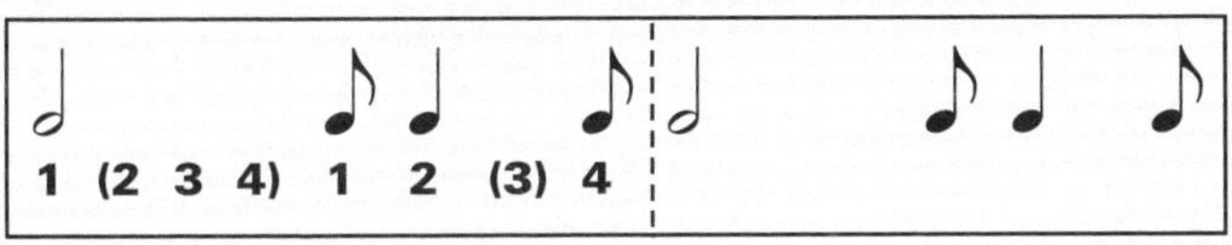


No. 7

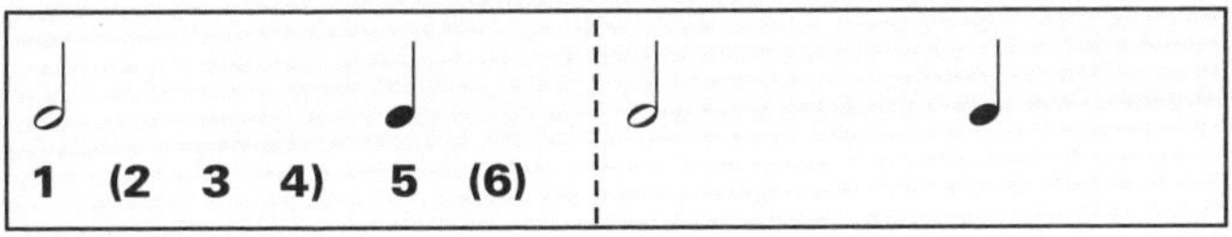


No. 8

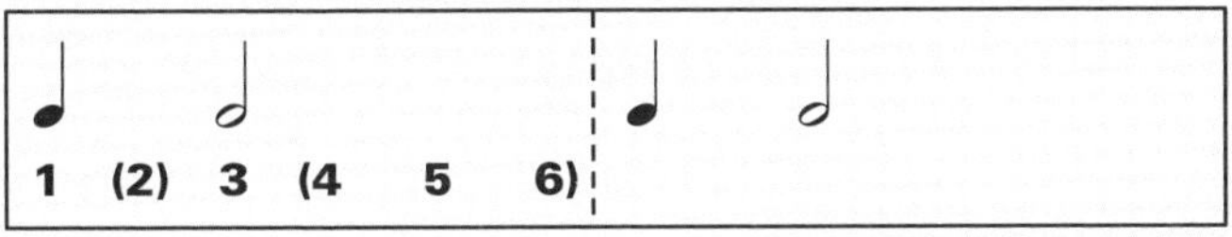


No. 9

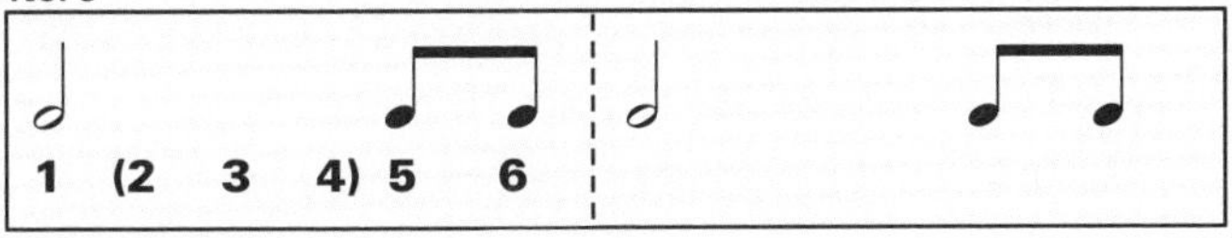

# Dotted Minims

A dotted minim has a hollow notehead, a stem and a dot but no flag or beam.

A dotted minim is worth six quavers or three crotchets. If you are counting in quavers, a minim will take up the same length of time as six quavers. If you are counting in crotchets, a minim lasts three crotchets.

As with ordinary minims, practise clapping dotted minims in two ways. First, count quavers, clapping every six quavers: count '1 2 3 4 5 6 1 2 3 4 5 6...' and clap every time you say '1'.

Secondly, count in crotchets, clapping every three crotchets: count '1 2 3 1 2 3....' and clap each time you say '1'.

Practise the rhythms on the following pages to familiarize yourself with this note value. Start slowly, counting in quavers. As you speed up, move on to counting in crotchets.

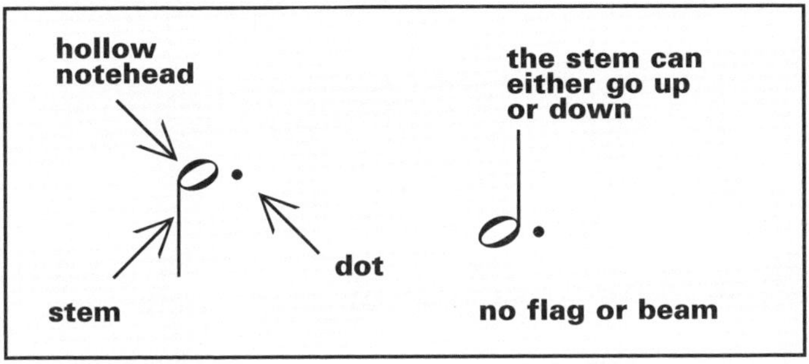


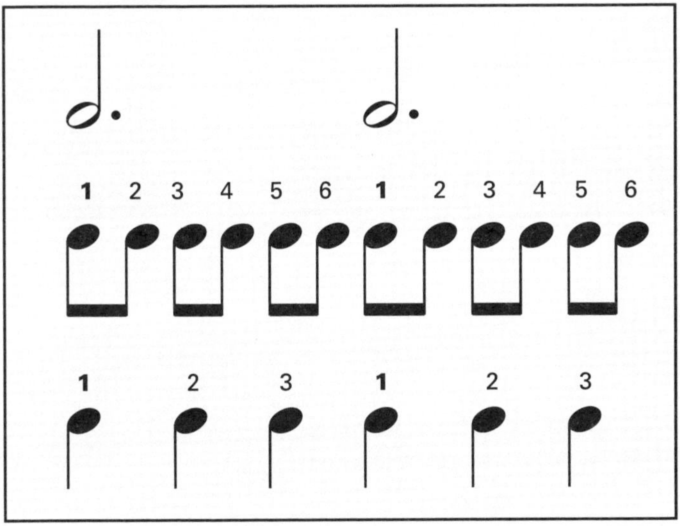


Pitch
Treble Clef
Base Clef
Rhythm
Play Along 1
ACC Accidentals
Key Sign
Scales
Chords
Other Chords
Play Along 2
Comp

# Dotted Minim Exercises

Clap these rhythms, following the same instructions as in previous exercises. Two different ways of counting are given under the notes. The first of these is for counting in quavers, while the second is for counting in crotchets. Practise both of these ways of counting.

**No. 1**

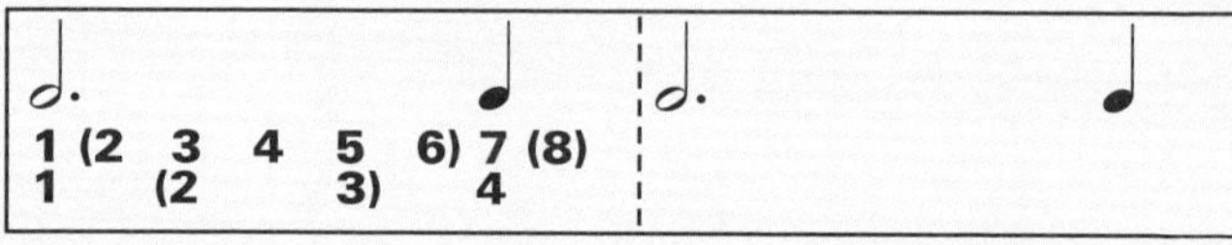


**No. 2**

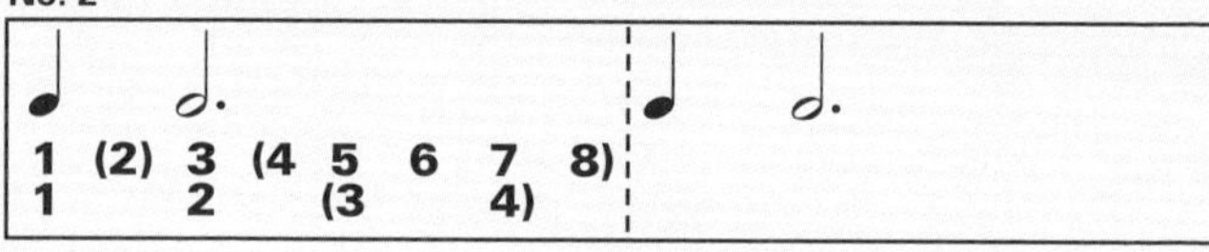


**No. 3**

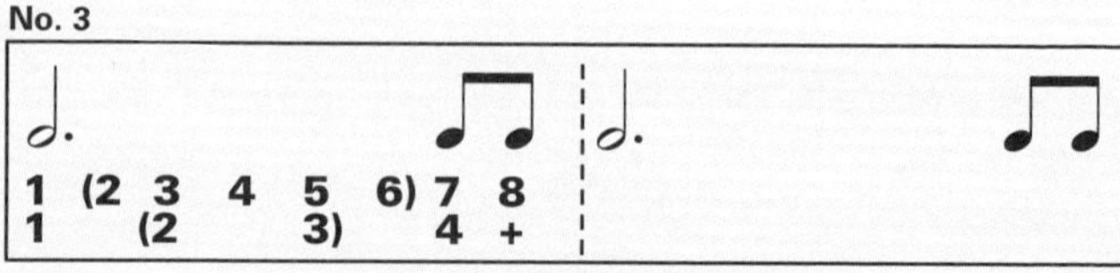


**No. 4**

No. 5

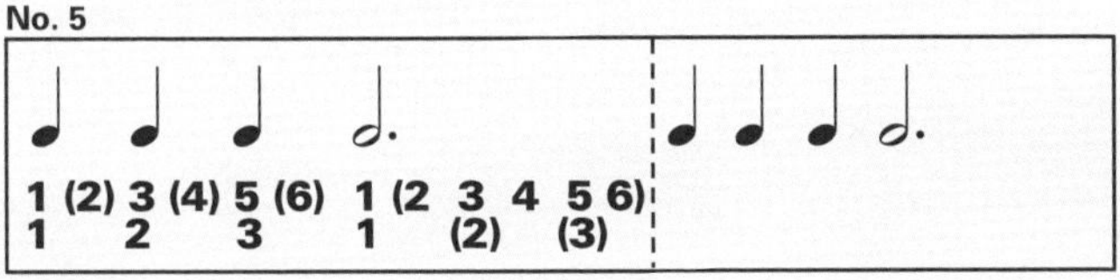


No. 6

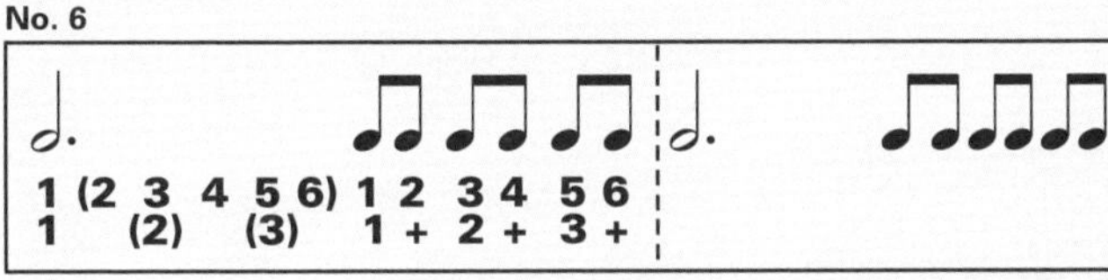


No. 7

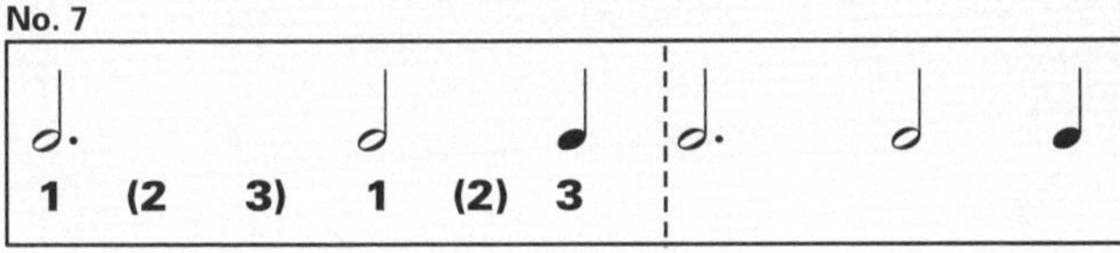


No. 8

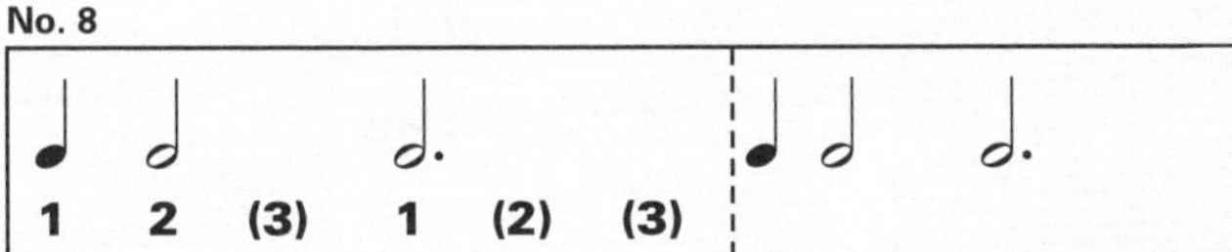


No. 9

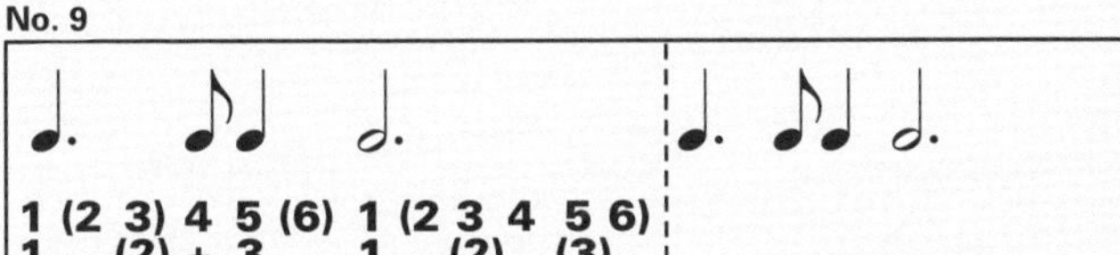

# Semibreves

The semibreve is the longest note value covered in this section. It consists of just a hollow notehead, with no stem, flag, beams or dots.

The semibreve is worth eight quavers, four crotchets or two minims. If you are counting in quavers, a semibreve will take up the same amount of time as eight quavers. If you are counting in crotchets, a semibreve lasts four crotchets. If you counting in minims, a semibreve lasts two minims.

Practise counting semibreves in three ways. First, count quavers, clapping every eight quavers: count '1 2 3 4 5 6 7 8 1 2 3 4 5 6 7 8...' and clap every time you say '1'.

Secondly, count in crotchets, clapping every four crotchets: count '1 2 3 4 1 2 3 4...' and clap each time you say '1'.

Finally, count in minims, clapping every two minims: count '1 2 1 2...' and clap each time you say '1'.

Practise the rhythms on the following pages to familiarize yourself with this note value. There are exercises counting in both quavers and crotchets.

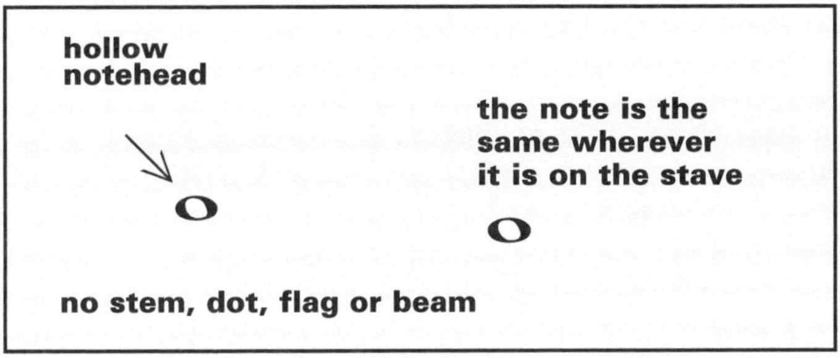
hollow
notehead
the note is the
same wherever
it is on the stave
no stem, dot, flag or beam

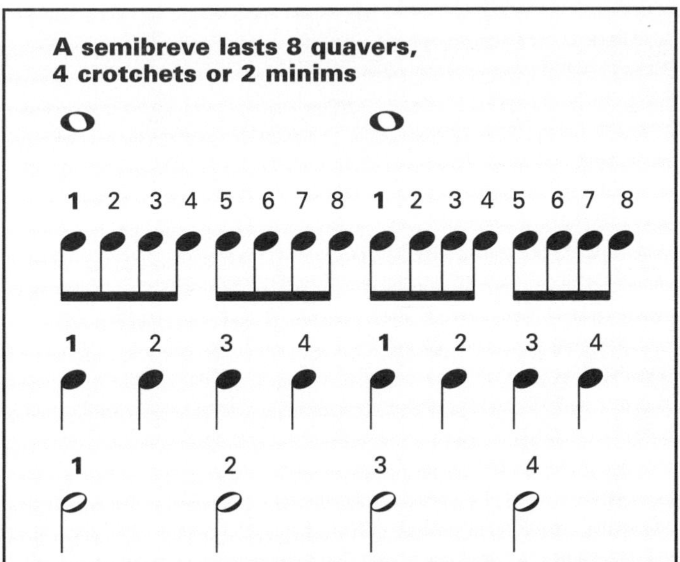
A semibreve lasts 8 quavers,
4 crotchets or 2 minims
1 2 3 4 5 6 7 8 1 2 3 4 5 6 7 8
1 2 3 4 1 2 3 4
1 2 3 4

# Semibreve Exercises

For the first half of the exercise, clap the rhythms in the boxes whilst counting out the numbers underneath, repeating this rhythm over and over again. Do not clap for numbers that are in brackets (or do a 'silent' clap). When ready, move on to the second half of each exercise, clapping the rhythms without the aid of the numbers written underneath.

**No. 1 (counting in quavers)**

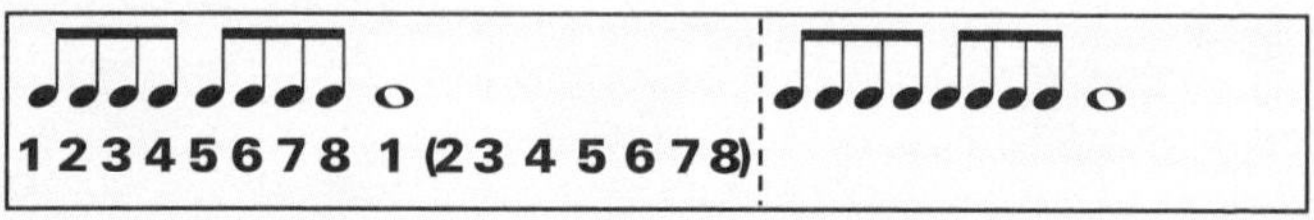


**No. 2 (counting in quavers)**

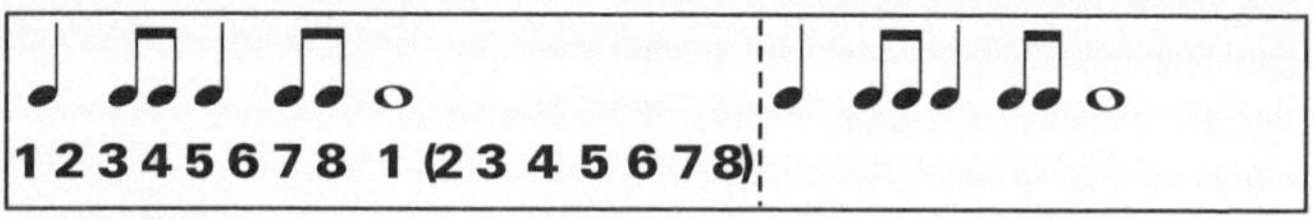


**No. 3 (counting in crotchets)**

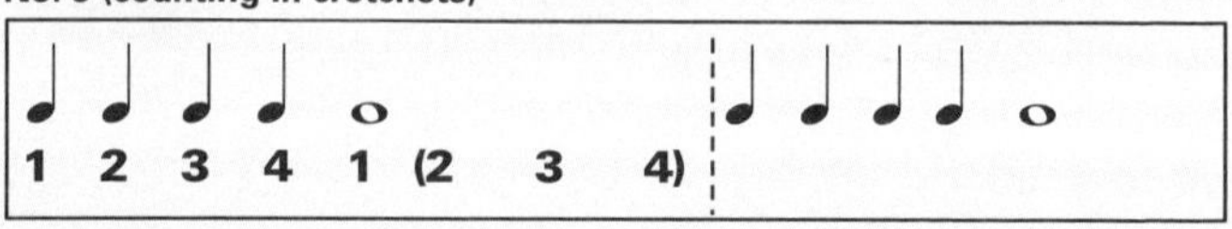


**No. 4 (counting in crotchets)**

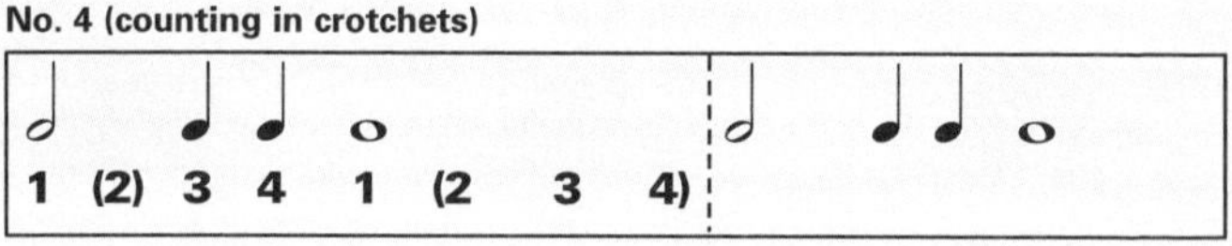

No. 5 (counting in crotchets)

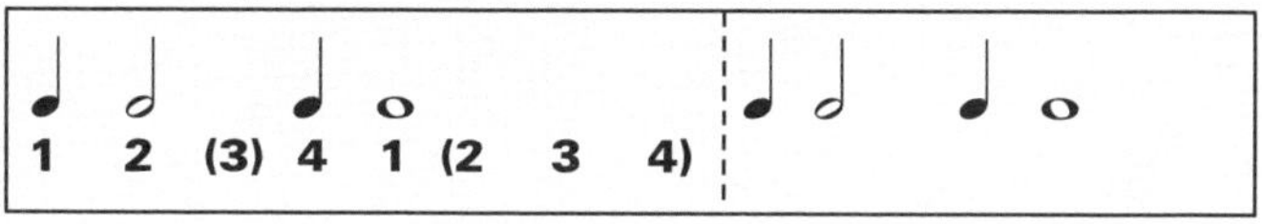


No. 6 (counting in crotchets)

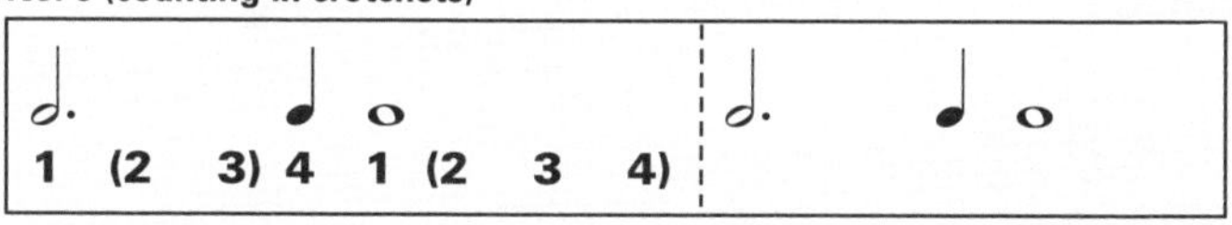


No. 7 (counting in quavers)

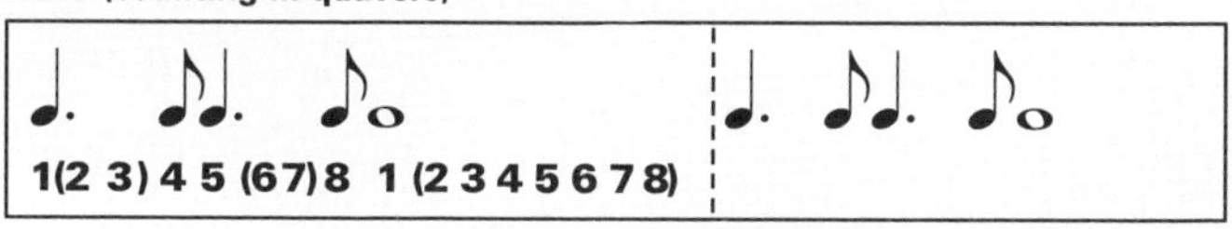


No. 8 (counting in quavers)

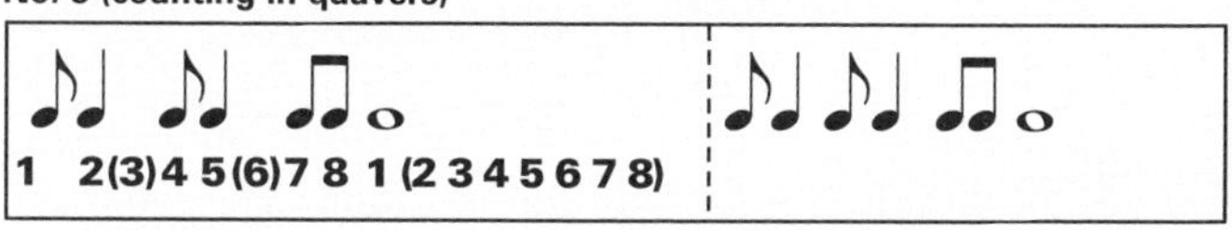


No. 9 (counting in quavers)

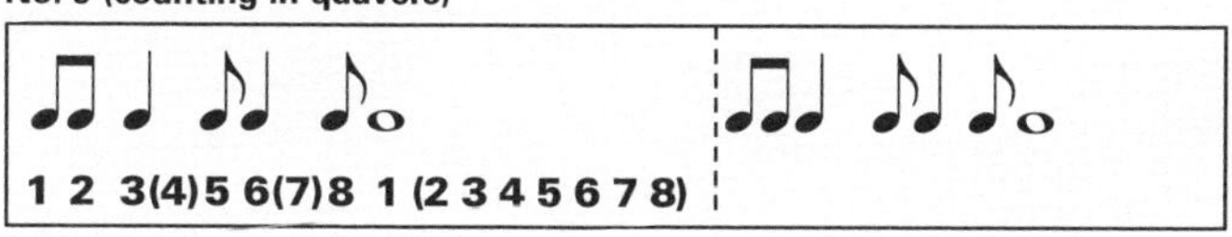

Pitch
Treble Clef
Bass Clef
Rhythm
Play Along 1
ACC Accidentals
Key Sign
Scales
Chords
Other Chords
Play Along 2
Comp

# Semiquavers

There are many note values shorter than quavers. The note value that is half as long as a quaver is called a semiquaver. It is written like a quaver, but with two flags or two beams instead of one. A semiquaver thus has a filled-in notehead, a stem, and either two flags or two beams.

Like quavers, neighbouring semiquavers can be joined together with beams. They can also be joined by beams to quavers and other short notes.

There are two semiquavers in a quaver, four semiquavers in a crotchet, eight semiquavers in a minim and sixteen semiquavers in a semibreve.

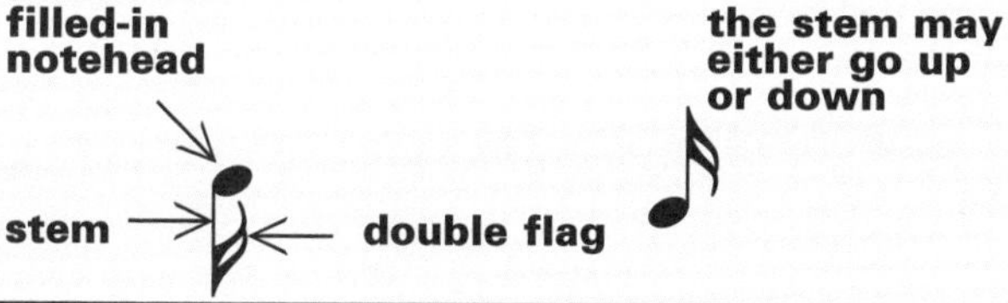


**semiquavers can be joined by beams to other semiquavers or quavers**

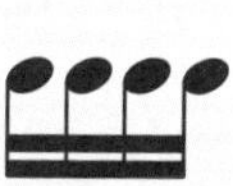

4 semiquavers joined by a double beam

2 semiquavers and a quaver joined by a double and single beam

semiquaver, quaver and semiquaver joined by a beam

**There are two semiquavers to a quaver and four semiquavers to a crotchet**

# Counting Semiquavers

To clap semiquavers while counting quavers, first count '1 and 2 and 1 and 2 and...', clapping on each word you say. Then keep clapping and counting at the same speed, but leave out the 'ands', leaving just '1 2 1 2...' You should be clapping twice to each number you say.

To clap semiquavers while counting crotchets, first repeat the phrase 'one-a-pen-ny two-a-pen-ny one-a-pen-ny two-a-pen-ny', clapping to every syllable. Keep repeating the phrase, but leave out each 'a-pen-ny' so that you are left with '1 2 1 2 1 2 1 2...' You should be clapping four times to each number you say.

Practise the rhythms on the following pages to get used to common semiquaver patterns. There are semiquaver exercises counting in both quavers and crotchets.

## Clapping semiquavers to a quaver pulse

**STEP 1:**

**clap:**

**say:** 1 and 2 and 1 and 2 and 1 and 2 and 1 and 2 and

**STEP 2:**

**clap:**

**say:** 1 2 1 2 1 2 1 2

## Clapping semiquavers to a crotchet pulse

**STEP 3:**

**clap:**

**say:** one-a-pen-ny two-a-pen-ny one-a-pen-ny two-a-pen-ny

**STEP 4:**

**clap:**

**say:** 1 2 1 2

Pitch
Treble Clef
Bass Clef
Rhythm
Play Along 1
ACC Accidentals
Key Sign
Scales
Chords
Other Chords
Play Along 2
Comp

# Semiquaver Exercises

These exercises are in three steps. For step one, clap repeated semiquavers and say the words and numbers underneath. In step two, clap the new rhythm and say the words underneath. For step three, clap the rhythm without saying the words. For exercises 1–5 count in quavers and in crotchets for 6–7.

The '+' sign represents the word 'and'

**No. 1** **STEP 1** **STEP 2** **STEP 3**

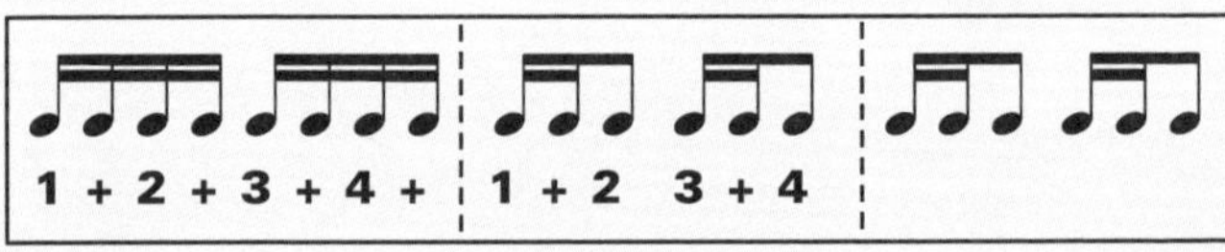


**No. 2**

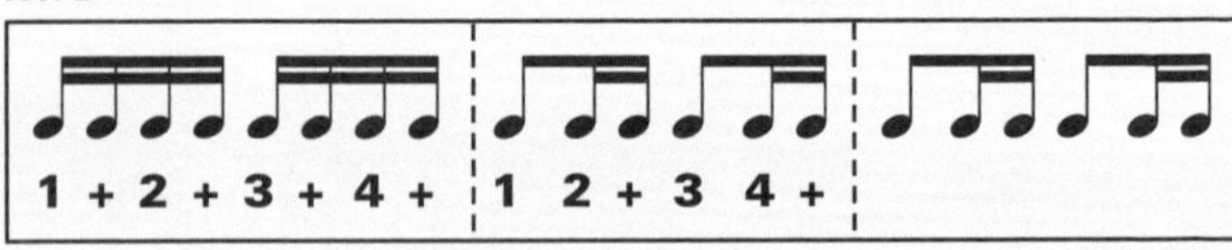


**No. 3**

No. 4

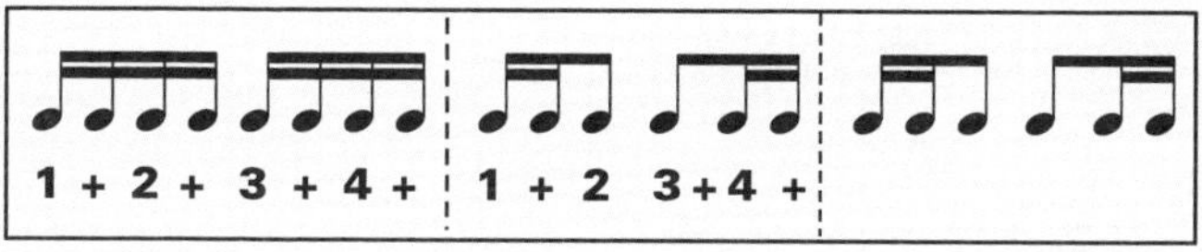


No. 5

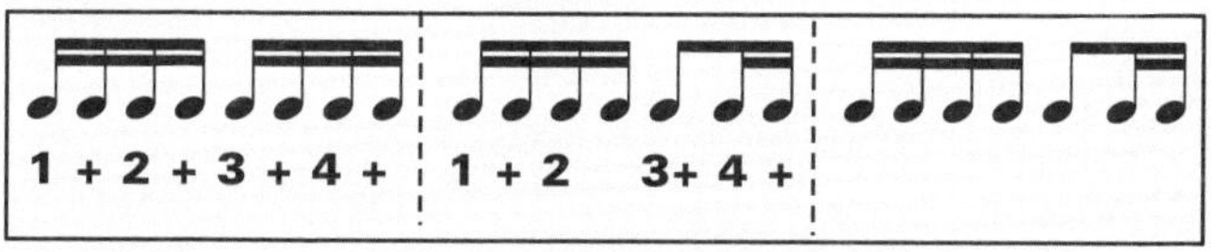


No. 6

No. 7

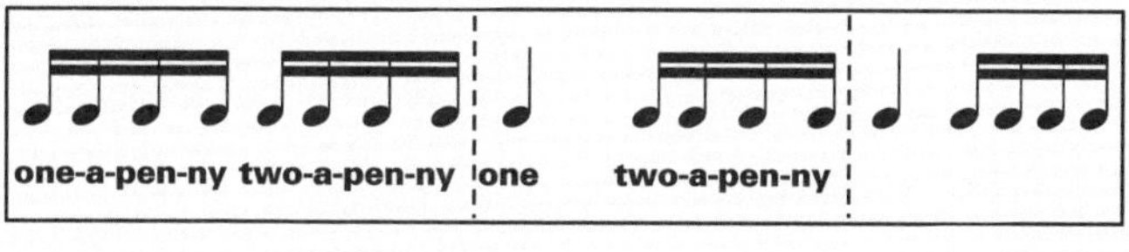

Pitch
Treble Clef
Bass Clef
Rhythm
Play Along 1
ACC Accidentals
Key Sign
Scales
Chords
Other Chords
Play Along 2
Comp

# Dotted Quavers

Just as a dot added to a crotchet or a minim extends that note value by a half, so adding a dot to a quaver extends the quaver from two semiquavers to three semiquavers in length.

Dotted quavers are often followed by a semiquaver to form a rhythm known as a 'dotted rhythm'. To clap this, repeat the numbers '1 2 3 4 1 2 3 4...' fairly fast and clap every time you say '1' and '4'.

Another common rhythm with dotted crotchets is called the 'Scotch snap' rhythm. Here, a semiquaver is followed by a dotted quaver. Repeat the numbers '1 2 3 4 1 2 3 4...' and clap every time you say '1' and '2'.

Practise the rhythms on the following pages to get used to common patterns involving dotted quavers.

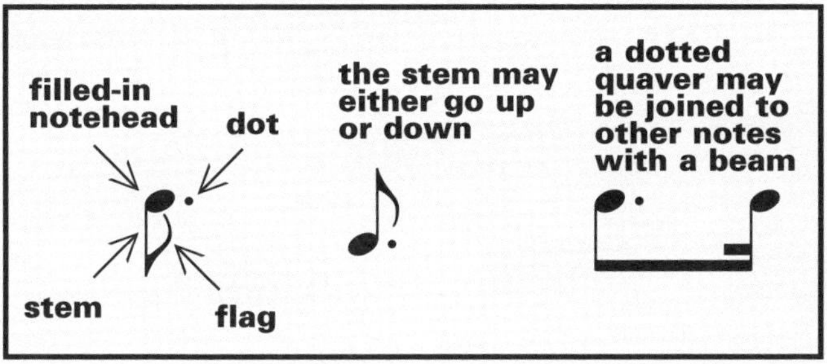


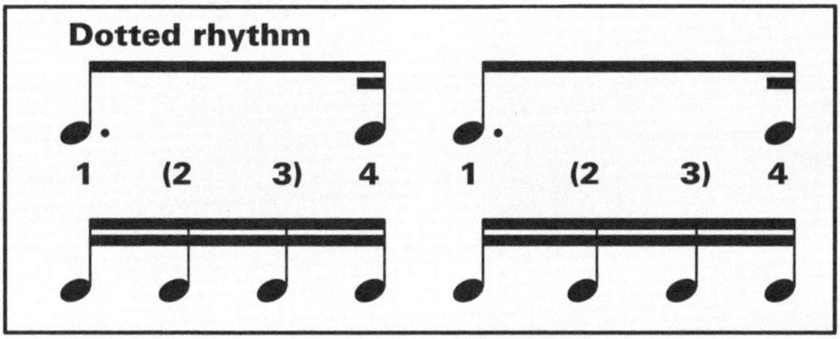

Pitch
Treble Clef
Bass Clef
Rhythm
Play Along 1
ACC Accidentals
Key Sign
Scales
Chords
Other Chords
Play Along 2
Comp

# Dotted Quaver Exercises

For the first half of each exercise, clap the rhythms in the boxes whilst counting out the numbers underneath, repeating this rhythm over and over again. Do not clap for numbers that are in brackets (or do a 'silent' clap). When ready, move on to the second half of each exercise, clapping the rhythms without the aid of the numbers written underneath.

No. 1

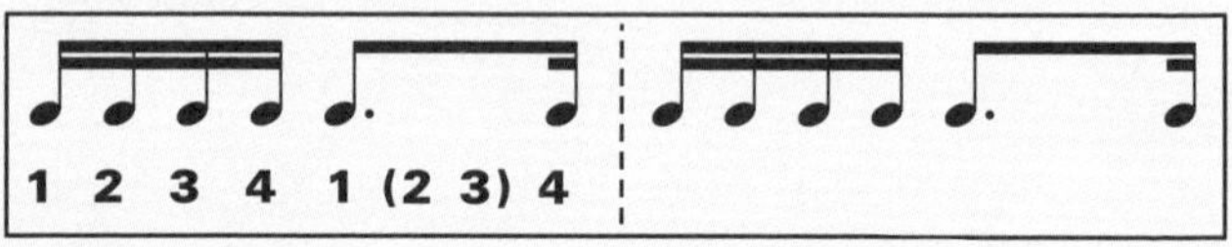


No. 2

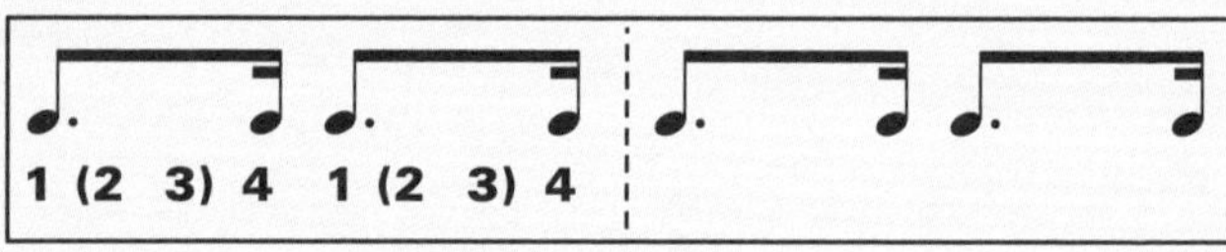


No. 3

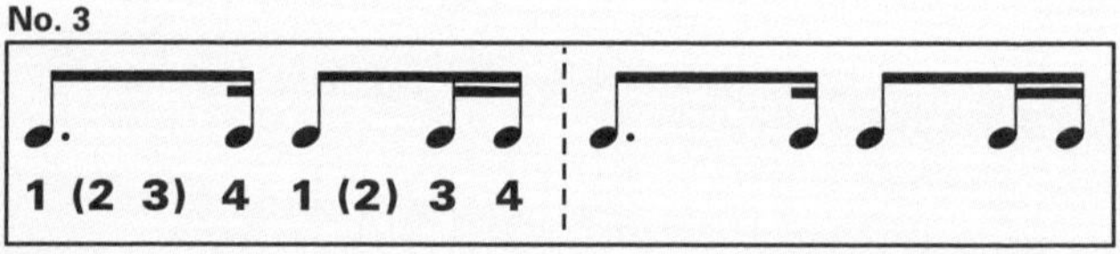


No. 4

No. 5

No. 6

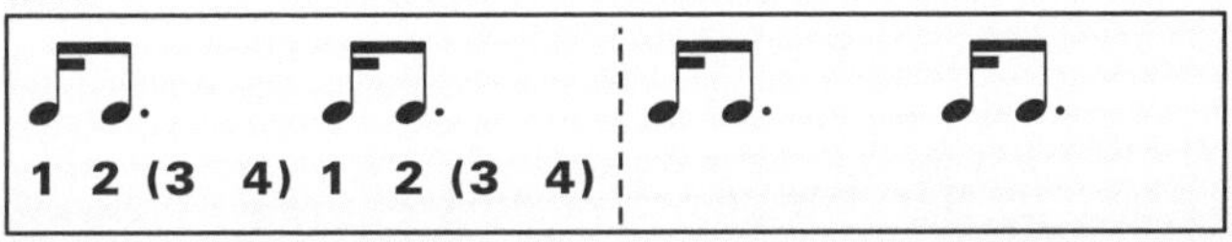


No. 7

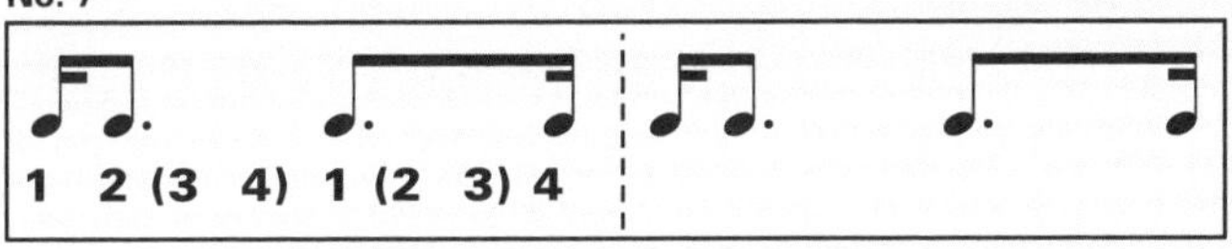


No. 8

No. 9

Pitch
Treble Clef
Bass Clef
Rhythm
Play Along 1
ACC Accidentals
Key Sign
Scales
Chords
Other Chords
Play Along 2
Comp

# Triplets

A triplet is a note value divided into three equal parts. Take a minim as an example. If you divide it into two, you get two crotchets. If you divide it into four, you get four quavers. There is no note value for dividing it into three, so three crotchets are written with a bracket and the number '3' written above or below them.

A note written as a triplet is always shorter than if the note was written normally. So quaver triplets are shorter and faster than ordinary quavers, crotchet triplets are shorter than ordinary crotchets and so on.

With triplets, the three triplets fit exactly into the next note value up. So three triplet crotchets fit into a minim, three quaver triplets fit into a crotchet and three semiquaver triplets fit into a quaver.

Notes to be played as triplets are shown with a bracket over or under the notes and the number three

Notes joined by a beam may just have the number and no bracket

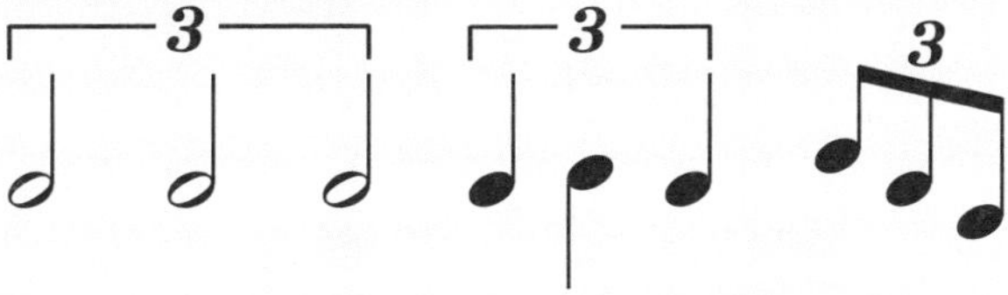


Three minim triplets fit into the time of a semibreve

Three crotchet triplets fit into the time of a minim

Three quaver triplets fit into the time of a crotchet

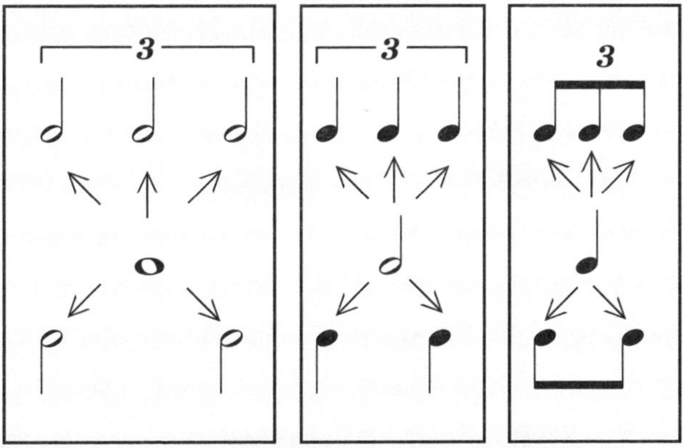


Three minim triplets last the same time as two normal minims

Three crotchet triplets last the same time as two normal crotchets

Three quaver triplets last the same time as two normal quavers

# Counting Triplets

Triplets can be confusing at first. A helpful way of learning them is to use the rhythm of certain words.

First set up a steady pulse: say '1 2 1 2 1 2...', clapping every time you say '1' (Intro step 1). Then, keep clapping at the same speed but instead of saying '1 2 1 2...', say 'fruit-cake fruit-cake...', clapping on the word 'fruit' (Intro step 2).

Still clapping at the same speed, replace the word 'fruitcake' with the word 'pineapple', so that you are saying 'pi-neap-ple pi-neap-ple...' clapping on the syllable 'pine'. Try to make each syllable of 'pineapple' the same length. You should now be speaking in triplets. Next, clap along to each syllable as you say it (No. 1 step 2). Finally, stop speaking but carry on clapping in the same rhythm (No. 1 step 3).

Other common triplet rhythms are included in No. 2 and No. 3: set up a steady pulse before each of these exercises following the steps in Intro.

Intro

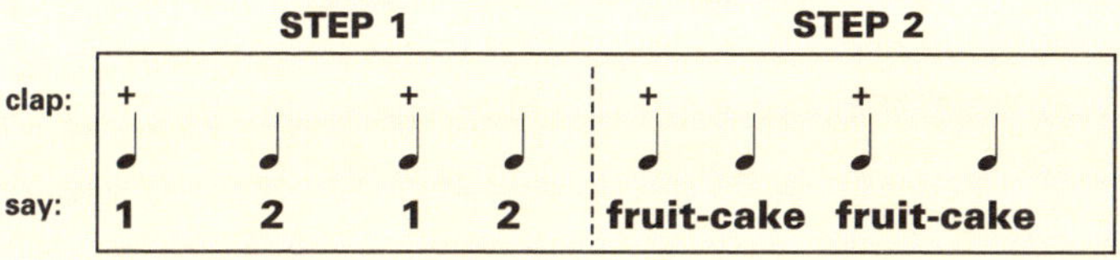


No. 1

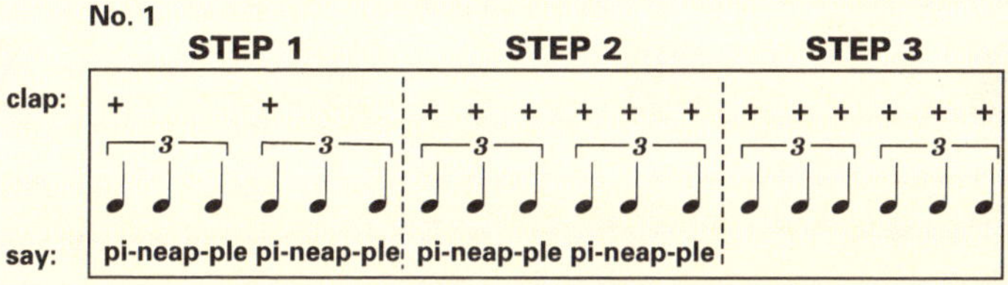


No. 2

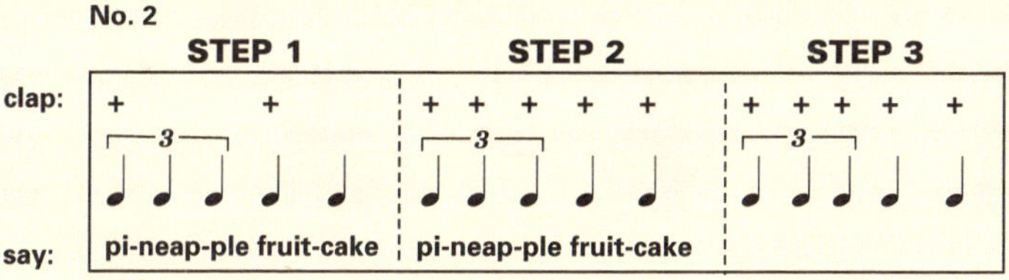


No. 3

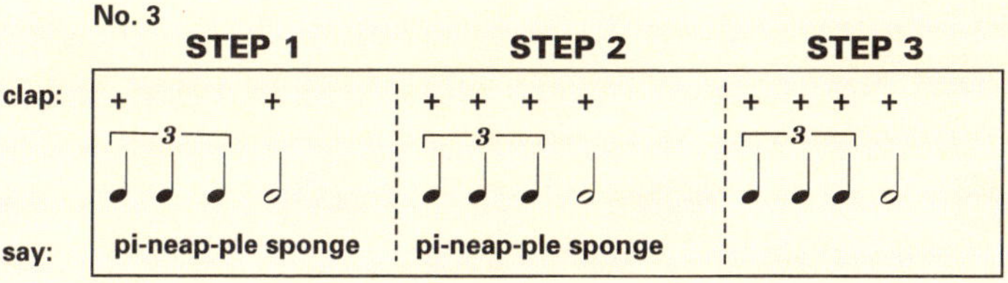

# Ties

When two or more notes are joined together, they are linked with a curved line called a tie.

The total length of the notes joined with a tie is the total of each individual note value involved. Notes of any value can be linked with ties, which can also cross barlines.

Ties tend to be used in three situations:

- to create a note value for which there is no single symbol
- to extend a note across a barline
- where the note value is easier to read if it is written as more than one tied note.

Before you attempt the exercises on the following pages, remind yourself of how many quavers each note value contains.

## A tie is a curved line linking two or more noteheads

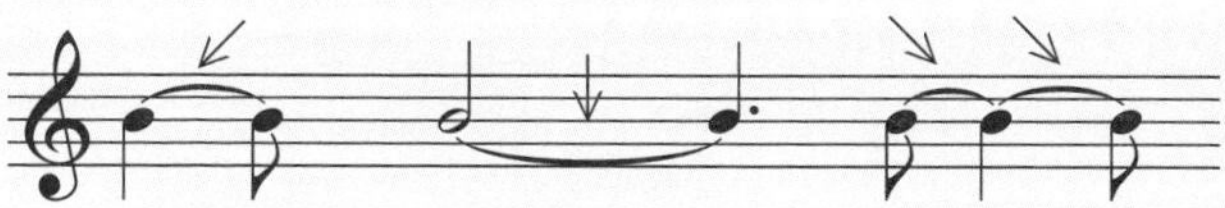


## Unusual note values can be written by tying notes together

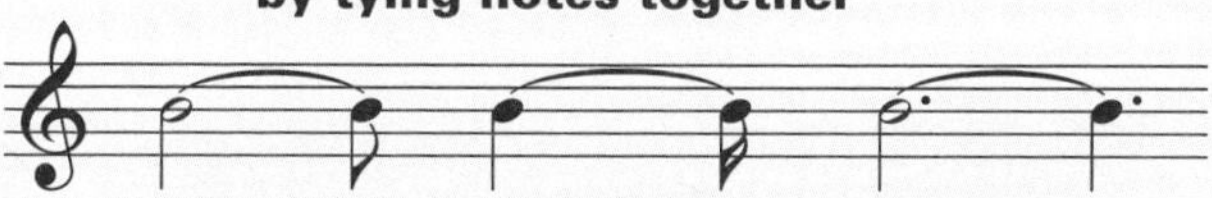


## Ties can join notes over barlines

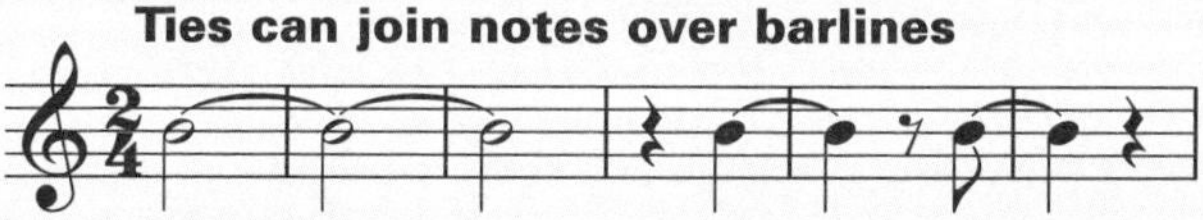


## The note values in a) are easier to count if written as in b)

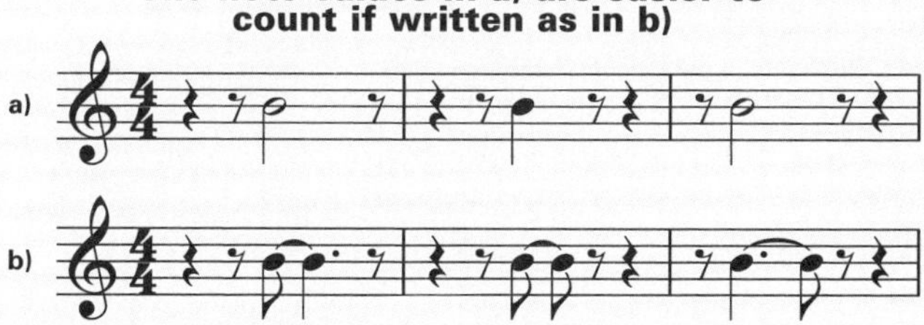

Pitch
Treble Clef
Bass Clef
Rhythm
Play Along 1
ACC Accidentals
Key Sign
Scales
Chords
Other Chords
Play Along 2
Comp

# Tied Note Exercises

## Write down the total number of quavers in each bar in the space provided

**Example**

(1 + 2) (1 + 1) (2 + 2) (4 + 4 + 1) (6 + 3)

3 2 4 9 9

1. 2. 3. 4. 5.

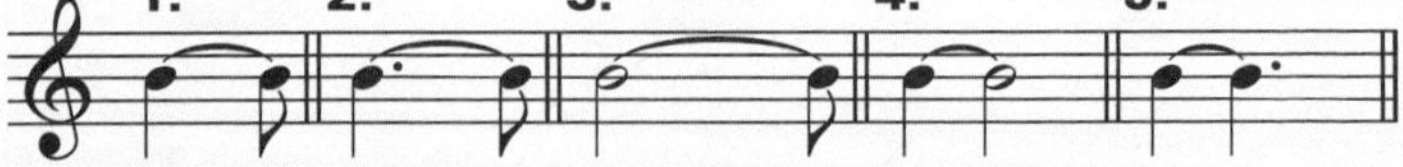

6. 7. 8. 9.

10. 11. 12. 13.

14. 15. 16. 17.

# Write one note value in each bar so that the tied notes in that bar add up to the total written below

Example 1: Answer: Example 2: Answer:

total: 5 quavers total: 3 crotchets

1. 2. 3. 4.

6 quavers 4 quavers 4 quavers 5 quavers

5. 6. 7. 8.

5 quavers 7 quavers 7 quavers 9 quavers

9. 10. 11. 12.

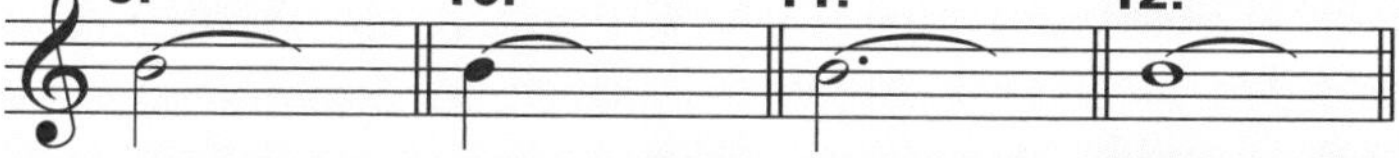

3 crotchets 5 crotchets 5 crotchets 7 crotchets

13. 14. 15.

6 quavers 11 quavers 11 quavers

# Rests

As well as notes, in music it is also essential to be able to indicate to the player the exact lengths of places where they should be silent. These spaces in the music are called 'rests'.

For each of the note values there is an equivalent rest. Rests come in three types: those that look like bricks (minim and semibreve), the crotchet rest, which is like a squiggle, and those that look like keys (quaver and semiquaver). Notice that rests have a set position on the stave.

Rests may be dotted in the same way that notes are, with the dot extending the rest's value by half. A dot placed after a crotchet rest, for example, will make that rest worth three quavers instead of two.

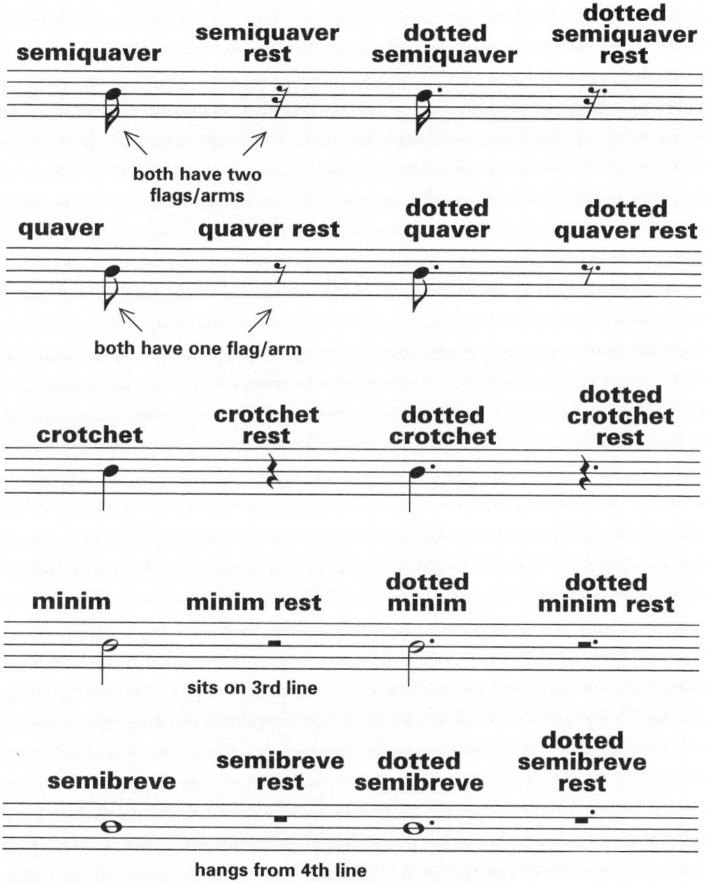
semiquaver
semiquaver rest
dotted semiquaver
dotted semiquaver rest
both have two flags/arms
quaver
quaver rest
dotted quaver
dotted quaver rest
both have one flag/arm
crotchet
crotchet rest
dotted crotchet
dotted crotchet rest
minim
minim rest
dotted minim
dotted minim rest
sits on 3rd line
semibreve
semibreve rest
dotted semibreve
dotted semibreve rest
hangs from 4th line

# Counting Rests

Rests are counted in the same way as notes. Work through these exercises, counting quavers and clapping when there is a note.

For the first half of each exercise, clap the rhythms in the boxes whilst counting out the numbers underneath, repeating this rhythm over and over again. Clap 'silently' for numbers in brackets. When ready, move on to the second half of each exercise, clapping the rhythms without the aid of the numbers written underneath.

No. 5

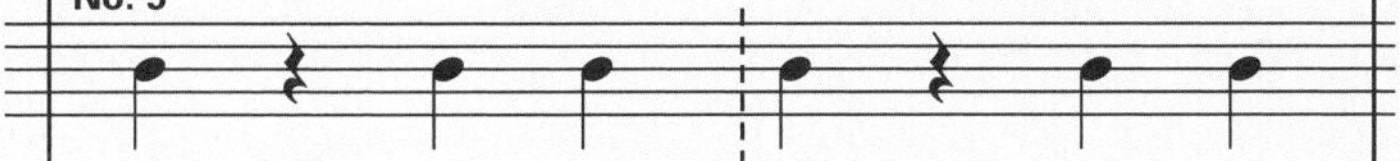

1 (2) 3 4

No. 6

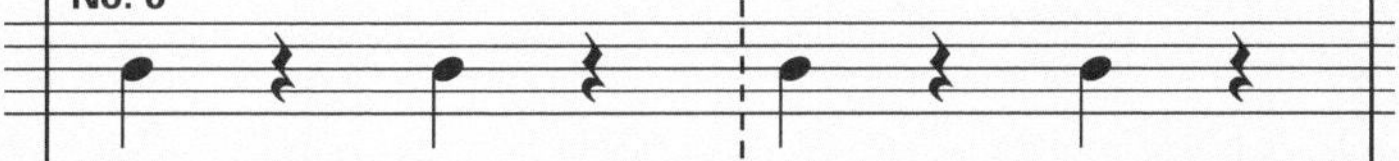

1 (2) 3 (4)

No. 7

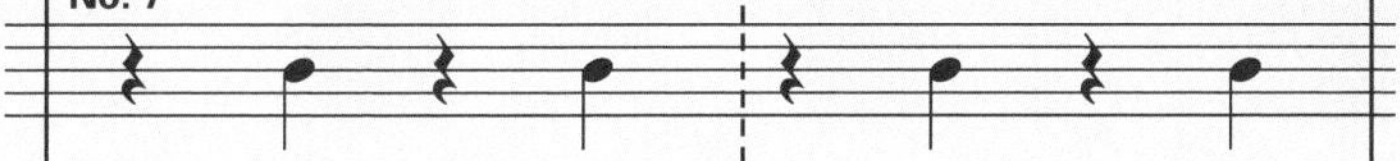

(1) 2 (3) 4

No. 8

1 (2) 3 4 (5 6 7) 8

No. 9

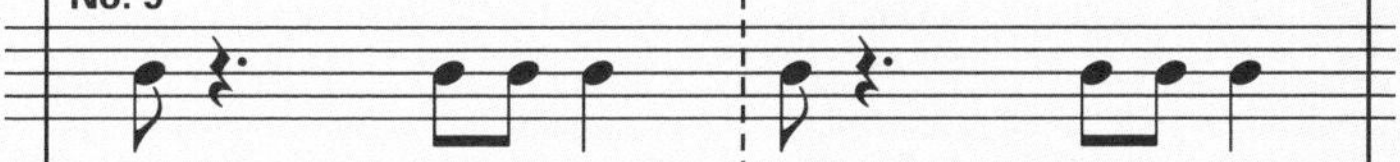

1 (2 3 4) 5 6 7 (8)

# Counting Rests

No. 10

No. 11

No. 12

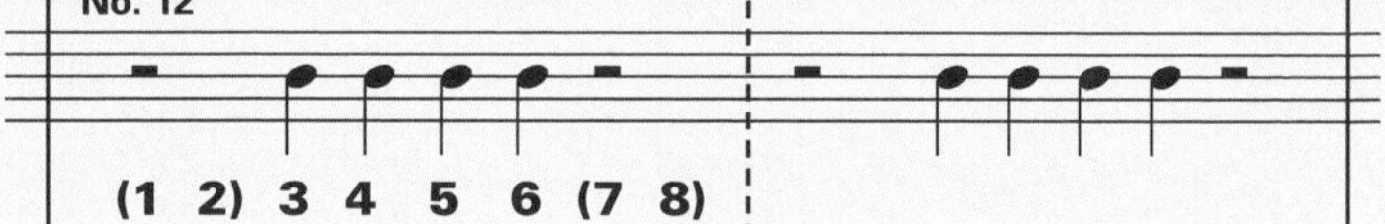


No. 13

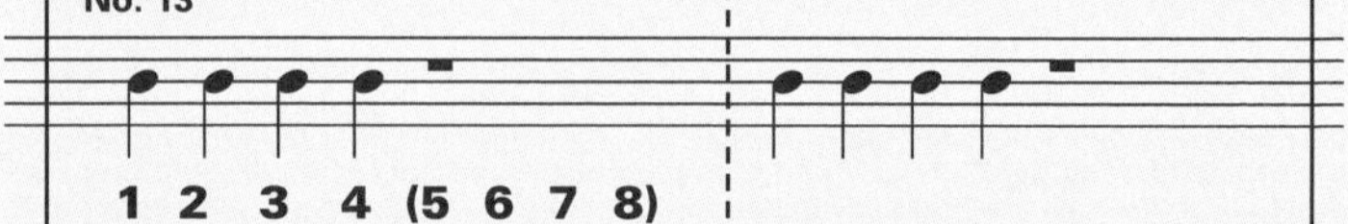


No. 14

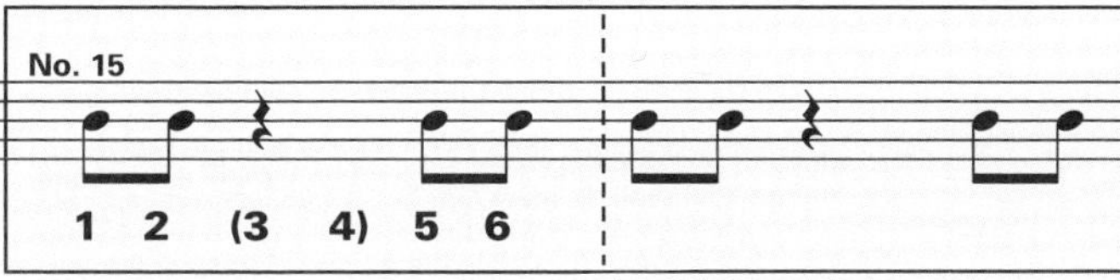
No. 15
1 2 (3 4) 5 6

No. 16
1 2 (3) 4 5 6

No. 17
1 (2 3 4) 5 6 (7) 8

No. 18
1 2 (3) 4 5 (6) 7 8

No. 19
1 (2 3) 4 5 (6 7 8)

# Time Signatures and Barlines

A large number of note values written in a row looks confusing, as it is easy to lose track of the main beat. To make things simpler, music is divided into short sections called bars that contain a manageable number of note values. In a lot of music, all the bars have the same number of beats in them, specified by two numbers written at the start of the music called a time signature.

There are two pieces of information in a time signature: how many beats there are in a bar, represented by the top number and which note value a beat should represent, indicated by the bottom number.

The bottom number is usually 8 (meaning a quaver or eighth note), 4 (a crotchet or quarter note) or 2 (a minim or half note). Occasionally it can be 16 (a semiquaver or sixteenth note) or 32 (a demisemiquaver or thirty-second note).

The top number can – in theory – be any number, but the most common are 2, 3, 4, 6, 9 and 12.

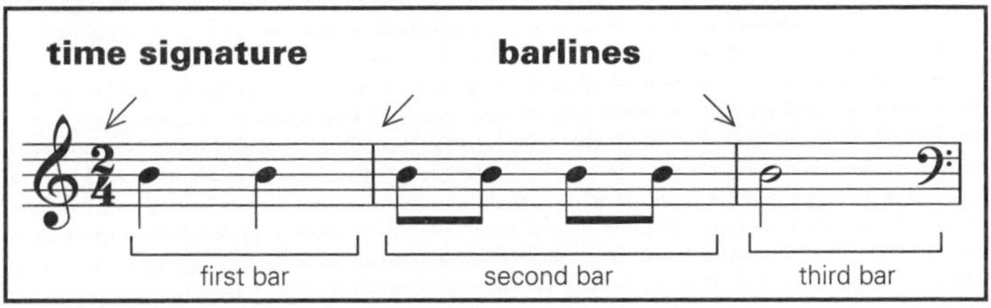


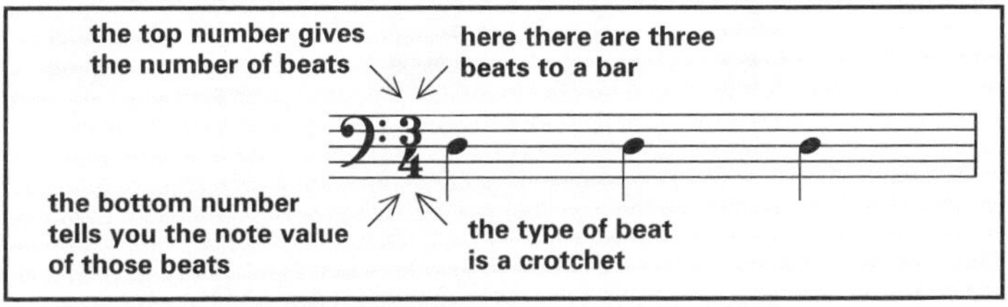


**What the bottom number of a time signature means:**

**2 = minim** (half-note)
**4 = crotchet** (quarter-note)
**8 = quaver** (eigth-note)
**16 = semiquaver** (sixteenth-note)

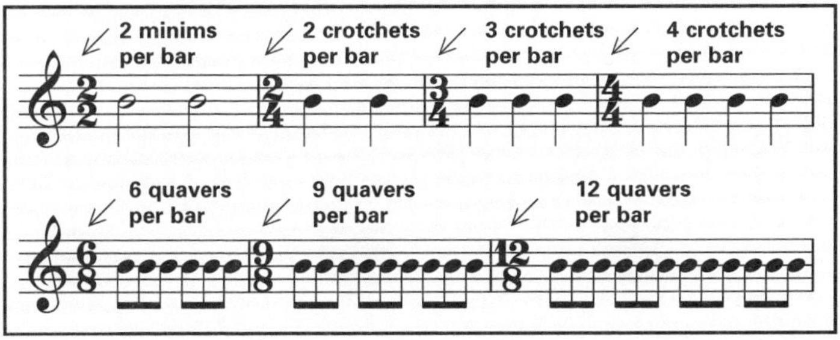

# Making Bars Add Up

Once the time signature has been given, each subsequent bar of music must contain that same number of beats until the end of the piece, or until a different time signature is used. For example, if the time signature is 4/4, the note values and rests in each bar must add up to four crotchets' worth of beats.

On the page opposite, write one note in each box so that all the notes in that bar add up to the same number of beats as the time signature.

**No. 1**
**time signature: 4 crotchets in a bar**

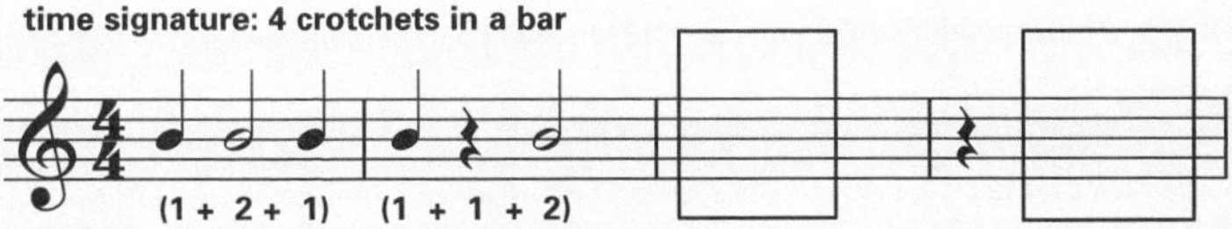


**each bar adds up to 4 crotchets (or 8 quavers)**

**No. 2**
**time signature: 3 crotchets in a bar**

**each bar adds up to 3 crotchets (or 6 quavers)**

**No. 3**
**time signature: 2 crotchets in a bar**

**each bar adds up to 2 crotchets (or 4 quavers)**

**No. 4**
**time signature: 6 quavers in a bar**

**each bar adds up to 6 quavers**

# Pulse

When you listen to a piece of music, there is usually a clear, regular beat that you could tap your foot to. Even when nothing happens on a certain beat, you can usually still 'feel' a beat.

If you listen more closely, one beat usually sounds more important than others, often giving a repeated pattern like '1 2 3 4 1 2 3 4' or '1 2 3 1 2 3'.

Time signatures tell you what sort of beat pattern the music has. In 2/4, 3/4 and 4/4, the pulse is the crotchet. The strongest beat of each bar is always the first, so in 2/4, there is a clear '1 2 1 2' pulse, with '1' being stronger than '2'. In 3/4, there is a '1 2 3 1 2 3' pulse, with again 1 being stronger than the other beats. In 4/4, the pulse is '1 2 3 4 1 2 3 4', with again 1 being strongest.

In 2/2, there is a minim pulse, the pattern being '1 2 1 2', with '1' being the important beat. Notice that although there are the same total of notes values in 2/2 and 4/4, you count '1 2 1 2' in 2/2 as opposed to '1 2 3 4 1 2 3 4' in 4/4.

In 3/2, there is again a minim pulse and you count '1 2 3 1 2 3', with a stress on '1'.

**In 4/4, 3/4 and 2/4, the main pulse is the crotchet**

**In these metres, each crotchet beat is slightly stressed, with the first beat of the bar stressed the most**

**In 2/2 and 3/2, the main pulse is the minim**

**In these metres, each minim beat is slightly stressed, with the first beat of the bar stressed the most**

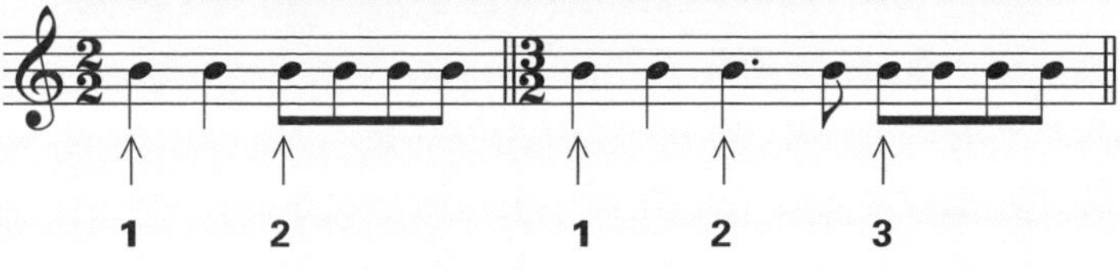

# Pulse – 6/8, 9/8

Time signatures like 6/8 and 9/8 are slightly different from the metres looked at so far. In these time signatures, there is a pulse of a dotted crotchet rather than a crotchet or minim. This means that that there are three shorter notes to each beat rather than 2 or 4, which gives the music a skipping effect. The lazy, swung rhythms of jazz and blues are often in 6/8.

To count 6/8, you could either repeat '1 2 3 4 5 6 1 2 3 4 5 6', with a stress on '1' and '4' or repeat '1 2 1 2', fitting 3 quavers to each beat. The effect of a 6/8 metre can be achieved by repeating the phrases 'Hig-gle-dy Pig-gle-dy Hig-gle-dy Pig-gle-dy' or 'One and a Two and a One and a Two and a'.

9/8 also has a dotted crotchet pulse, with three dotted crotchets to a bar. It could be counted as '1 2 3 4 5 6 7 8 9 1 2 3 4 5 6 7 8 9' with stresses on '1', '4' and '7' or '1 2 3 1 2 3' with three quavers to each beat.

**In 6/8, 9/8 and 12/8, the main pulse is the dotted crotchet**

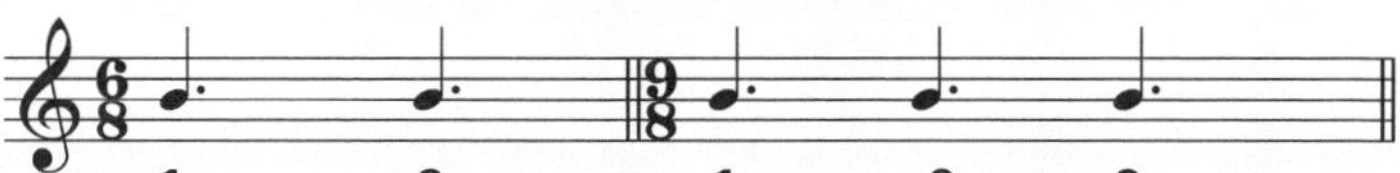


**In these metres, each dotted crotchet beat is slightly stressed, with the first beat of the bar stressed the most**

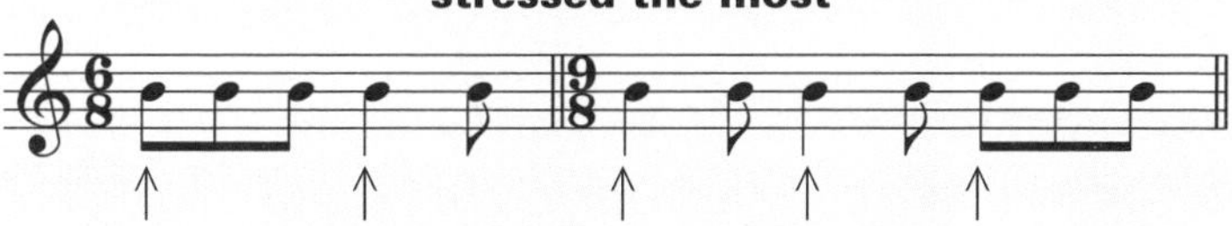


**You can also count these metres in quavers, stressing every third beat**

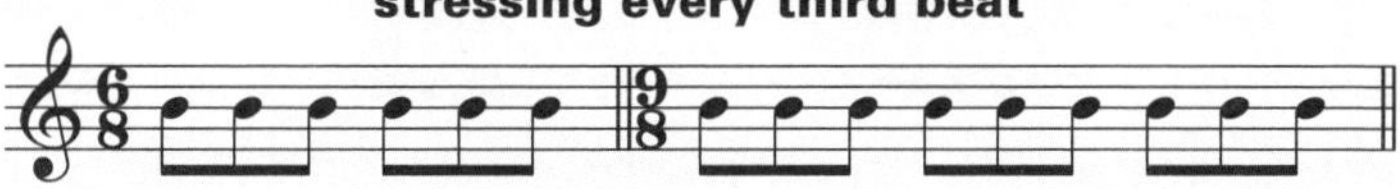

# Play Along – Putting Pitch and Rhythm Together

So far, we have looked at pitch and rhythm separately. The next step is to put these two together, so that you are reading pitch and rhythm at the same time. This will allow you to play melodies.

The most important thing when reading music is to get the rhythm right. The exercises in this section will start with the rhythm of well-known melodies and gradually add in the pitches.

To learn each piece, use the following steps:

1. Clap through the rhythm
2. Play though the rhythm on one note
3. Find the notes on your instrument
4. Play the melody

Gradually increase the speed until you reach the appropriate tempo before moving to the next step.

Treble clef exercises are on the left, bass on the right.

# Big Ben

1. Clap through the rhythm
2. Play the rhythm on one note, as written.
   Make sure you hold on to notes for their full value

**Quite fast (♩ = 100)**

3. Find the notes on your instrument
4. Play the melody

Notes used: 

**Quite fast (♩ = 100)**

**Quite fast (♩ = 100)**

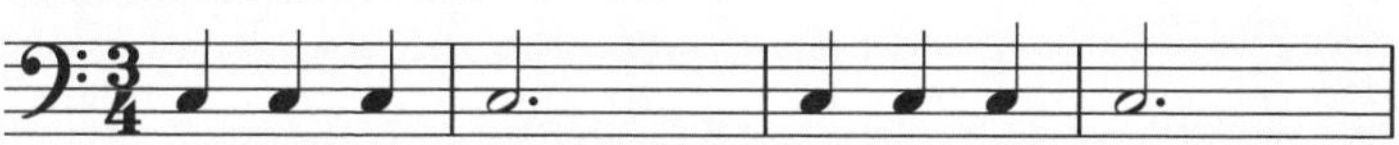

1 2 3 1 (2) (3) 1 2 3 1 (2) (3)

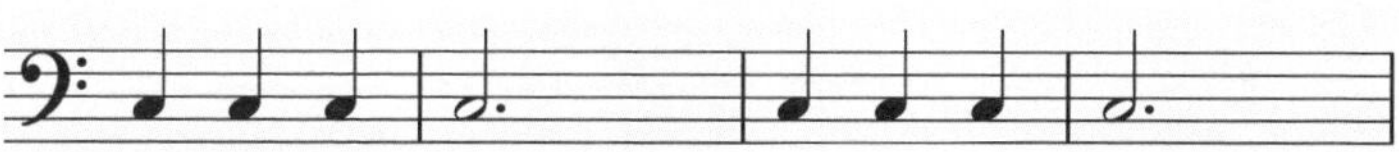

1 2 3 1 (2) (3) 1 2 3 1 (2) (3)

Notes used: 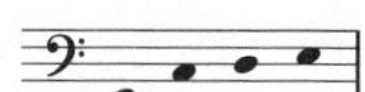

**Quite fast (♩ = 100)**

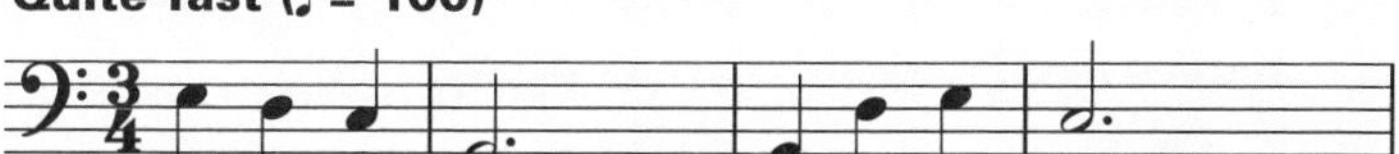

1 2 3 1 (2) (3) 1 2 3 1 (2) (3)

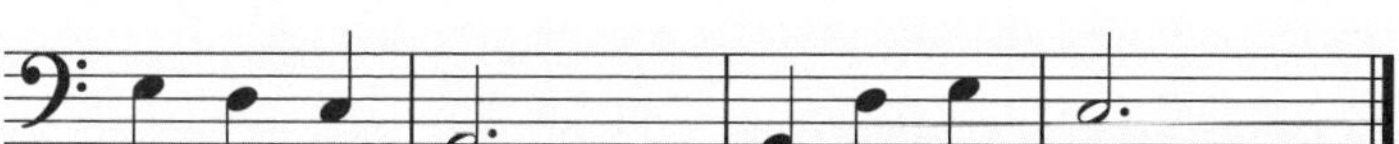

1 2 3 1 (2) (3) 1 2 3 1 (2) (3)

# Yankee Doodle

1. Clap through the rhythm
2. Play the rhythm on one note, as written.
   Make sure you hold on to notes for their full value

**Quite fast (♩ = 100)**

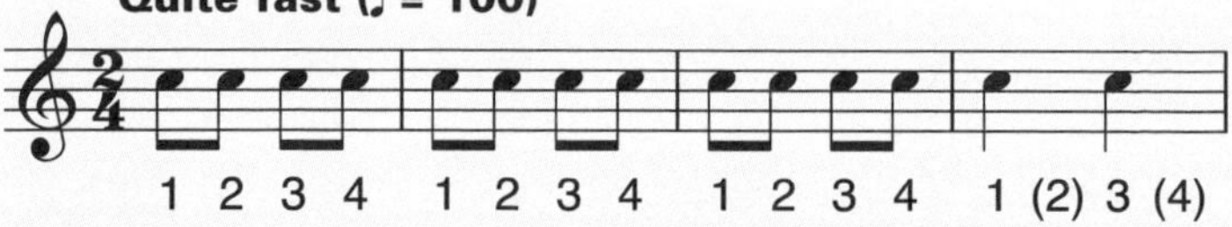

3. Find the notes on your instrument
4. Play the melody

Notes used:

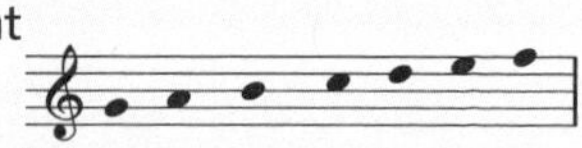

**Quite fast (♩ = 100)**

**Quite fast (♩ = 100)**

1 2 3 4 1 2 3 4 1 2 3 4 1 (2) 3 (4)

1 2 3 4 1 2 3 4 1 2 3 4 1 (2) 3 (4)

Notes used: 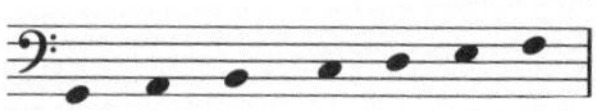

**Quite fast (♩ = 100)**

1 2 3 4 1 2 3 4 1 2 3 4 1 (2) 3 (4)

1 2 3 4 1 2 3 4 1 2 3 4 1 (2) 3 (4)

Pitch
Treble Clef
Bass Clef
Rhythm
Play Along 1
ACC Accidentals
Key Sign
Scales
Chords
Other Chords
Play Along 2
Comp

# Il Est Ne, Le Divin Enfant (French traditional)

Notes used: 

**Quite fast (♩ = 100)**

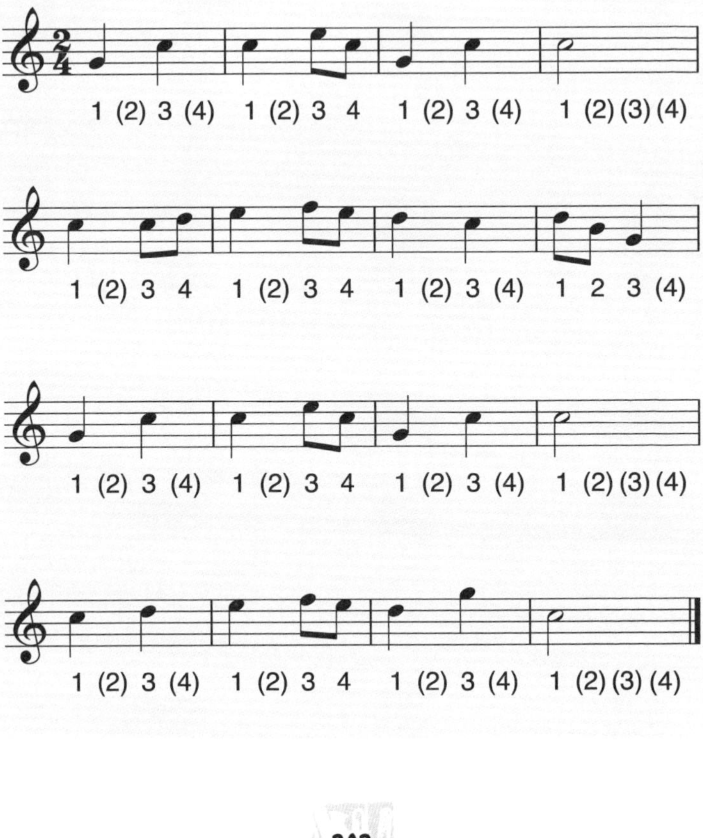

Notes used: 

**Quite fast (♩ = 100)**

1 (2) 3 (4) 1 (2) 3 4 1 (2) 3 (4) 1 (2) (3) (4)

1 (2) 3 4 1 (2) 3 4 1 (2) 3 (4) 1 2 3 (4)

1 (2) 3 (4) 1 (2) 3 4 1 (2) 3 (4) 1 (2) (3) (4)

1 (2) 3 (4) 1 (2) 3 4 1 (2) 3 (4) 1 (2) (3) (4)

# Ode to Joy

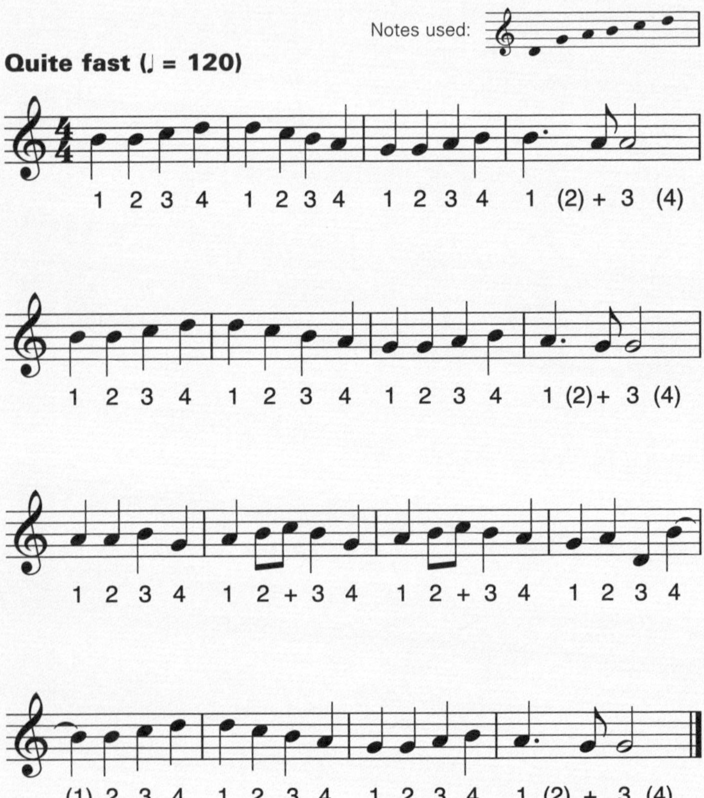
Notes used:
Quite fast (♩ = 120)
1 2 3 4 1 2 3 4 1 2 3 4 1 (2) + 3 (4)
1 2 3 4 1 2 3 4 1 2 3 4 1 (2)+ 3 (4)
1 2 3 4 1 2 + 3 4 1 2 + 3 4 1 2 3 4
(1) 2 3 4 1 2 3 4 1 2 3 4 1 (2) + 3 (4)

Notes used: 

**Quite fast (♩ = 120)**

# Camptown Races

## Play Along 1

Notes used:

**Fast (♩ = 140)**

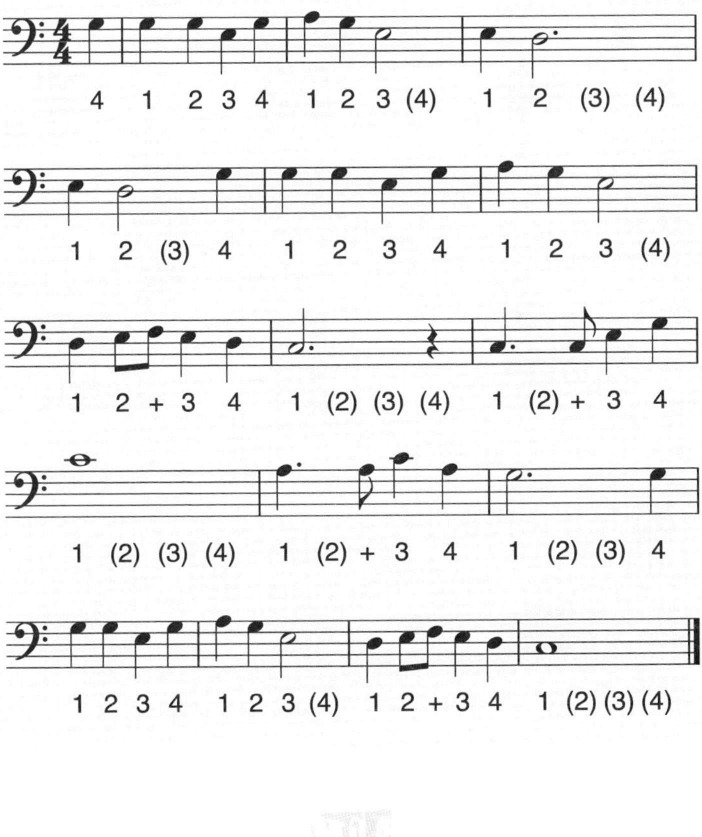

# Once in Royal David's City

Notes used: 

**Quite fast (♩ = 120)**

Notes used:

**Quite fast (♩ = 120)**

# O Come, O Come, Emmanuel

Notes used: 

**Moderately (♩ = 88)**

4 1 2 3 4 1 2 3 4 1 (2) (3) 4 1 2 3 4

1 2 3 4 1 (2) (3) 4 1 2 3 4 1 (2) 3 4

1 (2) (3) 4 1 2 3 4 1 2 3 4 1 (2) (3) 4 1 (2) (3) 4

1 (2) (3) 4 1 2 3 4 1 2 3 4 1 2 3 4 1 2 3

Notes used:

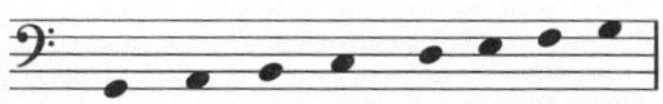

**Moderately (♩ = 88)**

# When the Saints Come Marching In

Notes used: 

**Moderately (♩ = 90)**

Notes used: 

**Moderately (♩ = 90)**

# God Save the Queen

Notes used: 

**Moderately (♩ = 80)**

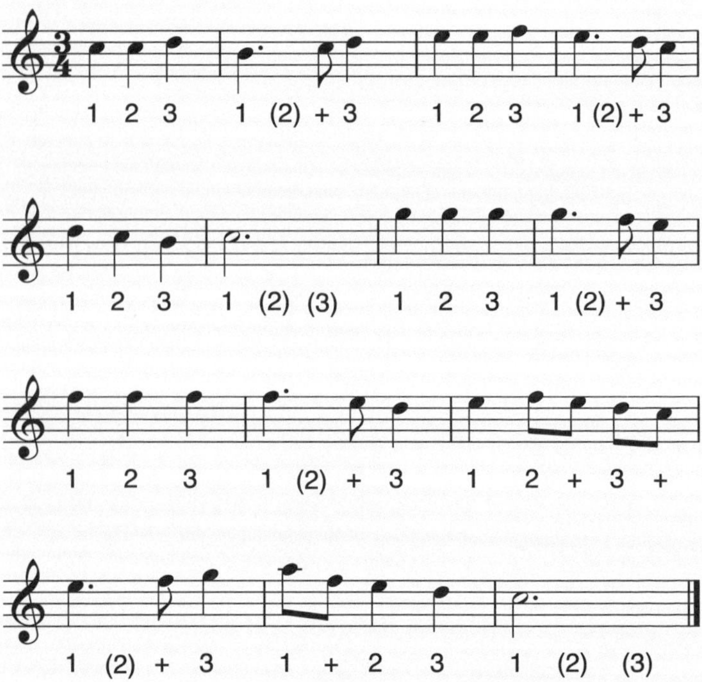

Notes used: 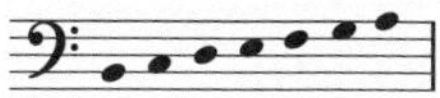

**Moderately (♩ = 80)**

# Scarborough Fair

Notes used:

**Quite fast (♩ = 110)**

Notes used: 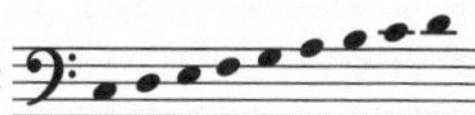

**Quite fast (♩ = 110)**

# Land of My Fathers

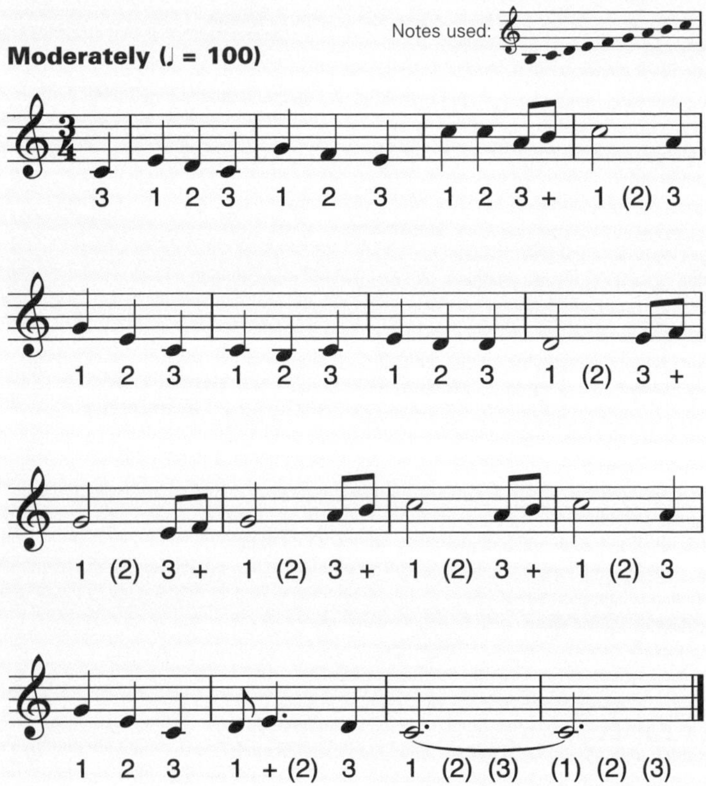

Notes used: 

**Moderately (♩ = 100)**

3 1 2 3 1 2 3 1 2 3 + 1 (2) 3

1 2 3 1 2 3 1 2 3 1 (2) 3 +

1 (2) 3 + 1 (2) 3 + 1 (2) 3 + 1 (2) 3

1 2 3 1 + (2) 3 1 (2) (3) (1) (2) (3)

# Happy Birthday

Notes used: 

**Moderately (♩ = 100)**

Notes used: 

**Moderately (♩ = 100)**

# The Battle Hymn of the Republic

Notes used:

**Moderately (♩ = 90)**

Notes used: 

**Moderately (♩ = 90)**

1 (2) + 3 4 1 (2) 3 (4)

1 (2) + 3 4 1 (2) 3 (4)

1 (2) + 3 4 1 (2) 3 4

1 2 3 4 1 (2) (3) (4)

# Green Bushes (English)

Notes used: 

**Quite fast (♩ = 120)**

Notes used: 

**Quite fast (♩ = 120)**

Pitch
Treble Clef
Bass Clef
Rhythm
Play Along 1
ACC Accidentals
Key Sign
Scales
Chords
Other Chords
Play Along 2
Comp

# For He's a Jolly Good Fellow

Notes used: 

**Quickly (♩. = 90)**

Notes used:

**Quickly (♩. = 90)**

Pitch
Treble Clef
Bass Clef
Rhythm
Play Along 1
ACC Accidentals
Key Sign
Scales
Chords
Other Chords
Play Along 2
Comp

# Sumer is Icumen In (Medieval)

Notes used: 

**Quite fast (♩ = 110)**

Notes used: 

**Quite fast (♩ = 110)**

Pitch
Treble Clef
Bass Clef
Rhythm
Play Along 1
ACC Accidentals
Key Sign
Scales
Chords
Other Chords
Play Along 2
Comp

# Come, All Ye Jolly Shepherds (Scottish)

## Play Along 1

Notes used: 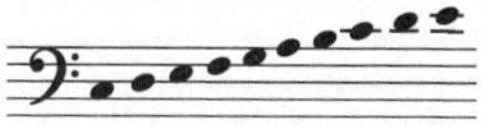

**Quite fast (♩ = 110)**

# Accidentals

So far, we have only looked at melodies which use the white notes of the keyboard or the notes of the C major scale.

You will probably have noticed that there are other notes besides these. In fact, there are twelve different musical notes. These form a scale called the chromatic scale, where each note is a semitone apart from the next one.

A semitone is the gap between adjacent notes on a keyboard or between adjacent fret positions on a guitar: F is a semitone higher than E and B is a semitone lower than C.

Pitch
Treble Clef
Bass Clef
Rhythm
Play Along 1
ACC Accidentals
Key Sign
Scales
Chords
Other Chords
Play Along 2
Comp

# The Chromatic Scale

You can see the chromatic scale most clearly on a keyboard. If you take the notes middle C to the C an octave higher, there are seven white notes and five black notes. Mostly the notes alternate between white and black notes, but there are two places where there are two white notes next to each other.

How are these extra black notes written on the stave? As all the lines and spaces have been used up on white notes, black notes are notated by writing symbols in front of ordinary line and space notes. These symbols are called accidentals.

# The chromatic scale on a keyboard

**any 12 notes next to each other on a keyboard form a chromatic scale**

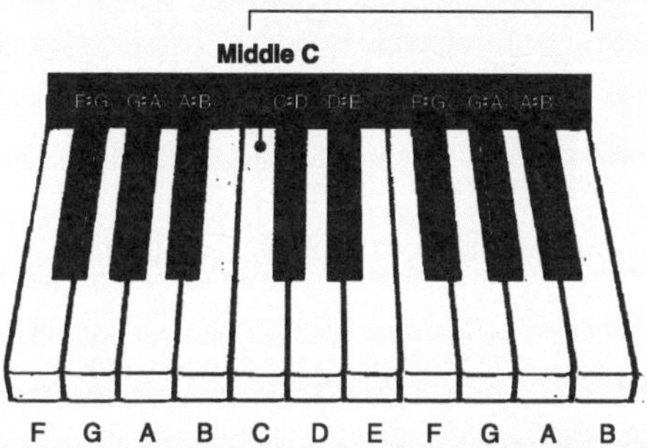


# The same chromatic scale written on the stave

**Black notes are notated by placing accidentals before space or line notes**

each note is separated from the next one by a semitone

# The same chromatic scale written in TAB

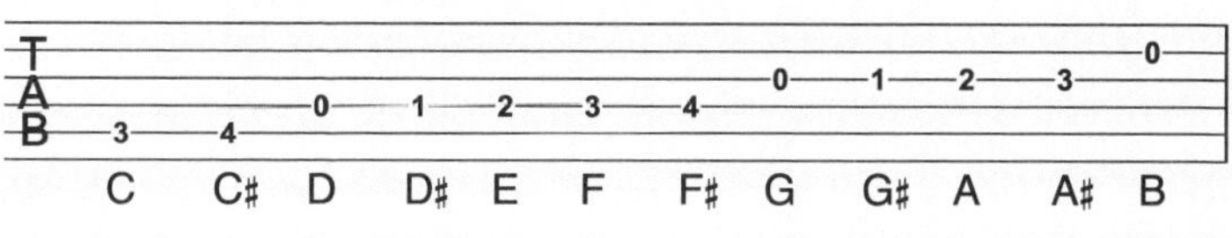


Pitch
Treble Clef
Bass Clef
Rhythm
Play Along 1
ACC Accidentals
Key Sign
Scales
Chords
Other Chords
Play Along 2
Comp

# Sharps

First let's look at sharps. If a sharp symbol is written immediately before a notehead, the pitch of that note is raised by a semitone. If you are playing a keyboard, that note will be the next black or white note to the right. If you are playing a guitar, a sharpened note is one fret higher up the fingerboard.

Looking again at the piano keyboard, you will also notice that the notes do not alternate between white and black. In two places in each octave, there are two white notes next to each other: E and F and B and C. What happens if an E or a B is sharpened?

An E sharp is actually the same note as an F. B sharp is the same note as a C. So if you come across an E sharp, play an F, and if you see a B sharp, play a C.

Note that once a sharp sign has been used in a bar, it lasts for the rest of the bar. So if you have an F sharp early in a bar and see the same F without a sharp sign later in the bar, you need to play it as an F sharp.

**a sharp before a note raises that note by a semitone** ♯

**sharps are written immediately to the left of a note:**

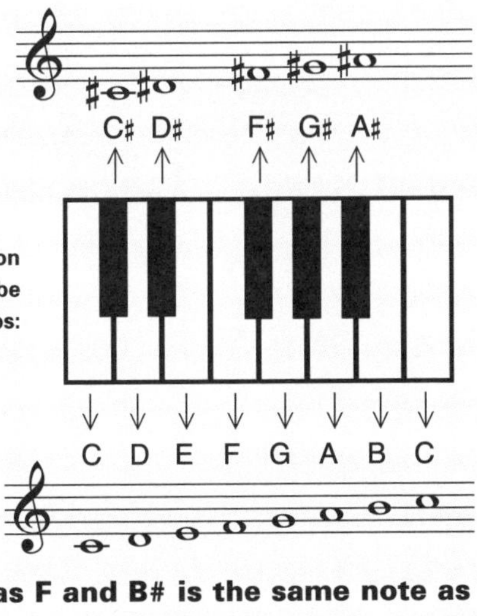


**the black notes on a keyboard can be written as sharps:**

**E♯ is the same note as F and B# is the same note as C:**

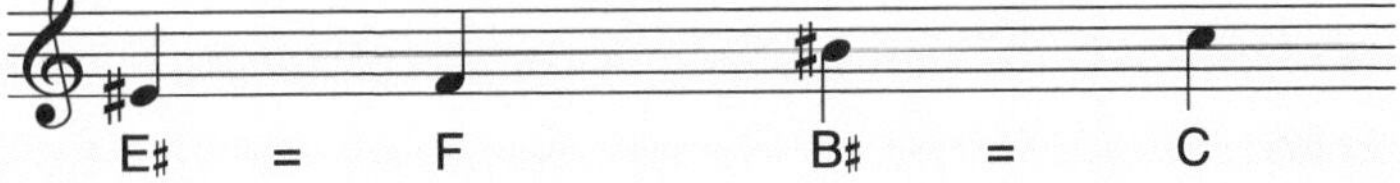

# Flats

The second accidental is the flat. This is the opposite of a sharp: if a note has a flat before it, the note is lowered by a semitone. On the keyboard, you would play the black or white note immediately to the left. On the guitar, you would play the note one fret lower, or one fret nearer to the neck of the instrument.

What happens when an F flat or a C flat is written? On a keyboard, they have no black note immediately to their left. This case is similar to that with E sharps and B sharps: a semitone lower than F is E, so if you see an F flat, you play an E. If you see a C flat, you play a B.

As with sharps, once a flat appears, it lasts for the rest of the bar.

**the flat symbol lowers a note by a semitone** ♭

**flats are written immediately to the left of a note:**

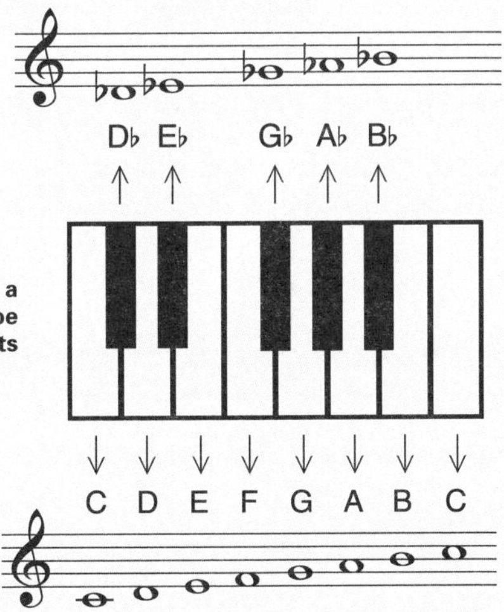


the black notes on a keyboard can be written as flats

**F♭ is the same note as E and C♭ is the same note as B:**

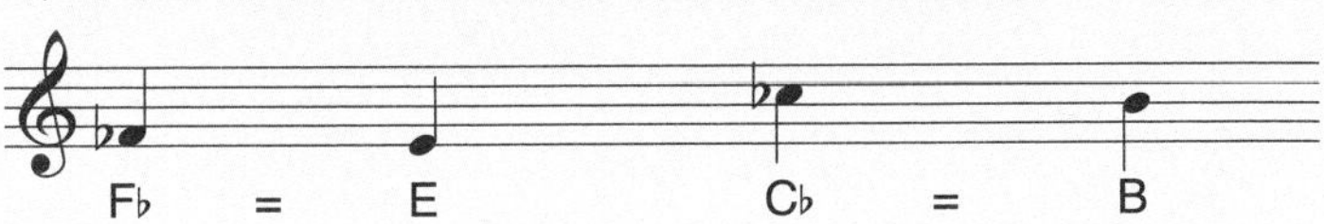

# Naturals, Double Sharps and Double Flats

The third accidental is the natural. The natural sign is used to cancel a sharp or flat from earlier in a bar, or from a previous bar. A natural before a note instructs you to play the note exactly as it is without any sharps or flats. So the note 'F natural' is exactly the same as 'F'.

As with flats and sharps, a natural lasts for the rest of the bar in which it appears.

Two less common accidentals are the double sharp and double flat. A double sharp before a note means that you play the note two semitones higher (two notes to the right on a piano keyboard, two fret positions higher on a guitar).

A double flat before a note means that you play the note two semitones lower (two notes to the left on a piano keyboard, two frets lower on a guitar).

You are only likely to see these last two symbols in quite advanced music.

**a natural symbol before a note tells you that note should be played as it is: ♮**

**naturals are written immediately to the left of a note:**

**natural signs are only needed if the same note earlier in the bar or in the bar before has been sharpened or flattened:**

**these naturals cancel the earlier B♭ A♭ and F♯**

**a double sharp raises a note by two semitones: 𝄪**

**a double flat lowers a note by two semitones: 𝄫**

# Sharps or Flats?

You might have noticed that the black notes of the keyboard can be written in two different ways: as a sharp and a flat. B flat, for instance, is the same note as A sharp. F sharp is the same as G flat. These alternative ways of 'spelling' notes are known as enharmonic spellings. So, for example, F sharp is the enharmonic of G flat, and D flat is the enharmonic of C sharp.

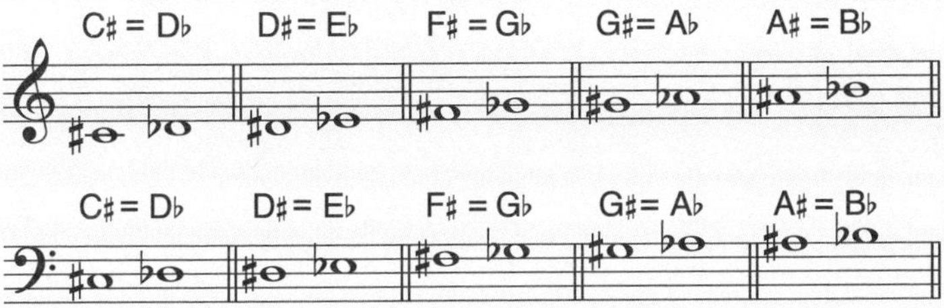


## Re-write these notes using sharps:

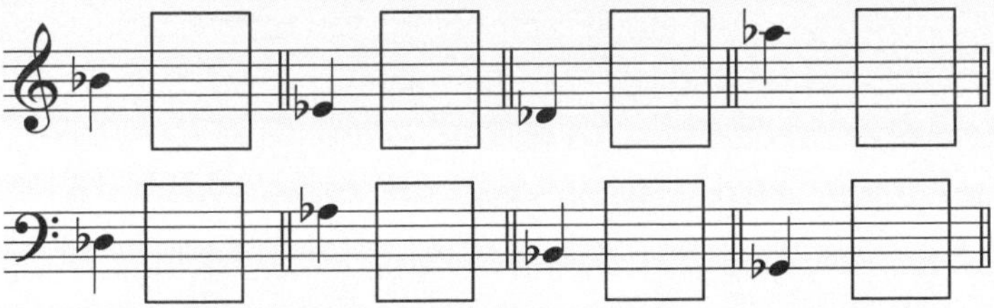

## Re-write these notes using flats:

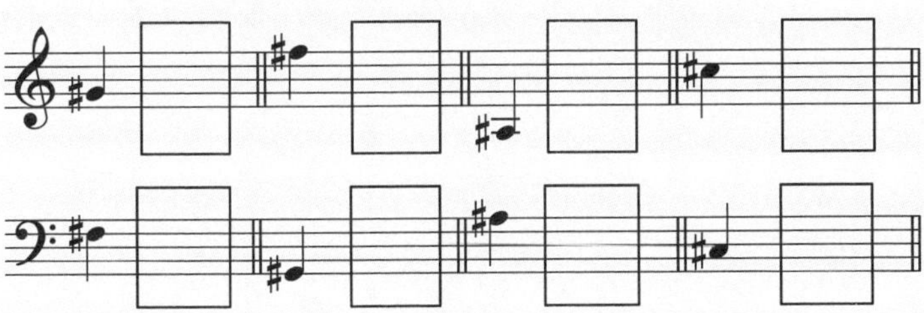

# Intervals

All the melodies in Play Along 1 are written just using white notes. If you wanted to write one of these melodies one note higher, the obvious thing to do might be to move each note up to the next line or space. However, if you try playing the result, you will find that the melody sounds wrong. Why is this?

The notes of the C major scale have a specific interval pattern. An interval is the size of the gap between two notes. As mentioned before, the smallest gap is called a semitone: this is the distance between notes that are right next to each other like C and C sharp, E and F or A and B flat. On the keyboard this is the interval between two keys that are next to each other; on the guitar, a semitone is the next fret.

**the same tune written one note higher on the stave**

**these notes sound wrong**

## a semitone

**a semitone is the smallest step between notes on the keyboard**

## a tone

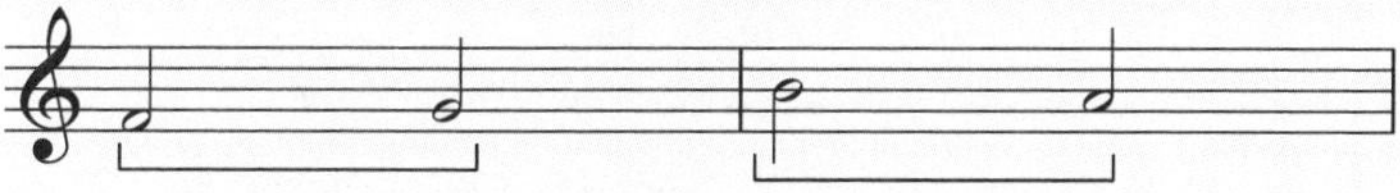

**a tone is the same as two semitones**

Pitch
Treble Clef
Bass Clef
Rhythm
Play Along 1
ACC Accidentals
Key Sign
Scales
Chords
Other Chords
Play Along 2
Comp

# Interval Patterns

The notes of C major make up a specific pattern of tones and semitones: Tone Tone Semitone Tone Tone Tone Semitone. (TTSTTTS). Starting from C and following this interval pattern, you get the notes C D E F G A B. This group of notes make up the 'key' of C major.

To write out a melody in another key, for instance D major, you need to keep the same interval pattern, or the melody will sound 'wrong'. This will mean making some of the notes sharp or flat so that the pattern of intervals stays the same.

In a scale starting on D, the interval pattern TTSTTTS gives you the notes D E F sharp G A B C sharp. If you rewrite the melody one step higher on the stave but changing any F's to F sharps and C's to a C sharps, you will find that it now sounds right.

## the interval pattern of the notes of C major

## the same interval pattern starting on D: this gives the notes of D major

## the tune rewritten in D major

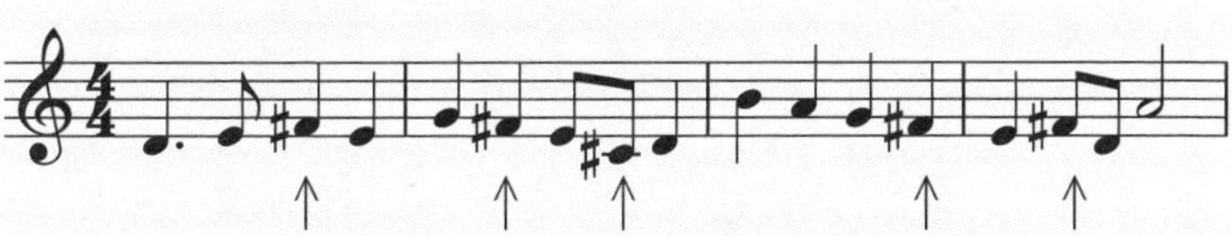

now that these notes have been changed to the notes of D major, the tune sounds correct

Pitch
Treble Clef
Bass Clef
Rhythm
Play Along 1
ACC Accidentals
Key Sign
Scales
Chords
Other Chords
Play Along 2
Comp

# Key Signatures

To tell you which key the music is in, a key signature is written at the start of the stave, just after the clef. Unlike the time signature, which is written once at the beginning, a key signature is written at the start of every stave.

# What Is a Key Signature?

The key signature contains one or more sharps or flats written on lines and spaces: these tell you that these notes are always to be played as sharps or flats, whichever octave they appear in.

From the number of sharps or flats, you can work out the key of the music.

If the natural version is required of a note that is flattened or sharpened in the key signature, a natural sign needs to be written before that note.

## Key signatures are written at the beginning of a stave after the clef and before the time signature

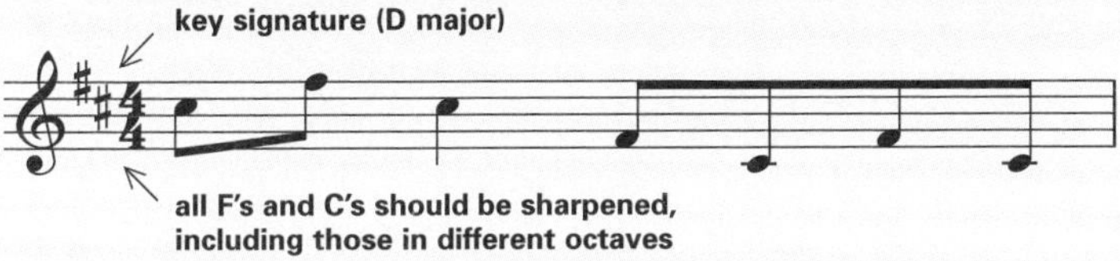


the actual notes to be played:

## Natural signs need to be used if an unaltered version of a note in the key signature is to be played

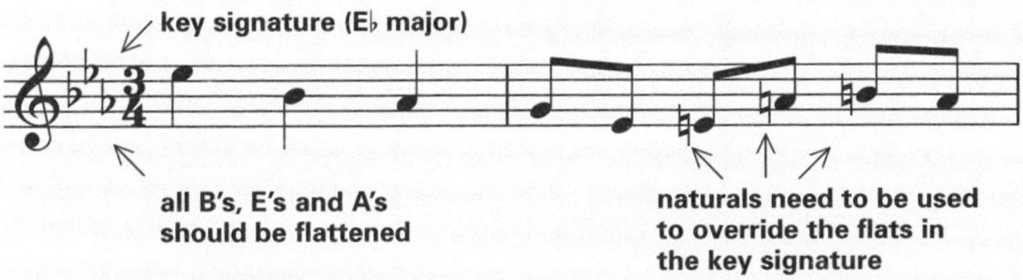


the actual notes to be played:

Pitch
Treble Clef
Bass Clef
Rhythm
Play Along 1
ACC Accidentals
Key Sign
Scales
Chords
Other Chords
Play Along 2
Comp

# Remembering Sharp Key Signatures

Each white and black note – C, C sharp, D and so on – has its own scale with its own particular numbers of sharps or flats. This sounds daunting, but fortunately there is a logical pattern which can be remembered fairly easily.

In key signatures with sharps, the sharps always follow a set order. The first sharp in the key signature is always F sharp. The second is always C sharp and the sequence continues: G sharp, D sharp, A sharp, E sharp and B sharp. This can be remembered by the first letters of this phrase:

**F**ather **C**harlie **G**oes **D**own **A**nd **E**nds **B**attle

To work out the key in a sharp key signature, look at the final sharp of the key signature. The note one semitone higher than this is the major key of the key signature.

So a key signature of three sharps will have as its final sharp G ('Goes'). A semitone higher than G sharp is A, so A major is the major key with this key signature.

**The sharps in a key signature always follow the same order:**

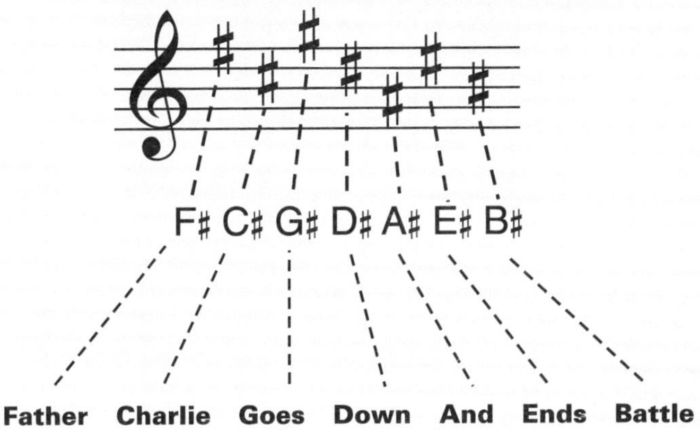


**The major key of a particular key signature is one semitone higher than the final sharp in the key signature**

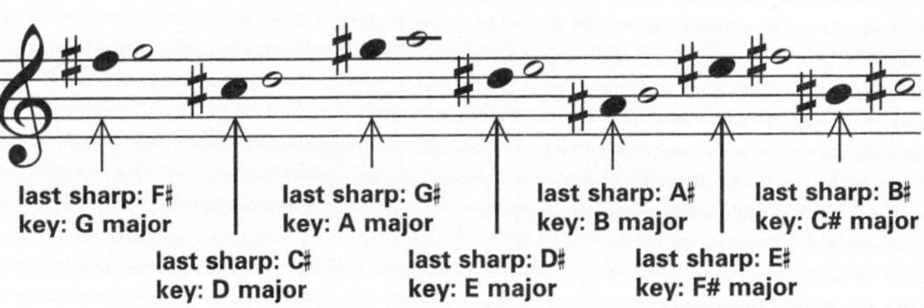

Pitch
Treble Clef
Bass Clef
Rhythm
Play Along 1
ACC Accidentals
Key Sign
Scales
Chords
Other Chords
Play Along 2
Comp

# Remembering Flat Key Signatures

Flat key signatures have a similar pattern. The order of flats in a flat key signature is the reverse of that in a sharp key signature. The first flat is always B flat, the second E flat, then A flat, D flat, G flat, C flat, F flat. They can be remembered by reversing the 'Father Charlie' phrase:

**B**attle **E**nds **A**nd **D**own **G**oes **C**harlie's **F**ather

The home note of a flat key signature is the same note as the second last flat in the key signature.

For example, in a key signature of five flats, the second last flat in the signature is D flat ('Down'). So D flat major is the key with this key signature. Obviously, this only works if the key signature has two or more flats, so you have to remember that F major has one flat.

**The flats in a flat key signature always follow a particular order:**

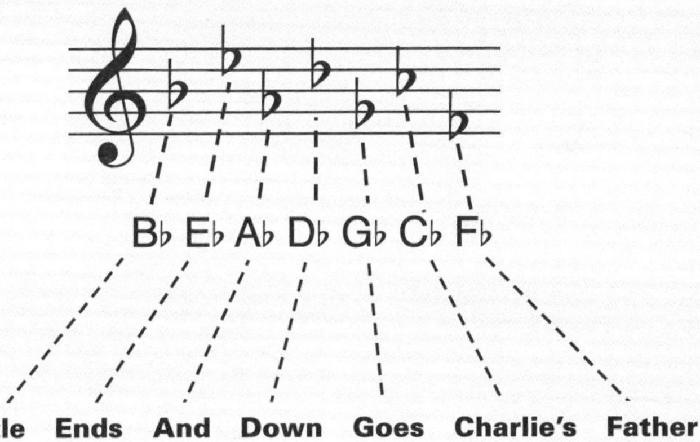


**The major key of a particular flat key signature is the same as the second last flat in that key signature**

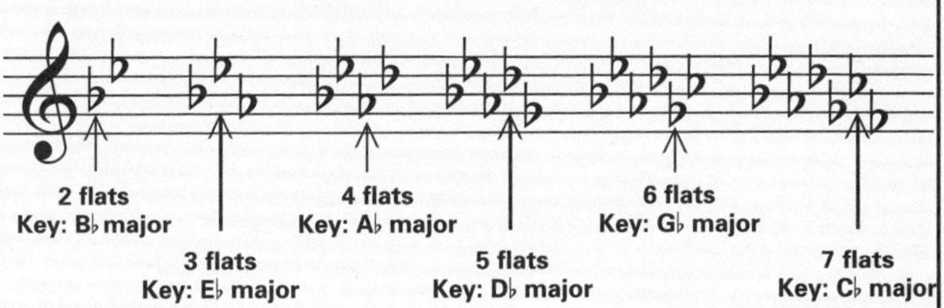

# No Sharps or Flats

## C major or A minor: treble clef

**No notes are sharpened or flattened unless accidentals are used on individual notes**

### Melody in C major

### Melody in A minor

# C major or A minor: bass clef

**No notes are sharpened or flattened unless accidentals are used on individual notes**

## Melody in C major

## Melody in A minor

# One Sharp

## G major or E minor: treble clef

♯

**F's are sharpened.**
**These notes:** **are played as these notes.**

### Melody in G major: all notes marked '+' are sharpened

### Melody in E minor: all notes marked '+' are sharpened

# G major or E minor: bass clef

♯

F's are sharpened.
These notes: are played as these notes.

## Melody in G major: all notes marked '+' are sharpened

## Melody in E minor: all notes marked '+' are sharpened

# Two Sharps

## D major or B minor: treble clef

F's and C's are sharpened.
These notes: are played as these notes.

### Melody in D major: all notes marked '+' are sharpened

### Melody in B minor: all notes marked '+' are sharpened

# D major or B minor: bass clef

**F's and C's are sharpened.**
**These notes:** **are played as these notes:**

## Melody in D major: all notes marked '+' are sharpened

## Melody in B minor: all notes marked '+' are sharpened

# Three Sharps

## A major or F♯ minor: treble clef

F's, C's and G's are sharpened.
These notes: are played as these notes:

### Melody in A major: all notes marked '+' are sharpened

### Melody in F♯ minor: all notes marked '+' are sharpened

# A major or F♯ minor: bass clef

**F's, C's and G's are sharpened.**
**These notes:** **are played as these notes:**

## Melody in A major: all notes marked '+' are sharpened

## Melody in F♯ minor: all notes marked '+' are sharpened

# Four Sharps

## E major or C♯ minor: treble clef

**F's, C's, G's and D's are sharpened.**
**These notes:** **are played as these notes:**

### Melody in E major: all notes marked '+' are sharpened

### Melody in C♯ minor: all notes marked '+' are sharpened

## E major or C♯ minor: bass clef

**F's, C's, G's and D's are sharpened.**
**These notes: are played as these notes:**

### Melody in E major: all notes marked '+' are sharpened

### Melody in C♯ minor: all notes marked '+' are sharpened

Pitch
Treble Clef
Bass Clef
Rhythm
Play Along 1
ACC Accidentals
Key Sign
Scales
Chords
Other Chords
Play Along 2
Comp

Pitch
Treble Clef
Bass Clef
Rhythm
Play Along 1
ACC Accidentals
Key Sign
Scales
Chords
Other Chords
Play Along 2
Comp

# Five Sharps

## B major or G♯ minor: treble clef

F's, C''s, G's, D's and A's are sharpened.

These notes: are played as these notes:

### Melody in B major: all notes marked '+' are sharpened

### Melody in G♯ minor: all notes marked '+' are sharpened

# B major or G♯ minor: bass clef

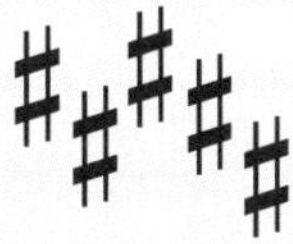

**F's, C"s, G's, D's and A's are sharpened.**
**These notes:** **are played as these notes:**

## Melody in B major: all notes marked '+' are sharpened

## Melody in G♯ minor: all notes marked '+' are sharpened

# Six Sharps

## F♯ major or D♯ minor: treble clef

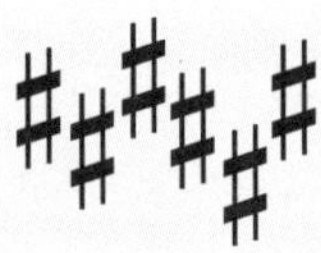

**F's, C's, G's, D's, A's and E's are sharpened.**
**These notes:** **are played as these notes:**

## Melody in F♯ major: all notes marked '+' are sharpened

## Melody in D♯ minor: all notes marked '+' are sharpened

# F♯ major or D♯ minor: bass clef

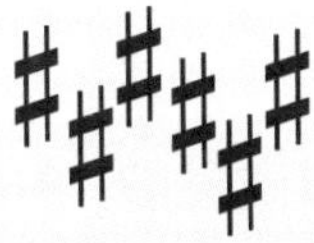

**F's, C's, G's, D's, A's and E's are sharpened.**
**These notes:** **are played as these notes:**

## Melody in F♯ major: all notes marked '+' are sharpened

## Melody in D♯ minor: all notes marked '+' are sharpened

# One Flat

## F major or D minor: treble clef ♭

**B's are flattened.**
**These notes:** **are played as these notes:**

### Melody in F major: all notes marked '+' are flattened

### Melody in D minor: all notes marked '+' are flattened

# F major or D minor: bass clef

**B's are flattened.**
**These notes:** **are played as these notes:**

## Melody in F major: all notes marked '+' are flattened

## Melody in D minor: all notes marked '+' are flattened

# Two Flats

## B♭ major or G minor: treble clef

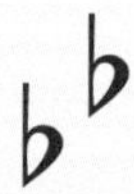

B's and E's are flattened.
These notes: are played as these notes:

### Melody in B♭ major: all notes marked '+' are flattened

### Melody in G minor: all notes marked '+' are flattened

# B♭ major or G minor: bass clef

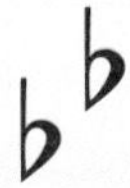

**B's and E's are flattened.**
**These notes:** **are played as these notes:**

## Melody in B♭ major: all notes marked '+' are flattened

## Melody in G minor: all notes marked '+' are flattened

# Three Flats

## E♭ major or C minor: treble clef

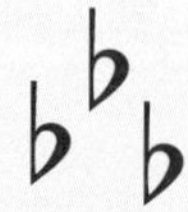

**B's, E's and A's are flattened.**
**These notes:** **are played as these notes:**

**Melody in E♭ major: all notes marked '+' are flattened**

**Melody in C minor: all notes marked '+' are flattened**

# E♭ major or C minor: bass clef

**B's, E's and A's are flattened.**
**These notes:** **are played as these notes:**

## Melody in E♭ major: all notes marked '+' are flattened

## Melody in C minor: all notes marked '+' are flattened

# Four Flats

## A♭ major or F minor: treble clef

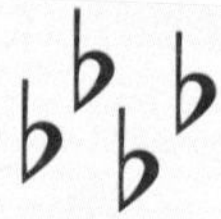

**B's, E's, A's and D's are flattened.**
**These notes: are played as these notes:**

### Melody in A♭ major: all notes marked '+' are flattened

### Melody in F minor: all notes marked '+' are flattened

# A♭ major or F minor: bass clef

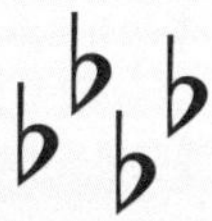

**B's, E's, A's and D's are flattened.**
**These notes:** **are played as these notes:**

## Melody in A♭ major: all notes marked '+' are flattened

## Melody in F minor: all notes marked '+' are flattened

# Five Flats

## D♭ major or B♭ minor: treble clef

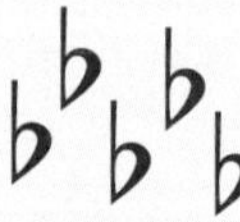

B's, E's, A's, D's and G's are flattened.
These notes: are played as these notes:

### Melody in D♭ major: all notes marked '+' are flattened

### Melody in B♭ minor: all notes marked '+' are flattened

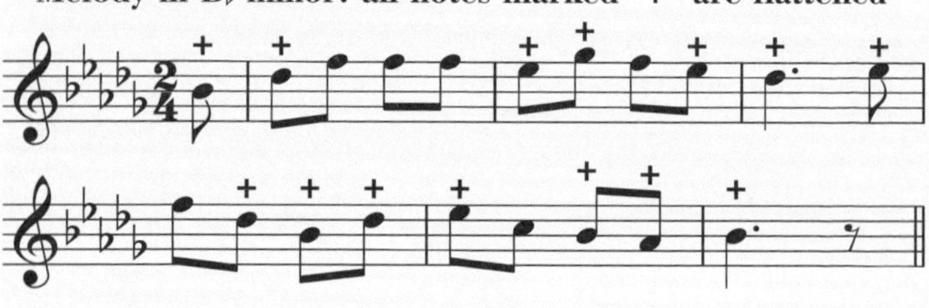

## D♭ major or B♭ minor: bass clef

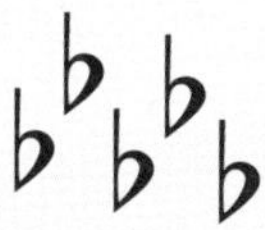

**B's, E's, A's, D's and G's are flattened.**

**These notes:** **are played as these notes:**

### Melody in D♭ major: all notes marked '+' are flattened

### Melody in B♭ minor: all notes marked '+' are flattened

# Six Flats

## G♭ major or E♭ minor: treble clef

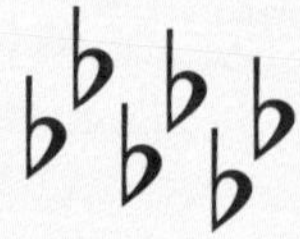

B's, E's, A's, D's, G's and C's are flattened.

These notes: are played as these notes:

### Melody in G♭ major: all notes marked '+' are flattened

### Melody in E♭ minor: all notes marked '+' are flattened

## G♭ major or E♭ minor: bass clef

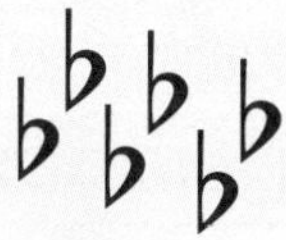

**B's, E's, A's, D's, G's and C's are flattened.**
**These notes: are played as these notes:**

### Melody in G♭ major: all notes marked '+' are flattened

### Melody in E♭ minor: all notes marked '+' are flattened

# Scales

What is a scale? A scale is a series of notes that form a stepwise pattern going up or down. There are many types of scales, but the most common are major and minor scales. Major scales are often said to sound 'happy' and minor scales to sound 'sad'. Each key signature has its own major and a minor scale, so there are 12 major and 12 minor scales.

Different types of scale have their own interval patterns. Minor scales come in two types: melodic minor scales are different going up to coming down, while harmonic minor scales are the same going up and down.

Scales are very important in music. Most melodies are based on major and minor scales in some way, so the more confident you are with the scales in this section, the more easily you will be able to play melodies.

The most common scales are C, D, E, F, G, A (major and minor) and B flat and E flat majors. When learning scales, start with the scales with fewest accidentals first. You may not come across the more difficult scales (those like F sharp major, with many accidentals) but they are included for completeness.

# C

## C major and C minor scales: treble clef

### C major

### C minor (melodic)

### C minor (harmonic)

# C

## C major and C minor scales: bass clef

### C major

### C minor (melodic)

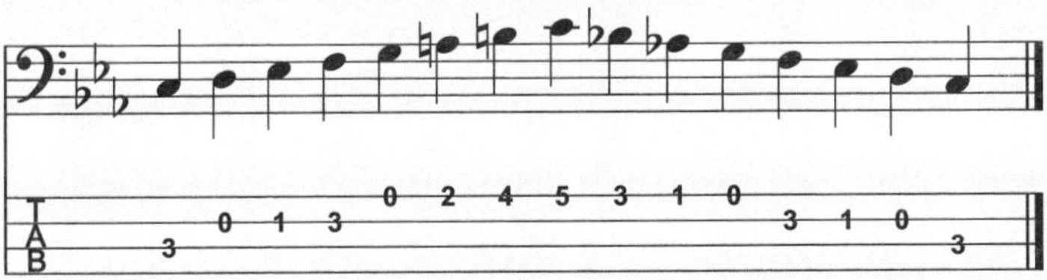

### C minor (harmonic)

# D♭/C♯

## D♭ major and C♯ minor scales: treble clef

### D♭ major

### C♯ minor (melodic)

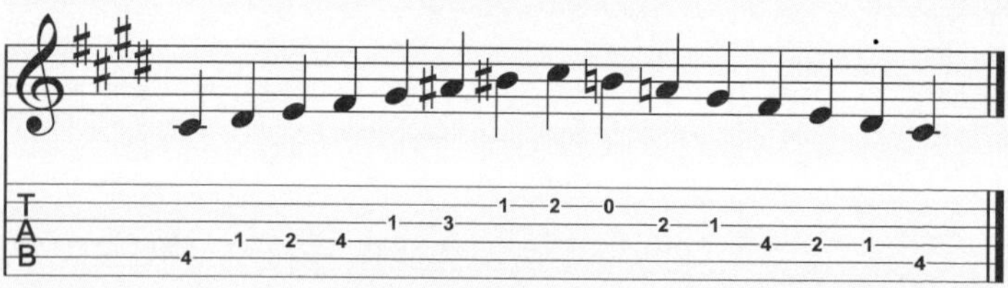


### C♯ minor (harmonic)

# D♭/C♯

## D♭ major and C♯ minor scales: bass clef

### D♭ major

### C♯ minor (melodic)

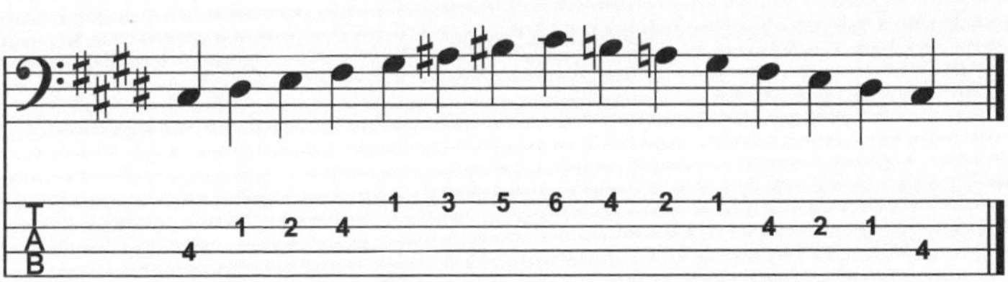


### C♯ minor (harmonic)

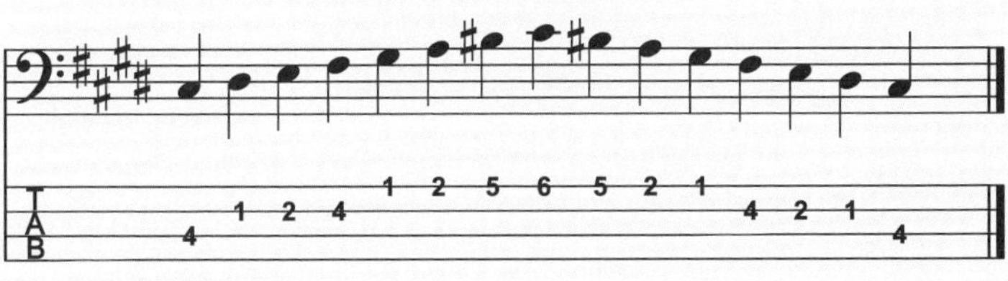

# D

## D major and D minor scales: treble clef

### D major

### D minor (melodic)

### D minor (harmonic)

# D

## D major and D minor scales: bass clef

### D major

### D minor (melodic)

### D minor (harmonic)

# E♭

## E♭ major and E♭ minor scales: treble clef

### E♭ major

### E♭ minor (melodic)

### E♭ minor (harmonic)

# E♭

## E♭ major and E♭ minor scales: bass clef

### E♭ major

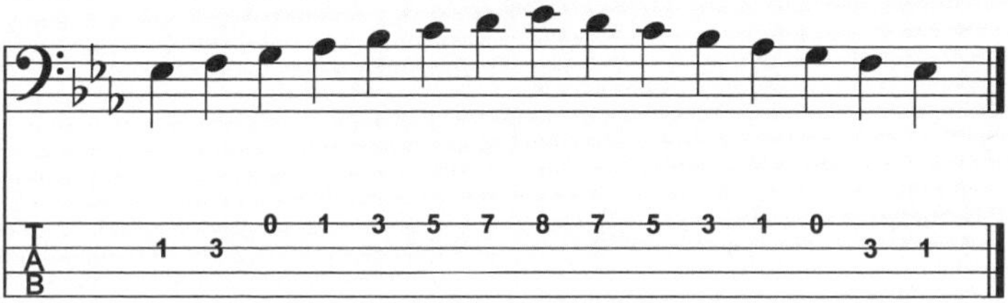

### E♭ minor (melodic)

### E♭ minor (harmonic)

# E

## E major and E minor scales: treble clef

### E major

### E minor (melodic)

### E minor (harmonic)

# E

## E major and E minor scales: bass clef

### E major

### E minor (melodic)

### E minor (harmonic)

# F

## F major and F minor scales: treble clef

### F major

### F minor (melodic)

### F minor (harmonic)

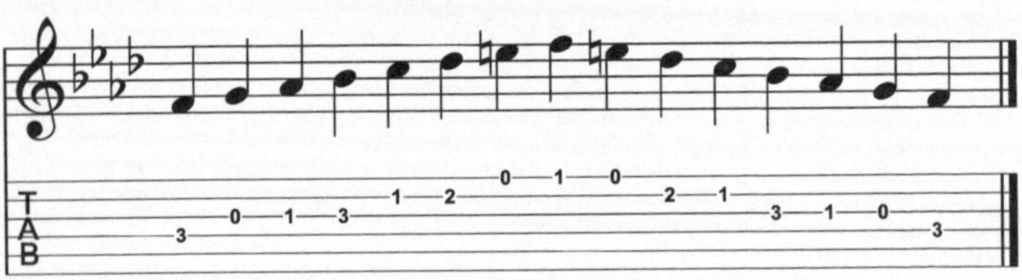

# F

## F major and F minor scales: bass clef

### F major

### F minor (melodic)

### F minor (harmonic)

# F♯

## F♯ major and F♯ minor scales: treble clef

### F♯ major

### F♯ minor (melodic)

### F♯ minor (harmonic)

# F♯

## F♯ major and F♯ minor scales: bass clef

### F♯ major

### F♯ minor (melodic)

### F♯ minor (harmonic)

Pitch
Treble Clef
Bass Clef
Rhythm
Play Along 1
ACC Accidentals
Key Sign
Scales
Chords
Other Chords
Play Along 2
Comp

# G

## G major and G minor scales: treble clef

### G major

### G minor (melodic)

### G minor (harmonic)

# G

## G major and G minor scales: bass clef

### G major

### G minor (melodic)

### G minor (harmonic)

Pitch
Treble Clef
Bass Clef
Rhythm
Play Along 1
ACC Accidentals
Key Sign
Scales
Chords
Other Chords
Play Along 2
Comp

# A♭/G♯

## A♭ major and G♯ minor scales: treble clef

### A♭ major

### G♯ minor (melodic)

### G♯ minor (harmonic)

# A♭/G♯

## A♭ major and G♯ minor scales: bass clef

### A♭ major

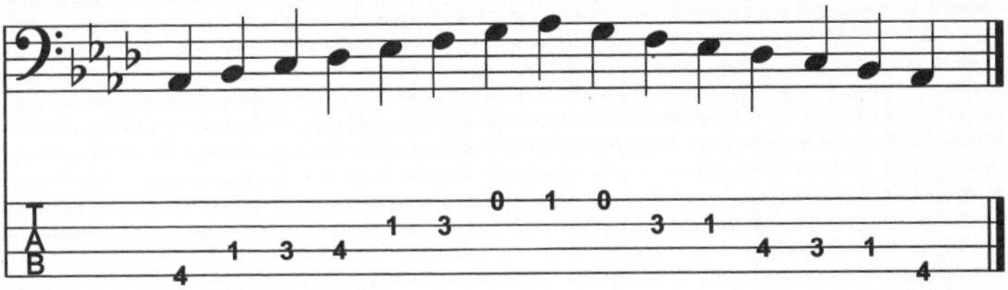

### G♯ minor (melodic)

### G♯ minor (harmonic)

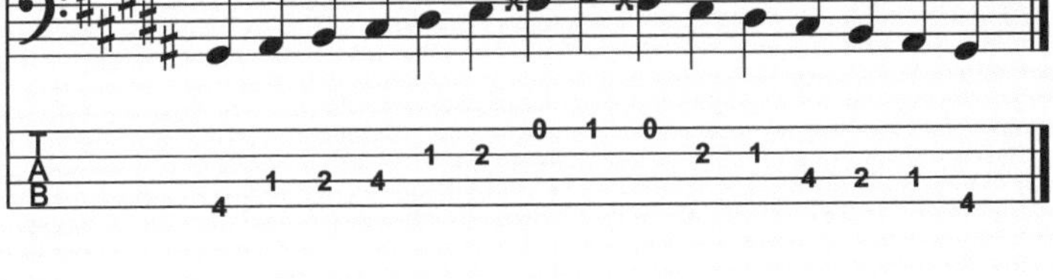

# A

## A major and A minor scales: treble clef

### A major

### A minor (melodic)

### A minor (harmonic)

# A

## A major and A minor scales: bass clef

### A major

### A minor (melodic)

### A minor (harmonic)

Pitch
Treble Clef
Bass Clef
Rhythm
Play Along 1
ACC Accidentals
Key Sign
Scales
Chords
Other Chords
Play Along 2
Comp

# B♭

## B♭ major and B♭ minor scales: treble clef

### B♭ major

### B♭ minor (melodic)

### B♭ minor (harmonic)

# B♭

## B♭ major and B♭ minor scales: bass clef

### B♭ major

### B♭ minor (melodic)

### B♭ minor (harmonic)

Pitch
Treble Clef
Bass Clef
Rhythm
Play Along 1
ACC Accidentals
Key Sign
Scales
Chords
Other Chords
Play Along 2
Comp

Pitch
Treble Clef
Bass Clef
Rhythm
Play Along 1
ACC Accidentals
Key Sign
Scales
Chords
Other Chords
Play Along 2
Comp

# B

## B major and B minor scales: treble clef

### B major

### B minor (melodic)

### B minor (harmonic)

# B

## B major and B minor scales: bass clef

### B major

### B minor (melodic)

### B minor (harmonic)

# Chords

So far, we have mainly looked at melodies, where just one note is played at a time. Of course, it is also possible to play more than one note at a time. When two or more notes are played simultaneously, they produce a chord. Chords usually contain three or more notes and are particularly useful for accompanying melodies.

Instruments that often need to play chords include keyboard, piano, synthesizer, guitar, banjo, ukelele, accordian, harp and vibraphone. Bowed string instruments like violins and cellos can also produce chords but not as easily. Many instruments, such as voice, wind and brass instruments, do not have chords written for them as they can only play one note at a time.

# Chord Symbol Notation

If you play a keyboard or guitar, you may have come across chord symbol notation, where a chord name, such as G (G major), C/E (C major with E as the lowest note) or C/G (C major with G as the lowest note) is written above the song lyrics.

Every chord has a unique sound. This comes not only from the notes within the chord, such as C, E and G in a C major chord, but also from the order that the notes appear from bottom to top (for instance E C G), from the register they are in (high, middle or low), the way they are spaced (wide apart or close together) and repeated (for instance having two C's in the chord rather than one). This is a lot of information to convey and chord symbols are not detailed enough for this. So the only way of writing down chords accurately is by using staff notation.

A C major chord consists of the notes C, E and G

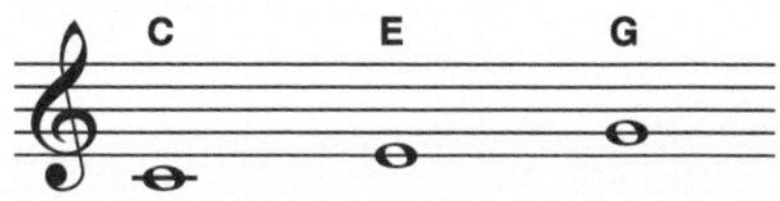


These three notes can appear in a different order from bottom to top

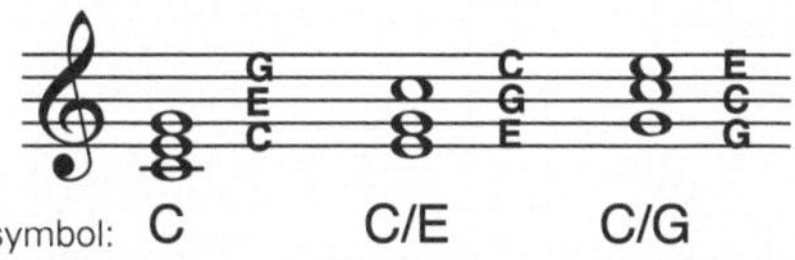


The chord can be written in different registers

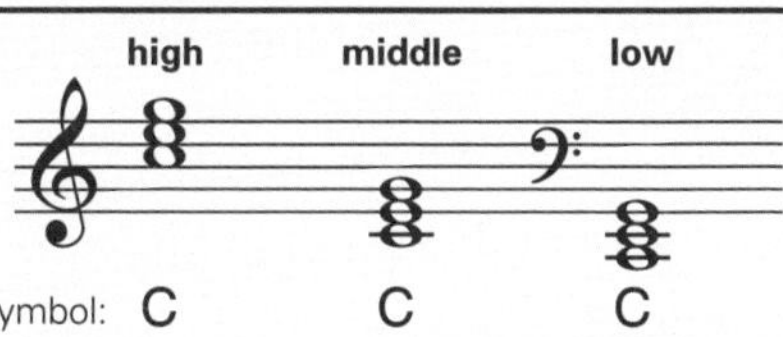


The chord can be spaced in different ways

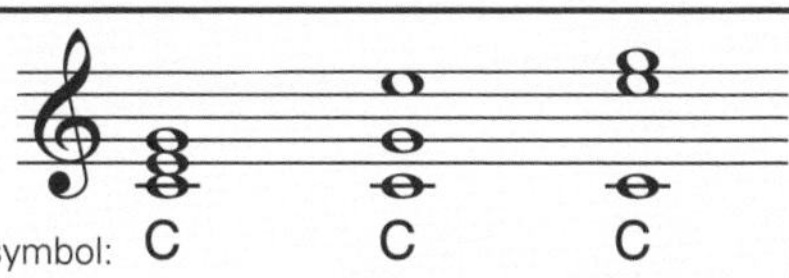


The chord can use the same note more than once

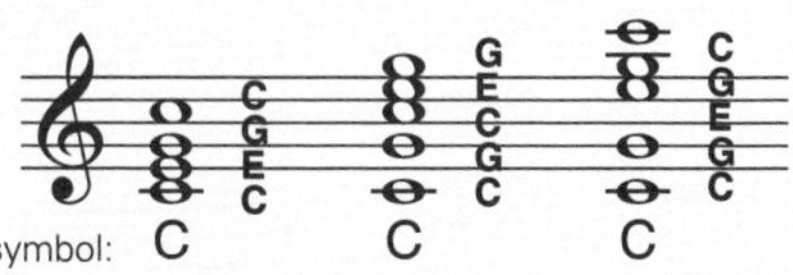

Pitch
Treble Clef
Bass Clef
Rhythm
Play Along 1
ACC Accidentals
Key Sign
Scales
Chords
Other Chords
Play Along 2
Comp

# Chords, Keys and Scales

Most music is in a key, for instance D major or G major. Generally speaking, music in a certain key mostly uses chords that are made up the notes of the scale of that key.

The simplest type of chord is called a triad and has three notes. You can find out the triads of a certain key, such as D major, by using that key's scale. First write out the ascending scale in that key. The first triad is built from the first, third and 5th notes of the scale, the second from the 2nd, 4th and 6th notes and so on. In other words, from the first note, you go two steps up the scale to find the second note and then two more steps to find the third.

Written on a stave, these triads have a distinctive look, as the three notes are written either on successive spaces or on successive lines. Triads with this close spacing are called root position triads

## Common D major chords are derived from the scale of D major

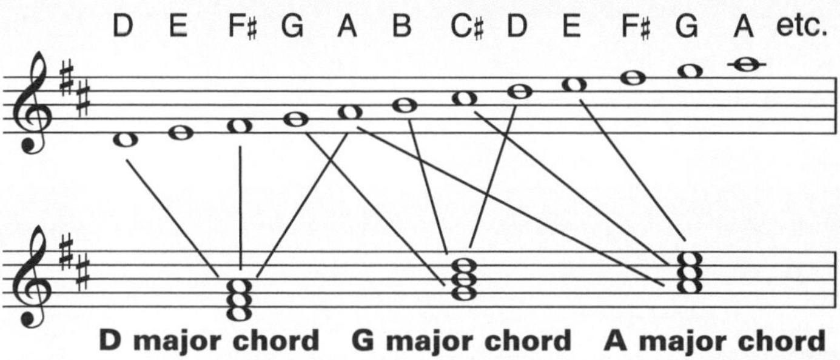


**Chords in a certain key can be worked out from the scale by selecting a note and finding the note two steps higher in the scale and the note two steps higher than that.**

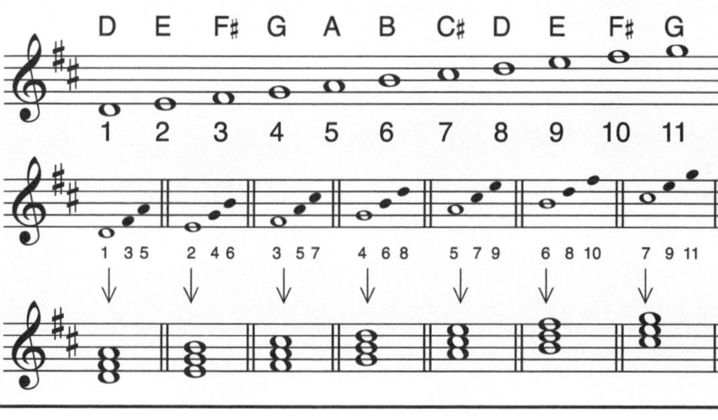

Pitch
Treble Clef
Bass Clef
Rhythm
Play Along 1
ACC Accidentals
Key Sign
Scales
Chords
Other Chords
Play Along 2
Comp

# C major

## Common chords: keyboard

**Chord I: C major**
**C, E and G**

**Chord V: G major**
**G, B and D**

**Chord IV: F major**
**F, A and C**

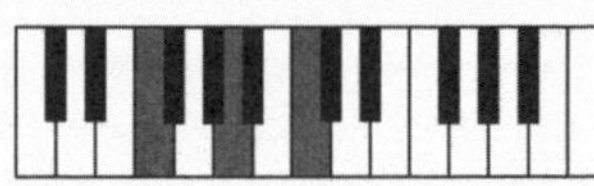

# C major

## Common chords: keyboard

**Chord VI: A minor**
**A, C and E**

**Chord II: D minor**
**D, F and A**

**chord Ic:**
**C major with G at the bottom**
**G, C and E**

# C major

## Common chords: guitar

**Chord I:**
**C major**
**C, E and G**

**Chord V:**
**G major**
**G, B and D**

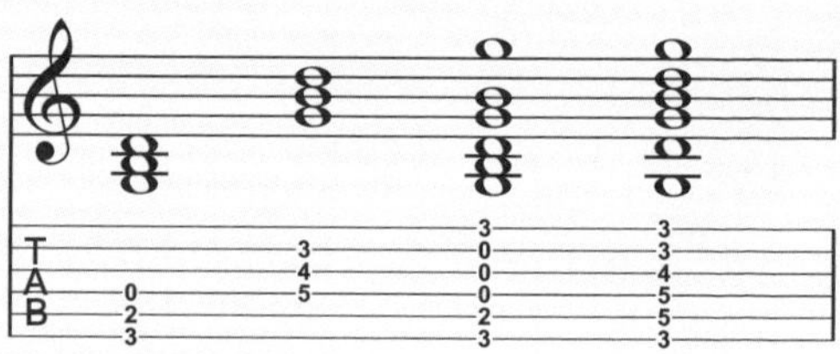

**Chord IV:**
**F major**
**F, A and C**

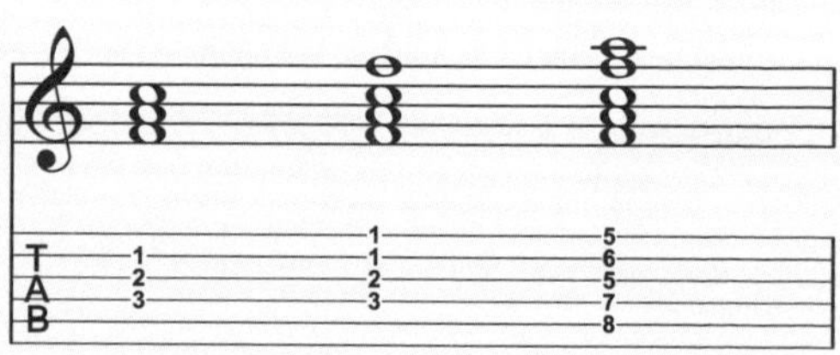

# C major

## Common chords: guitar

**Chord VI:**
**A minor**
**A, C and E**

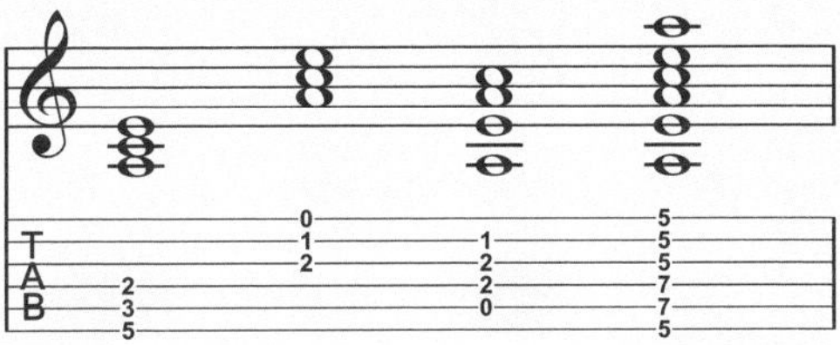

**Chord II:**
**D minor**
**D, F and A**

**Chord Ic:**
**C major/G**
**G, C and E**

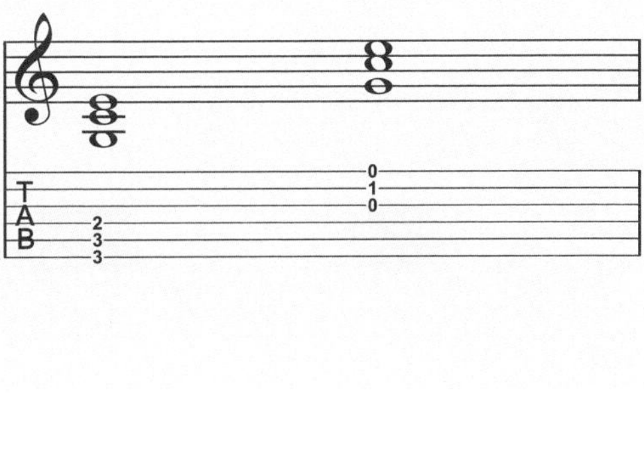

# C major

## Auld Lang Syne on keyboard

## 12-bar blues chord progression

# C major

## Auld Lang Syne on guitar

## 12-bar blues chord progression

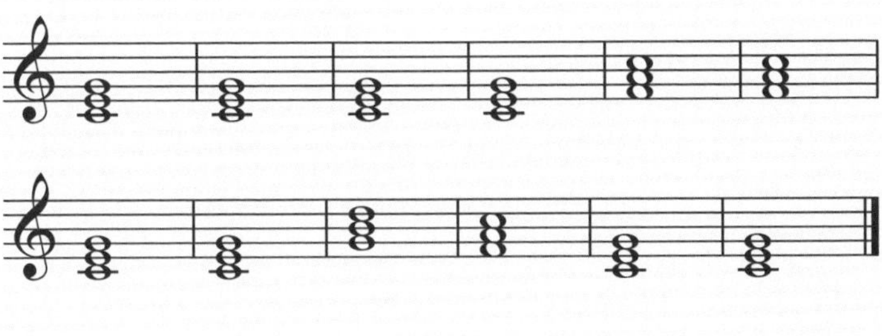

Pitch
Treble Clef
Bass Clef
Rhythm
Play Along 1
ACC Accidentals
Key Sign
Scales
Chords
Other Chords
Play Along 2
Comp

# G major

## Common chords: keyboard

**Chord I: G major**
**G, B and D**

**Chord V: D major**
**D, F♯ and A**

**Chord IV: C major**
**C, E and G**

# G major

## Common chords: keyboard

**Chord VI: E minor**
**E, G and B**

**Chord II: A minor**
**A, C and E**

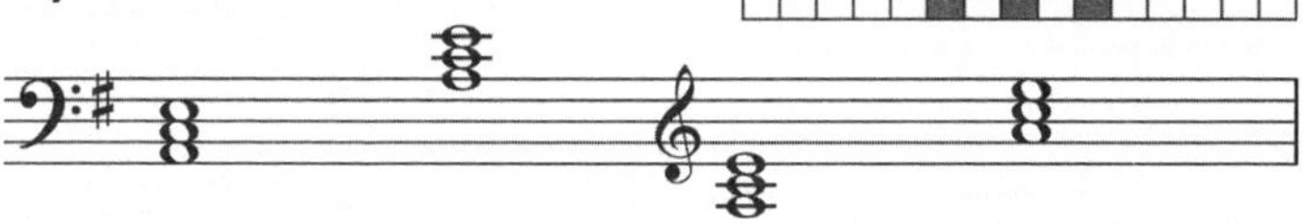

**Chord Ic:**
**G major with D at the bottom**
**D, G and B**

# G major

## Common chords: guitar

**Chord I:**
**G major**
**G, B and D**

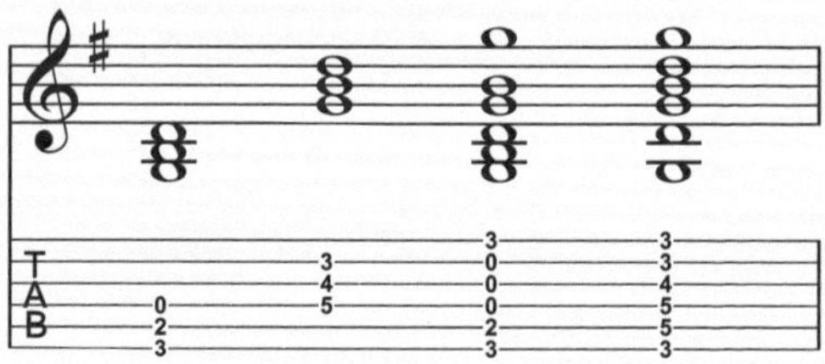

**Chord V:**
**D major**
**D, F♯ and A**

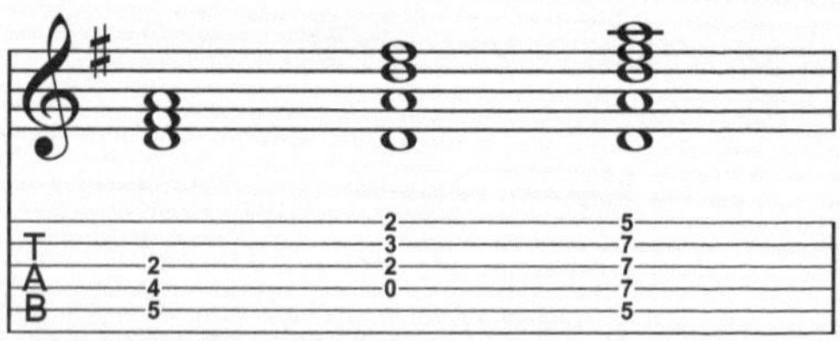

**Chord IV:**
**C major**
**C, E and G**

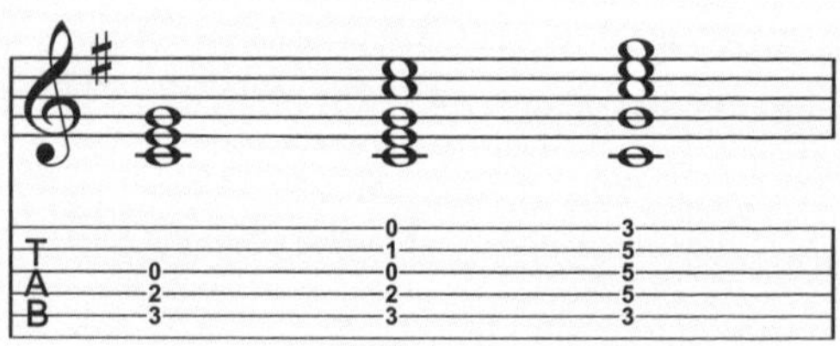

# G major

## Common chords: guitar

**Chord VI:**
**E minor**
**E, G and B**

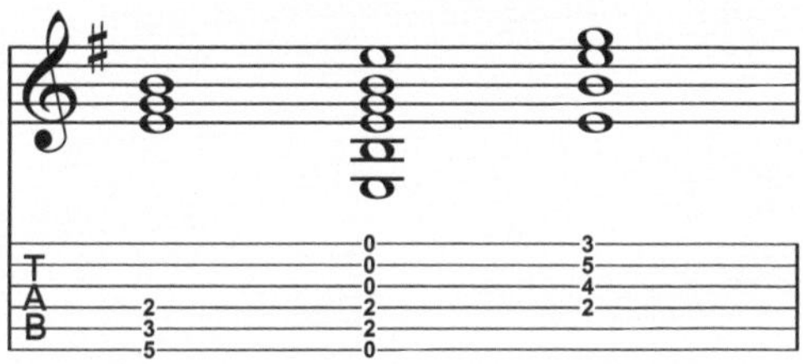

**Chord II:**
**A minor**
**A, C and E**

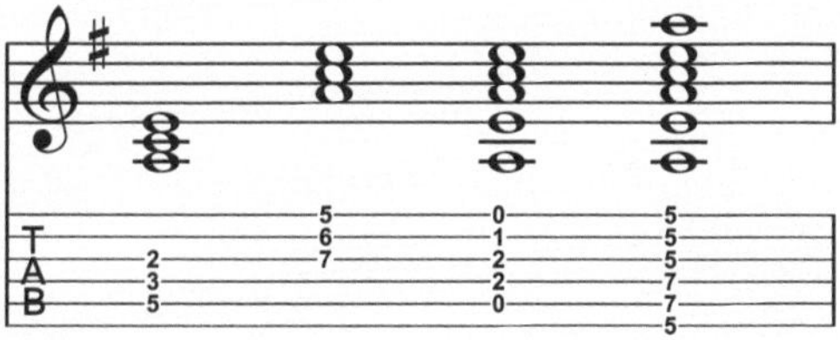

**Chord Ic:**
**G major with D**
**at the bottom**
**D, G and B**

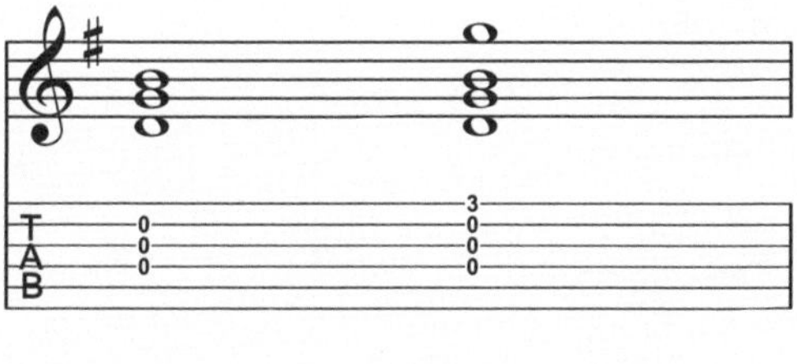

# G major

## Auld Lang Syne on keyboard

## 12-bar blues chord progression

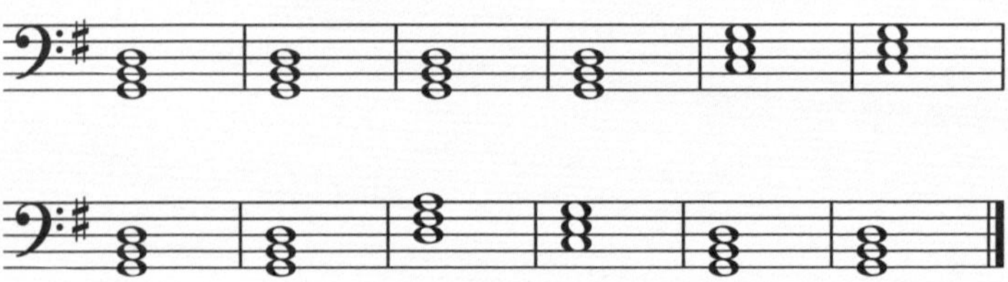

# G major

## Auld Lang Syne on guitar

## 12-bar blues chord progression

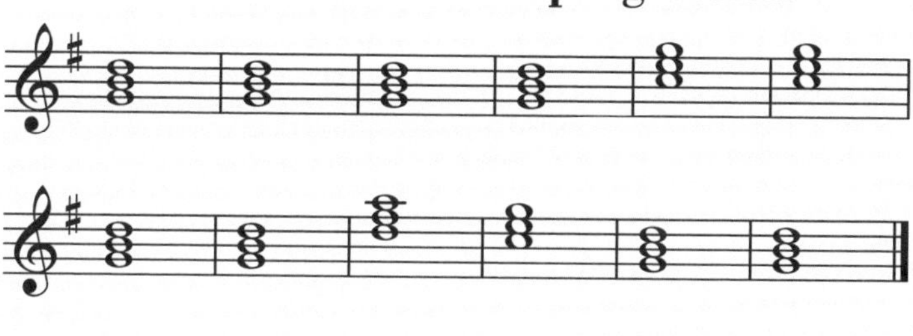

Pitch
Treble Clef
Bass Clef
Rhythm
Play Along 1
ACC Accidentals
Key Sign
Scales
Chords
Other Chords
Play Along 2
Comp

Pitch
Treble Clef
Bass Clef
Rhythm
Play Along 1
ACC Accidentals
Key Sign
Scales
Chords
Other Chords
Play Along 2
Comp

# F major

## Common chords: keyboard

**Chord I: F major**
**F, A and C**

**Chord V: C major**
**C, E and G**

**Chord IV: B♭ major**
**B♭, D and F**

# F major

## Common chords: keyboard

**Chord VI: D minor**
**D, F and A**

**Chord II: G minor**
**G, B♭ and D**

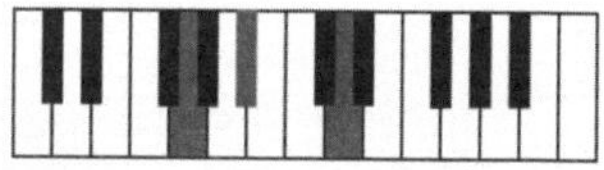

**Chord Ic:**
**F major with C at the bottom**
**C, F and A**

# F major

## Common chords: guitar

**Chord I:**
**F, A and C**

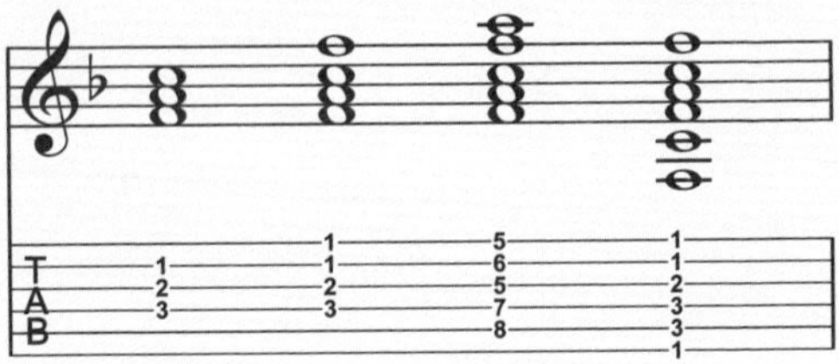


**Chord V:**
**C, E and G**

**Chord IV:**
**B♭, D and F**

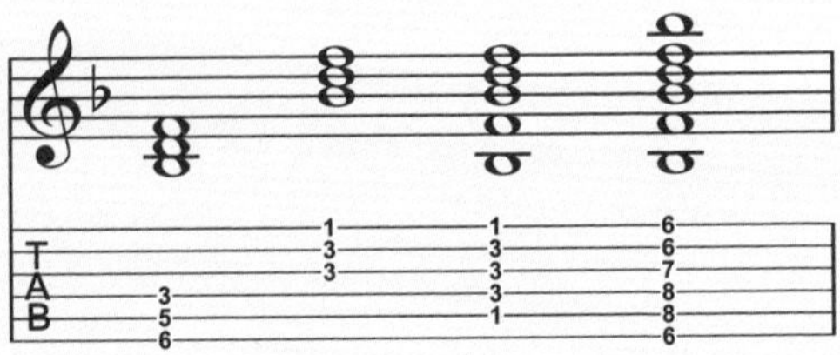

# F major

## Common chords: guitar

**Chord VI:**
**D, F and A**

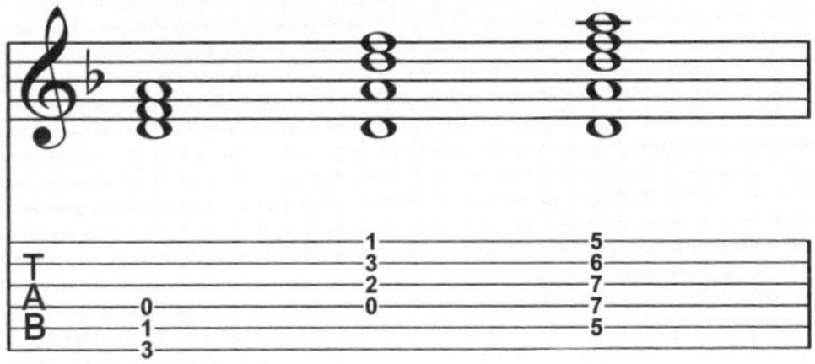

**Chord II:**
**G, B♭ and D**

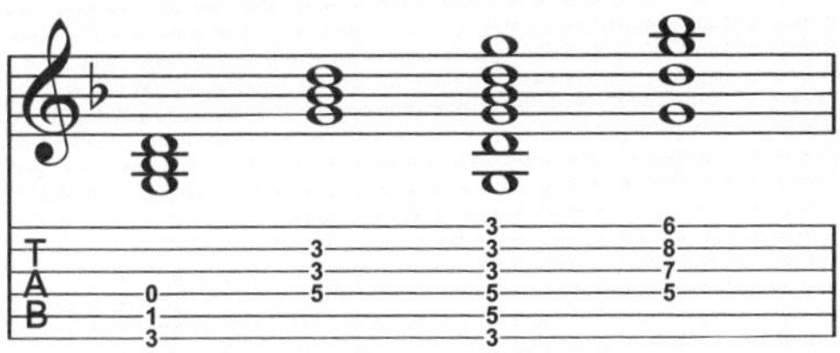

**Chord Ic:**
**F major with C at the bottom**
**C, F and A**

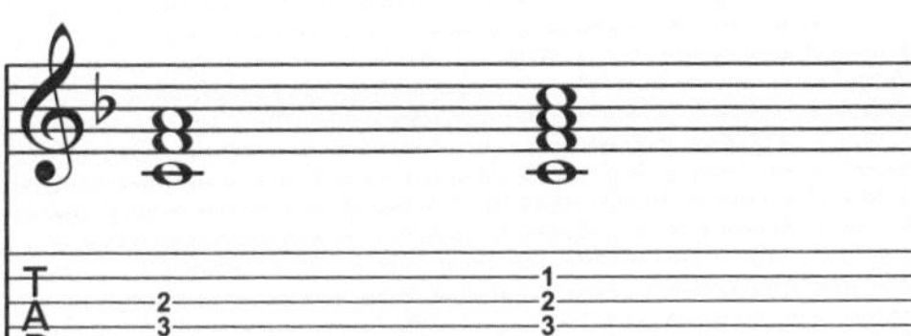

# F major

## Auld Lang Syne on keyboard

## 12-bar blues chord progression

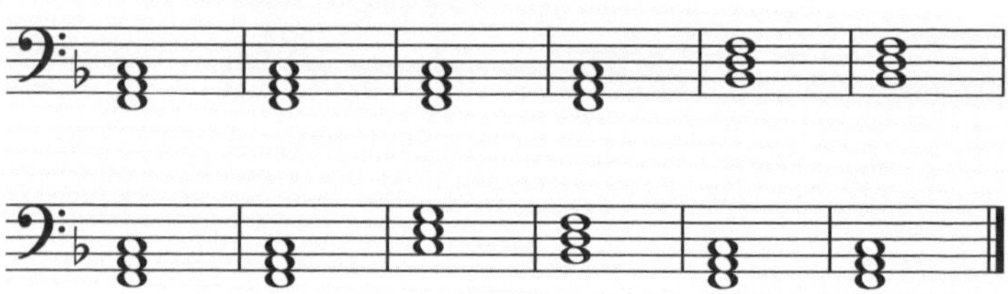

# F major

## Auld Lang Syne on guitar

## 12-bar blues chord progression

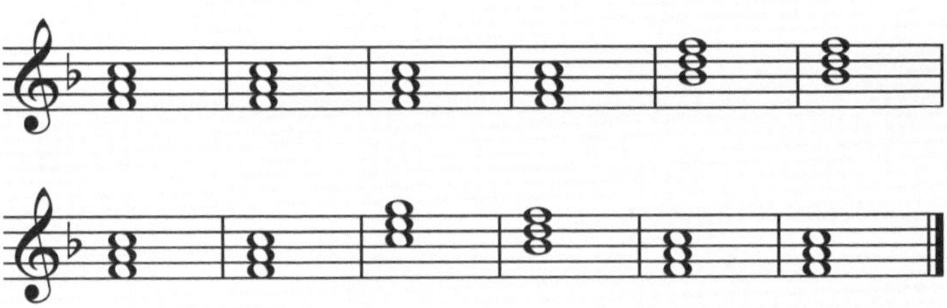

# C–C♯

**C major: C, E and G**

**C minor: C, E♭ and G**

**D♭ major: D♭, F and A♭**

**C♯ minor: C♯, E and G♯**

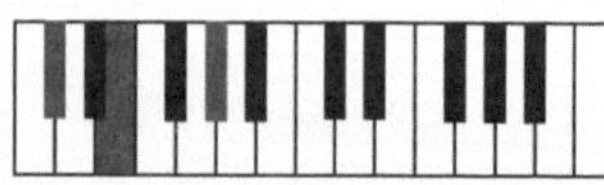

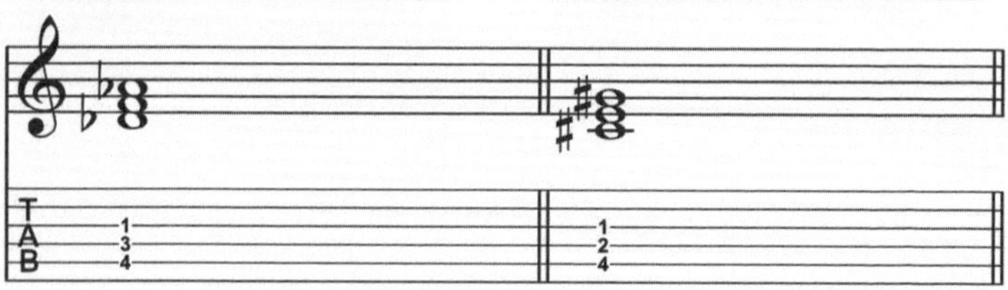

# D–E♭

**D major: D, F♯ and A**

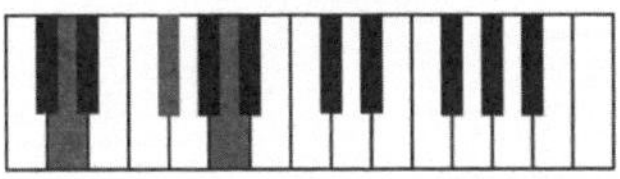

**D minor: D, F and A**

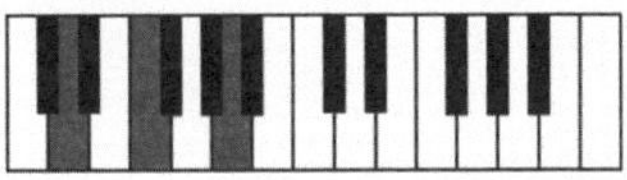

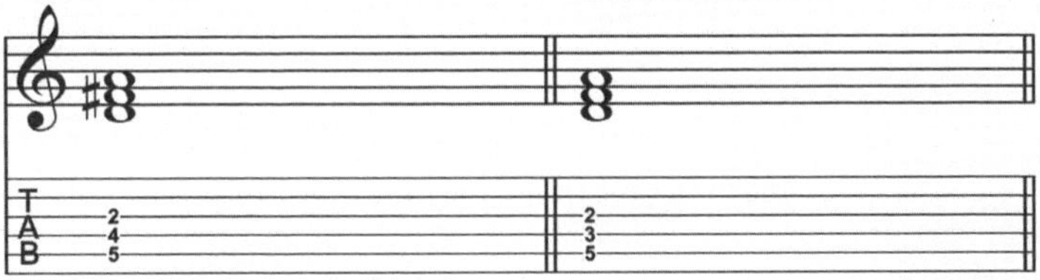


**E♭ major: E♭, G and B♭**

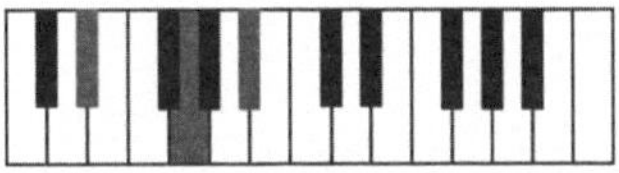

**E♭ minor: E♭, G♭ and B♭**

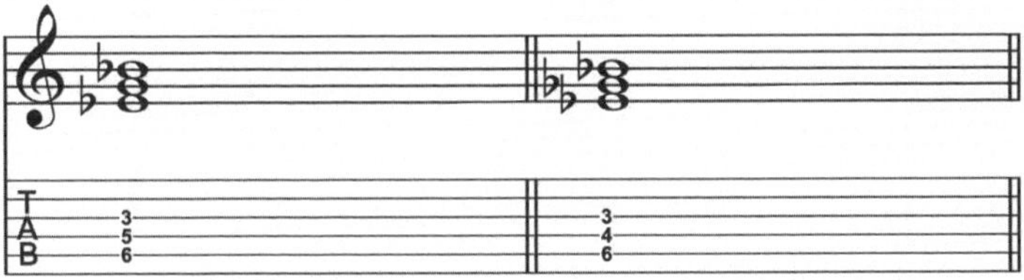

Pitch
Treble Clef
Bass Clef
Rhythm
Play Along 1
ACC Accidentals
Key Sign
Scales
Chords
Other Chords
Play Along 2
Comp

# E–F

**E major: E, G♯ and B** **E minor: E, G and B**

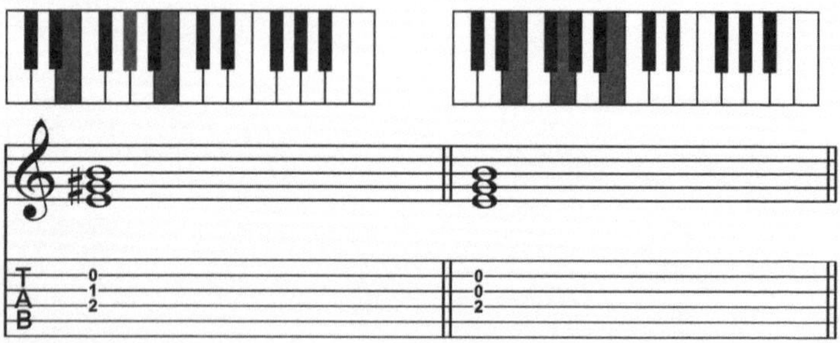

**F major: F, A and C** **F minor: F, A♭ and C**

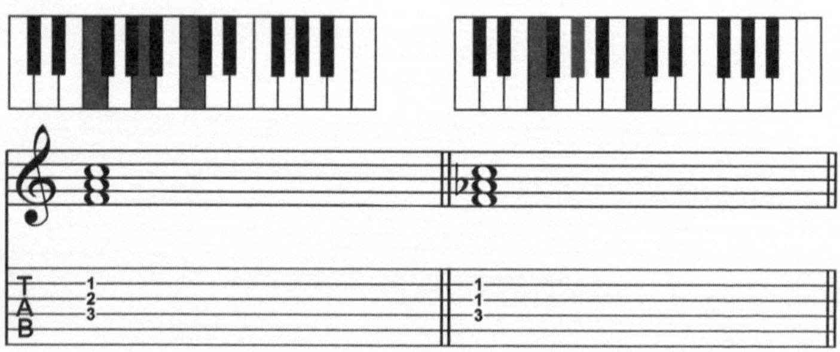

# F♯–G

**F♯ major: F♯, A♯ and C♯**

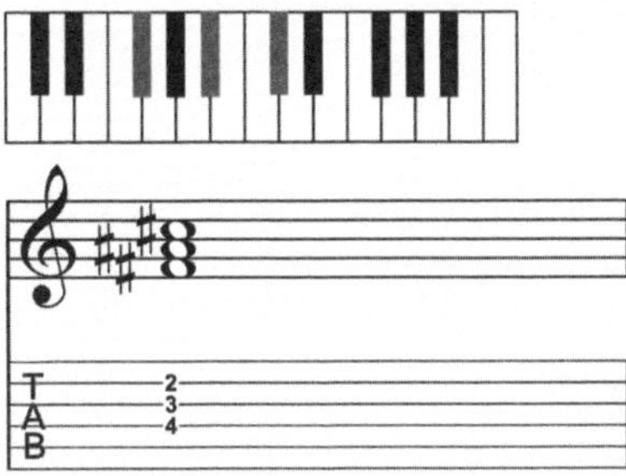


**F♯ minor: F♯, A and C♯**

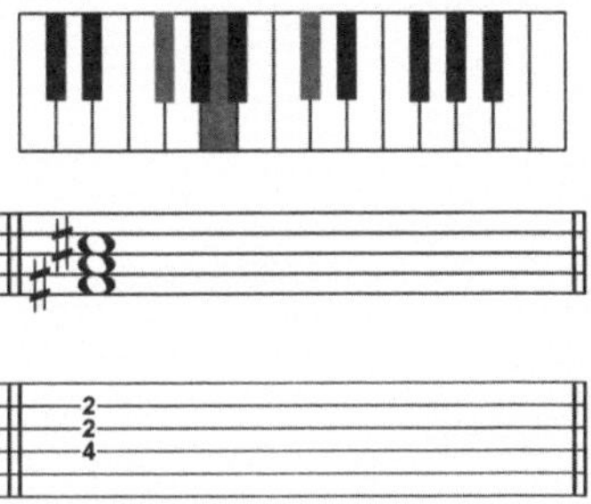


**G major: G, B and D**

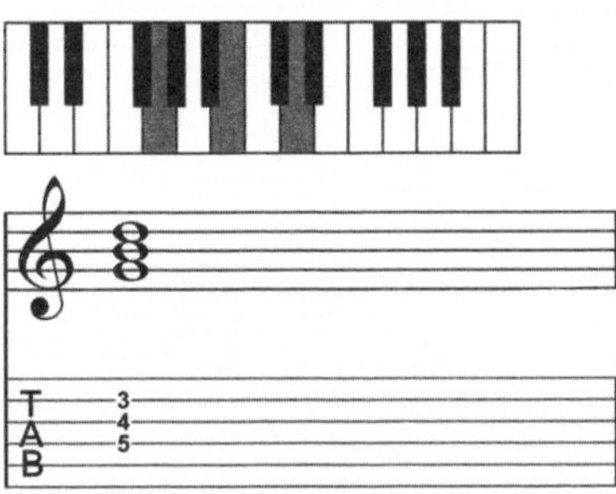


**G minor: G, B♭ and D**

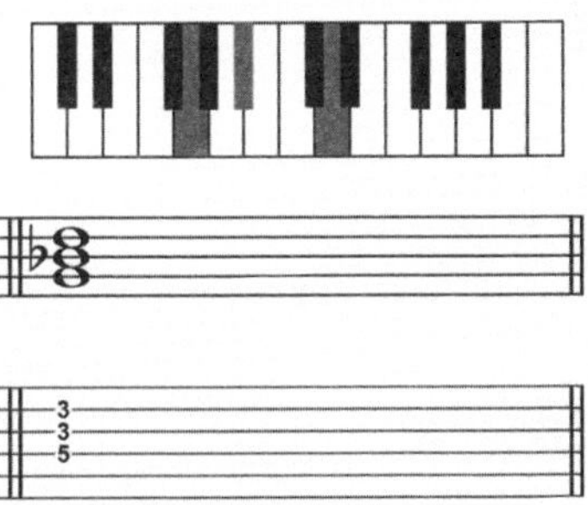

# G♯–A

**A♭ major: A♭, C and E♭** | **G♯ minor: G♯, B and D♯**

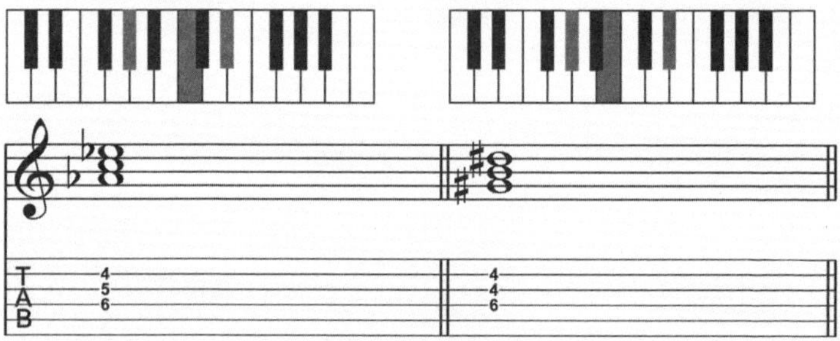


**A major: A, C♯ and E** | **A minor: A, C and E**

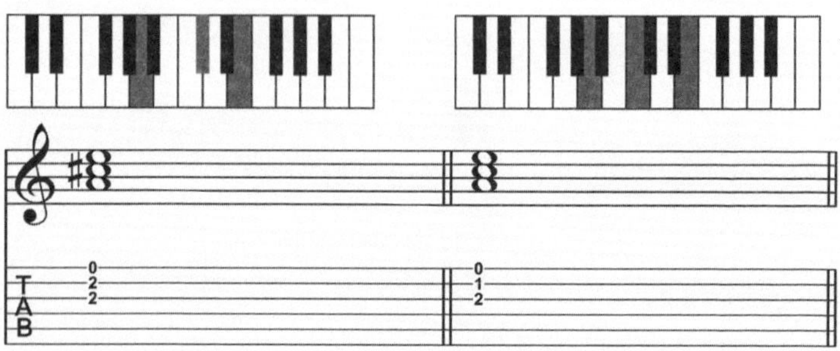

# B♭–B

**B♭ major: B♭, D and F**

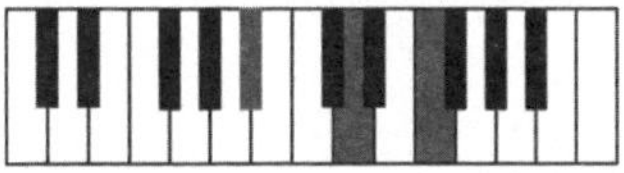

**B♭ minor: B♭, D♭ and F**

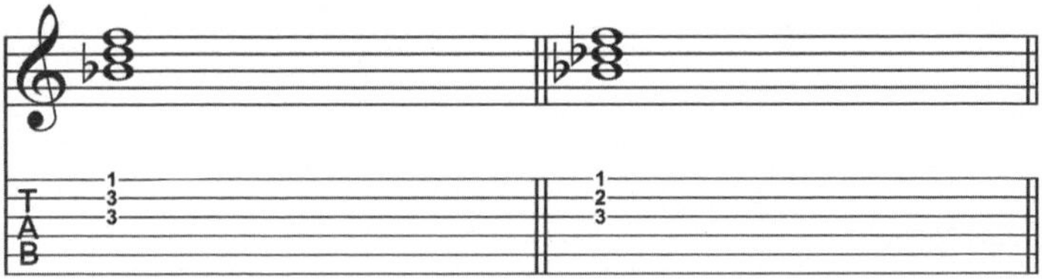


**B major: B, D♯ and F♯**

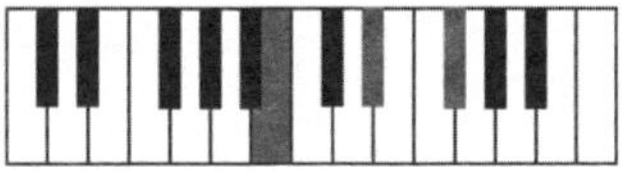

**B minor: B, D and F♯**

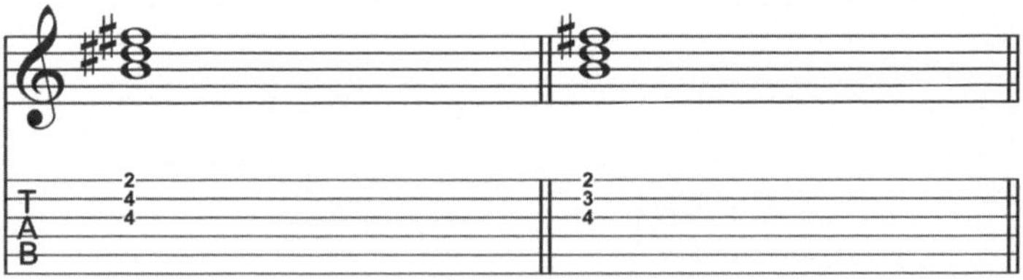

# Play Along 2

This second Play Along section will help you to improve your knowledge of keys, scales and, if you play a chordal instrument, chords. All the pieces are quite well-known, so you should find something you already know.

Learn the tunes in a similar way as in Play Along 1:

1. Clap the rhythm of the tune (you can write numbers under the music if it helps)
2. Play the rhythm on one note
3. Identify the key of the music, play through the notes of its scale and note the accidentals in the music
4. Play through the notes of the tune
5. Play through the notes of the tune to the rhythm.

To learn the chords on their own:

1. Clap the rhythm of the chordal part
2. Play the rhythm on one chord
3. Play through the chords, making sure you are using the accidentals in the key signature
4. Play through the chords in rhythm.

As always, start each step slowly and gradually speed up.

# Auld Lang Syne

**Moderately (♩ = 100)**

**tune: treble clef**
**chords: bass clef**

**Moderately (♩ = 100)** tune: bass clef

**Moderately (♩ = 100)** chords: treble clef

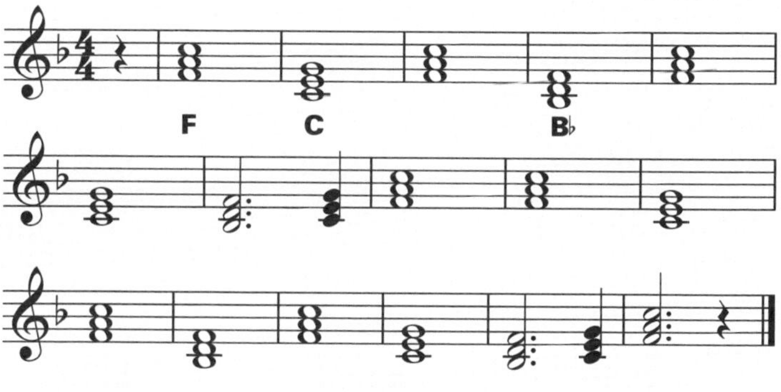

# New World Symphony

**Moderately (♩ = 100)**

**tune: treble clef**
**chords: bass clef**

## Play Along 2

**Moderately (♩ = 100)** tune: bass clef

**Moderately (♩ = 100)** chords: treble clef

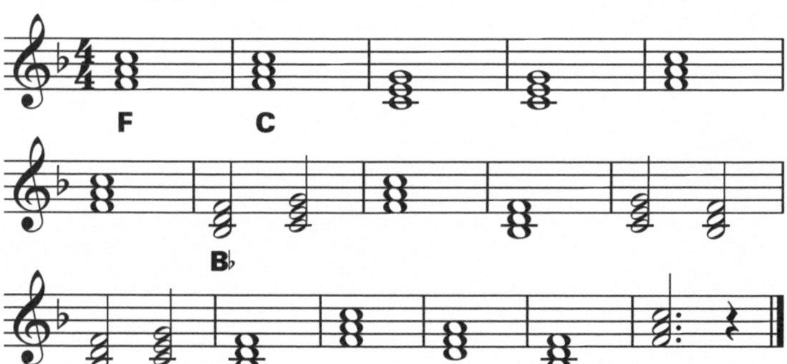

# Swing Low, Sweet Chariot

**Moderately (♩ = 100)**

**tune: treble clef**
**chords: bass clef**

**Moderately (♩ = 100)** **tune: bass clef**

**Moderately (♩ = 100)** **chords: treble clef**

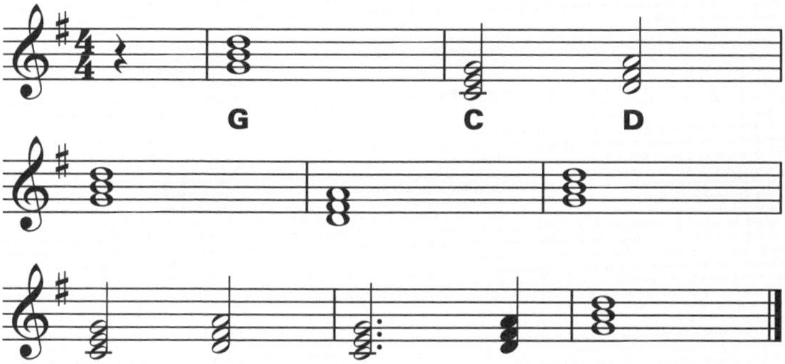


Pitch
Treble Clef
Bass Clef
Rhythm
Play Along 1
ACC Accidentals
Key Sign
Scales
Chords
Other Chords
Play Along 2
Comp

# Silent Night

**Quite slowly (♩. = 80)**

**tune: treble clef**
**chords: bass clef**

## Play Along 2

# Silent Night (cont.)

**Quite slowly (♩ = 80)** **tune: bass clef**

**Quite slowly (♩ = 80)**

chords: treble clef

# Battle Hymn of the Republic

**Moderately (♩ = 100)**

tune: treble clef
chords: bass clef

## Play Along 2

# Battle Hymn of the Republic (cont.)

**Moderately (♩ = 100)** **chords: treble clef**

# Waltzing Matilda

**Quickly (♩ = 90)**

**tune: treble clef**
**chords: bass clef**

# Waltzing Matilda (cont.)

**Quickly (♩ = 90)** **tune: bass clef**

**Quickly (♩ = 90)** **chords: treble clef**

# Greensleeves

**Quite slowly (♩. = 56)**

**tune: treble clef**
**chords: bass clef**

## Play Along 2

# Greensleeves (cont.)

**Quite slowly (♩. = 56)** **tune: bass clef**

## Play Along 2

**Quite slowly (♩. = 56)** chords: treble clef

# I Vow to Thee My Country

**Moderately (♩ = 100)**

tune: treble clef
chords: bass clef

## Play Along 2

# I Vow to Thee My Country (cont.)

**Moderately (♩ = 100)** **tune: bass clef**

**Moderately (♩ = 100)** **chords: treble clef**

# Jerusalem

**Moderately (♩ = 80)**

**tune: treble clef**
**chords: bass clef**

## Play Along 2

Pitch
Treble Clef
Bass Clef
Rhythm
Play Along 1
ACC Accidentals
Key Sign
Scales
Chords
Other Chords
Play Along 2
Comp

# Jerusalem (cont.)

**Moderately (♩ = 80)** tune: bass clef

**Moderately (♩ = 80)** chords: treble clef

# Compendium

## Transposing Instruments

| When these instruments read these notes: | These notes come out: |
|---|---|
| Clarinet in B♭, Trumpet in B♭ Soprano Saxophone | (a tone or 2 semitones lower) |

| | |
|---|---|
| Alto Saxophone in E♭ | (a major 6th or 9 semitones lower) |

| | |
|---|---|
| Tenor Saxophone in B♭ | (a major 9th or 14 semitones lower) |

| | |
|---|---|
| Baritone Saxophone in E♭ | (an octave and a minor 6th or 21 semitones lower) |

| | |
|---|---|
| French Horn in F | (a 5th or 7 semitones lower) |

**In addition, guitar, bass guitar and double bass sound an octave lower than written**

# Octave Signs & Other Clefs

| These written notes: | Produce these notes: |
| --- | --- |

this means 'play an octave higher'

this means 'play an octave lower'

**Alto clef** (used by viola)

**Tenor clef** (used by cello, bassoon and trombone)

Pitch
Treble Clef
Bass Clef
Rhythm
Play Along 1
ACC Accidentals
Key Sign
Scales
Chords
Other Chords
Play Along 2
Comp

# Instrument Ranges

## These are the comfortable written ranges of the instruments.

**Flute** **Oboe*** **Clarinet***

**Saxophone*** **Trumpet*** **French Horn***

**Violin*** **Viola*** **Recorder**

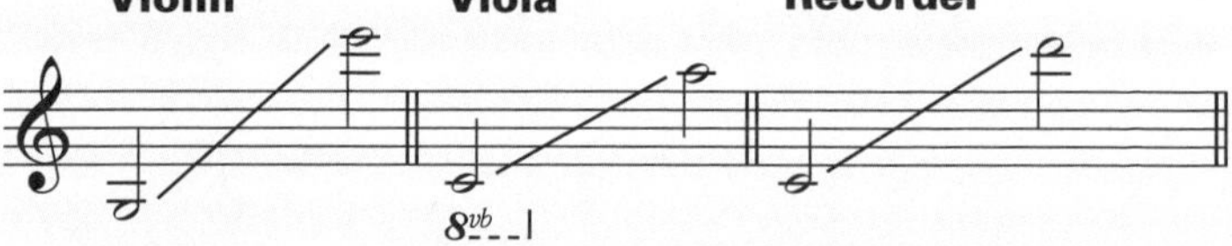


**Guitar*** **Soprano Voice*** **Alto Voice***

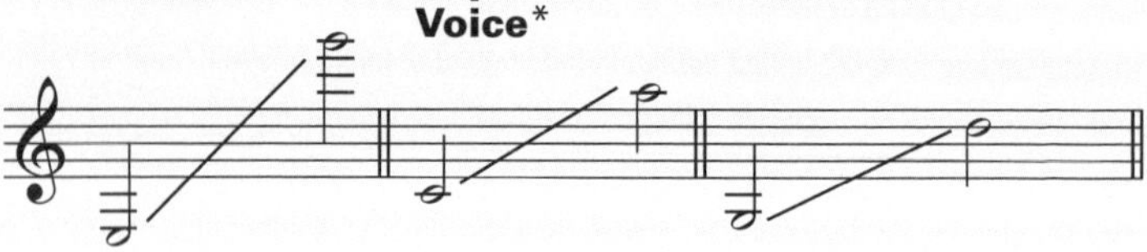

Instruments marked * can go higher and sometimes lower depending on the player or the instrument.

**Piano** | **Keyboard (5 Octaves)** | **Keyboard (4 Octaves)**

**Harp** | **Bassoon*** | **Trombone* and Euphonium***

**Tuba** | **Cello*** | **Double Bass***

**Bass Guitar*** | **Tenor Voice*** | **Bass Voice***

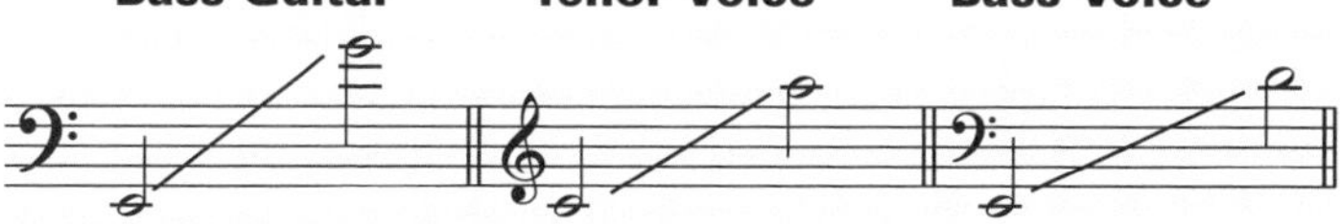

Pitch
Treble Clef
Bass Clef
Rhythm
Play Along 1
ACC Accidentals
Key Sign
Scales
Chords
Other Chords
Play Along 2
Comp

# TAB

**TAB, short for tablature, is a notation system for guitarists. It is based on the strings and frets of a guitar rather than actual notes.**

For six string guitars, it uses six lines, each of which represents one of the strings of the guitar.

On a guitar set to standard tuning, these strings are as follows:

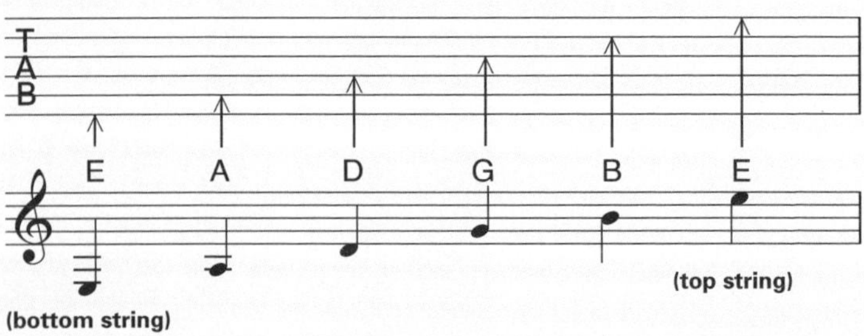

A number written on a line indicates that a note should be played on that string at that fret number. Numbers written directly above one another are to be played as chords.

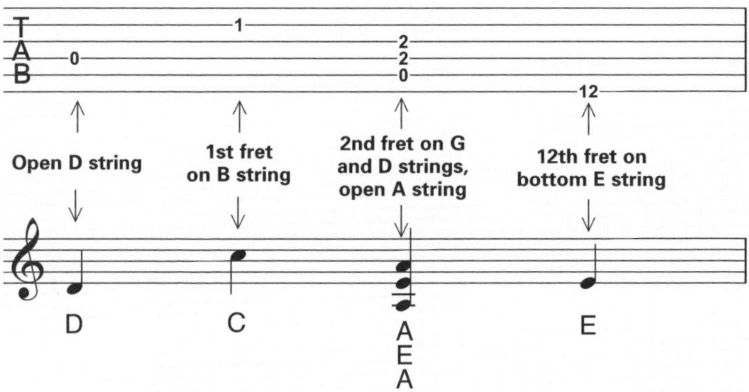


**0 indicates that an open string should be played.**
**Each fret position raises a string by a semitone.**

Pitch
Treble Clef
Bass Clef
Rhythm
Play Along 1
ACC Accidentals
Key Sign
Scales
Chords
Other Chords
Play Along 2
Comp

# TAB

Usually the rhythm of the music is written above the stave in notes which lack noteheads:

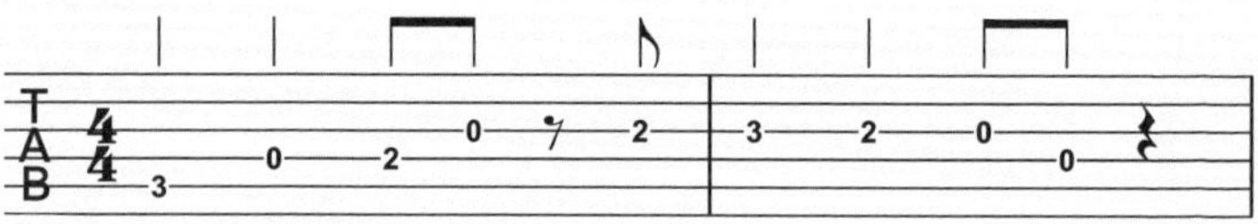


**this would be played as follows:**

In TAB notation for 4-string bass guitar, there are four lines.

In standard tuning, these represent the following notes:

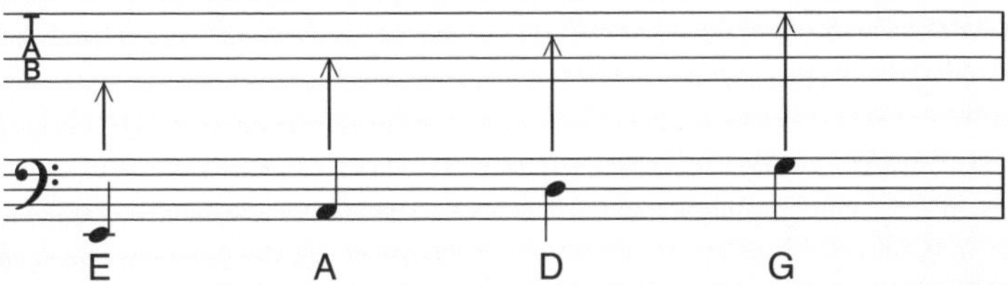


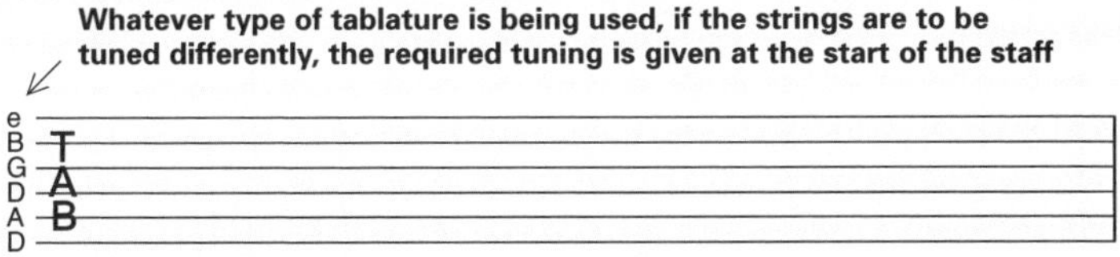


Pitch
Treble Clef
Bass Clef
Rhythm
Play Along 1
ACC Accidentals
Key Sign
Scales
Chords
Other Chords
Play Along 2
Comp

# Dynamics

**Dynamics are markings telling the player how loudly to play. They are usually written under the note(s) to which they refer.**

| Symbol | Italian term | Meaning |
|---|---|---|
| ***pp*** | pianissimo | very quiet |
| ***p*** | piano | quiet |
| ***mp*** | mezzo piano | fairly quiet |
| ***mf*** | mezzoforte | fairly loud |
| ***f*** | forte | loud |
| ***ff*** | fortissimo | very loud |
| $<$ | crescendo (cresc.) | getting louder |
| $>$ | diminuendo (dim.) | getting quieter |

# Articulation

**Articulation markings tell the player how to play the notes. They are usually written above or below the notehead(s).**

| Symbol | Italian term | Meaning |
|---|---|---|
| 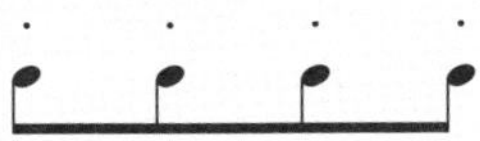 | staccato | short |
| 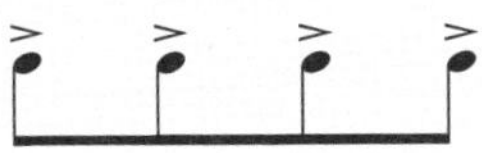 | accento | accented |
| 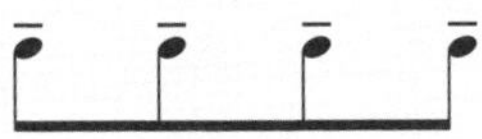 | tenuto | slightly stressed |
|  | legato | slurred; smoothly |
|  | sforzando | forced; very accented |
|  | fortepiano | loud attack then suddenly very quiet |

# Tempo

**Tempo markings tell the player how quickly to play. They are usually written above the stave(s).**

| Italian term | Meaning |
|---|---|
| lento or adagio | slowly |
| andante | at walking speed |
| moderato | at a moderate speed |
| allegretto | fairly fast |
| allegro | fast |
| presto | very fast |
| rit. or ritardando | slowing down |
| accel. or accelerando | getting faster |
| a tempo | at the original speed |
| più mosso | faster |
| meno mosso | slower |
| ad lib. or ad libitum | freely – the performer decides |

# Other Markings

| Marking | Explanation |
|---|---|
| trill | alternate between the note and the one above very quickly |

| Marking | Explanation |
|---|---|
| grace note or appoggiatura | play a short note just before the main note (it may be either just before or on the beat) |

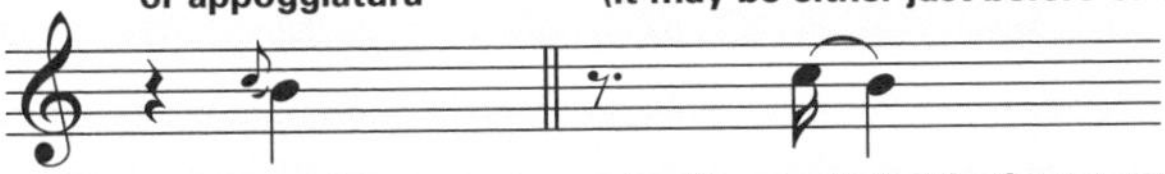

| Marking | Explanation |
|---|---|
| repeat marks | play the music inside the repeat signs twice |

| Marking | Explanation |
|---|---|
| pause | make the note last much longer than written (the exact length is up to the player) |

| Marking | Explanation |
|---|---|
| | repeat the previous bar |

| Marking | Explanation |
|---|---|
| D.C. al fine | go back to the beginning and play to the word 'fine' ('end') |
| D.C. al segno 𝄋 | go back to the beginning and play to the sign 𝄋 |

Pitch
Treble Clef
Bass Clef
Rhythm
Play Along 1
ACC Accidentals
Key Sign
Scales
Chords
Other Chords
Play Along 2
Comp

# Smaller Note Values

## A crotchet subdivided into smaller note values

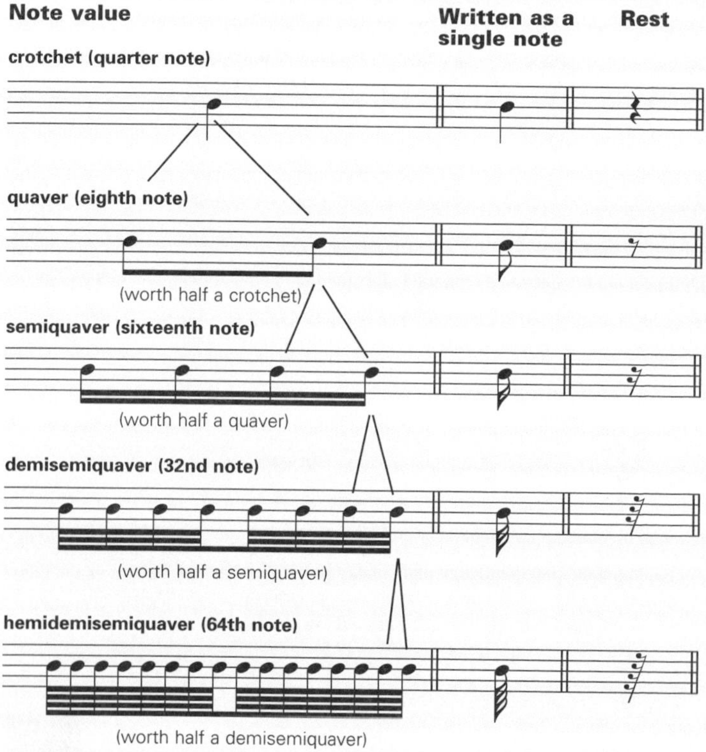

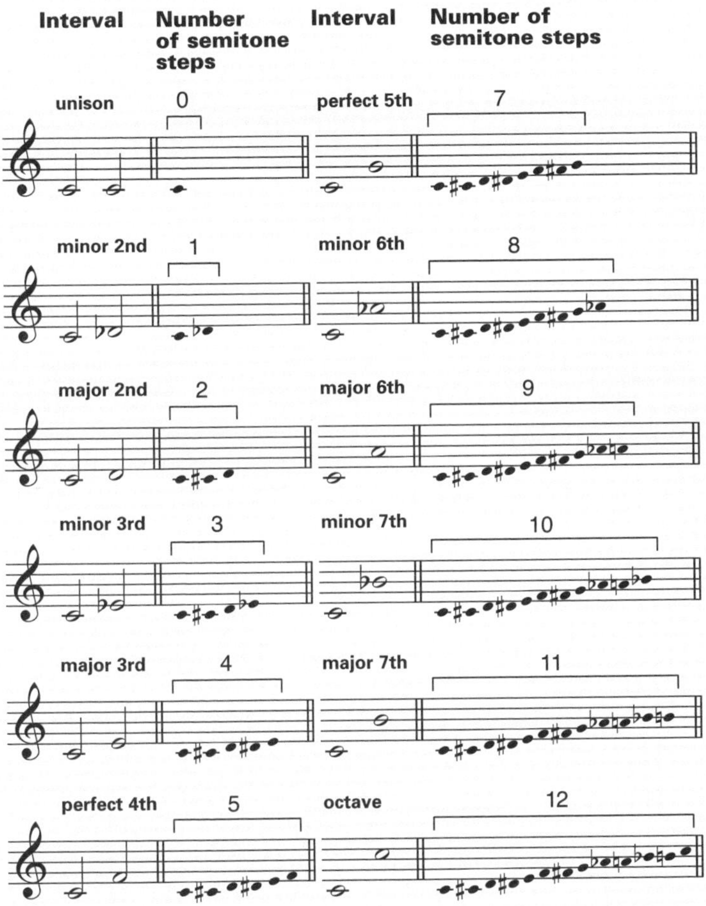
Interval
Number of semitone steps
Interval
Number of semitone steps
unison
0
perfect 5th
7
minor 2nd
1
minor 6th
8
major 2nd
2
major 6th
9
minor 3rd
3
minor 7th
10
major 3rd
4
major 7th
11
perfect 4th
5
octave
12

# Further Reading

Jackson, J., *Piano Chords*,
Flame Tree Publishing, 2007

Jackson, J., *Guitar Chords*,
Flame Tree Publishing, 2006

Jenkins, L. (ed.), *Musical Instruments Handbook*,
Flame Tree Publishing, 2006

*Concise Oxford Dictionary of Music*, OUP

Taylor, E., *Rudiments and Theory of Music*, ABRSM

# Internet Sites

www.abrsm.org

www.8notes.com/theory/

www.ibreathemusic.com/cat/3

flametreemusic.com

flametreepro.com